A Student's Guide to Academic and Professional Writing in Education

DATE DUE

A Student's Guide to Academic and Professional Writing in Education

Katie O. Arosteguy,
Alison Bright, and
Brenda J. Rinard

Foreword by Mya Poe

TEACHERS COLLEGE PRESS

TEACHERS COLLEGE | COLUMBIA UNIVERSITY

NEW YORK AND LONDON

Published by Teachers College Press, 1234 Amsterdam Avenue, New York, NY 10027

Copyright © 2019 by Teachers College, Columbia University

Cover design by Jeremy Fink

Permissions credit lines appear on pp. 34, 45, 84, and 159

Library of Congress Cataloging-in-Publication Data

Names: Arosteguy, Katie O., author. | Bright, Alison, author. | Rinard, Brenda J., author.
Title: A student's guide to academic and professional writing in education / Katie O. Arosteguy, Alison Bright, Brenda J. Rinard ; foreword by Mya Poe.
Description: New York : Teachers College Press, [2019] | Includes bibliographical references and index. |
Identifiers: LCCN 2019001980 (print) | LCCN 2019017005 (ebook) | ISBN 9780807777954 (ebook) | ISBN 9780807761236 (paperback : acid-free paper) | ISBN 9780807761854 (hardcover : acid-free paper)
Subjects: LCSH: Academic writing—Handbooks, manuals, etc. | Report writing—Handbooks, manuals, etc. | Education—Authorship—Handbooks, manuals, etc.
Classification: LCC LB2369 (ebook) | LCC LB2369 .A755 2019 (print) | DDC 808.06/6378—dc23
LC record available at https://lccn.loc.gov/2019001980

ISBN 978-0-8077-6123-6 (paper)
ISBN 978-0-8077-6185-4 (hardcover)
ISBN 978-0-8077-7795-4 (ebook)

Printed on acid-free paper
Manufactured in the United States of America

For all teachers past, present, and future. Thank you for the important work you do. Keep writing.

Katie, Alison, and Brenda

Contents

Foreword

The teaching of college-level writing has changed dramatically in the last 50 years. While first-year writing once dominated the attention of college-level educators, today writing in the disciplines is at the forefront of the teaching of writing in higher education. Writing in the disciplines invites faculty from across the university to draw on their disciplinary expertise in teaching students about textual apprenticeship. Education, just like chemical engineering or biology, has its specific ways of making meaning through texts. For undergraduates, the world of disciplinary writing is often murky, confusing, and downright odd. For aspiring teachers, that landscape is especially difficult as they learn their professional lives will be spent navigating the often competing forces of fellow teachers, students, parents, and community partners on one hand, and administrators and state legislators on the other. Thus, aspiring teachers need writing guidance from those who can provide transparent, grounded advice on the writing conventions of education. They need the kind of advice offered in *A Student's Guide to Academic and Professional Writing in Education.* In this guide, Katie Arosteguy, Alison Bright, and Brenda Rinard offer a rhetorically based, visually rich approach to learning the writing conventions used by professionals in education. With an eye toward educating students at the beginning of their careers, Arosteguy, Bright, and Rinard take education students from classroom writing into the world of professional writing. They demonstrate how purpose, audience, context, voice, and genre work in each case.

A Student's Guide to Academic and Professional Writing in Education does more than just describe writing conventions used in various educational contexts. Annotated examples show the principles they discuss. Peppered throughout the book is the kind of practical advice that novices need as they enter the profession—for example, stylistic choices that teachers need to consider when communicating with students. Exercises at the end of each chapter put into practice the lessons offered in each chapter.

In Part I: "Academic Writing," *A Student's Guide to Academic and Professional Writing in Education* offers students advice on composing reading responses, annotated bibliographies, and research papers. The advice on how to locate information is particularly useful because it provides students research strategies for finding information in education-related databases. And the advice does not stop there. The book goes on to show students how to read research, trace related ideas across sources, summarize sources, and critique those sources. Finally, with annotated samples of student texts, the guide connects student work to professional work, demystifying the relationship between professional and student texts.

Beyond writing with scholarly sources, a field-based writing chapter offers students advice on composing in genres such as field observations and interview-based educator profiles. And in a move that helps aspiring teachers see how they can marshal those sources for the purposes of teacher research, the authors explain how to combine data sources into a case study.

As students move into more advanced work, Part II: "Professional Writing" shows aspiring teachers how to connect curriculum plans to state standards without losing sight of the needs of the students in their own classrooms. Such an approach encourages teachers to assess what their students already know, what they already can do, and what they value before teachers design daily curricula. For teachers in training, such an approach, when combined with formative assessment, is critical in helping structure opportunities for success.

With advice on teaching philosophies, critical reflections in support of teaching portfolios, and policy proposals, Arosteguy, Bright, and Rinard offer writing advice that bridges what education majors learn in their college careers with what they will need to know as practicing teachers. The book illustrates concepts such as how to integrate theoretical and research-supported influences to articulate a pedagogical approach. In showing students how to write polices to propose educational change, this work demonstrates how to put research into practice.

At the heart of *A Student's Guide to Academic and Professional Writing in Education* is a commitment to the value of teachers' voices—that what teachers write matters, whether it be classroom writing, research writing, credential writing, or stakeholder writing. And it is this hopeful potential of teaching writing to aspiring teachers that underscores the value of teaching writing across the disciplines and into the community today.

—Mya Poe, director of the Writing Program, Northeastern University

Preface

Teachers are constantly writing. They design, execute, and assess curriculum; they articulate their approaches to teaching and then ground them in theory; they justify choices they make in lesson planning; they reflect on their teaching as well as on student learning; they communicate with diverse audiences on an everyday basis; and they use research to create plans for change. This book centers on the belief that the written voices of teachers matter, from the writing tasks they encounter on a daily basis that primarily affect their students to writing that has the power to effect change at the school, district, state, or national level.

Many of the ideas for this book arose out of pedagogical conversations we—three faculty members of the University Writing Program at the University of California, Davis—have had about the writing in education course we teach to undergraduates. When we started teaching the class years ago, we quickly realized there was no textbook for us to use, and with our various backgrounds and experience with/in education and writing studies, we worked to develop the course sequence reflected in this guide. Our approach is grounded in best practices in the education and writing studies fields. To inform this book, we conducted interviews with social science librarians and education professors, and we collected syllabi and assignments from faculty who teach education courses across the United States. We also collaborated with our own former students and education students across the country to gather a representative sample of the written work of preservice teachers, and we read widely in writing studies and genre theory to help illuminate different aspects of the writing process for our readers.

This guide is for students pursuing a career in education. They may be enrolled in an undergraduate, master's, or credential program focused on education and teaching. No matter what type of program they are in, or where they are in their career trajectory, however, they will need to understand that writing is part of teachers' intellectual work. Understanding the dynamic rhetorical situations associated with the field—and how high the stakes can be because students' learning hangs in the balance—is critical to writing effectively in education.

This guide will familiarize education students with some of the most common writing tasks they will encounter in the field of education, and equip them with the rhetorical strategies they'll need in order to write successfully for a variety of audiences and for a variety of purposes. While the strategies provided in this book undoubtedly will help students in their undergraduate and graduate education courses, our hope is that they will use this guide long after they receive their degree. Since *A Student's Guide to Academic and Professional Writing in Education* draws on information from the fields of both education *and* rhetoric and composition, with the objective of approaching education writing through a rhetorical lens, it will prepare students to navigate the research-to-practice, academic-to-professional continuum of writing in education.

This guide focuses on four major categories of writing in education: classroom writing, research writing, credential writing, and stakeholder writing. The categories move progressively from more common academic writing that education students will likely encounter in undergraduate classes (Part I) to the more specialized, professional writing they will encounter as practicing teachers (Part II).

Chapter 1 provides an overview of how and why educators write and explains what we mean by a rhetorical approach to writing in education. We stress the interconnected relationships among purpose, audience, context, voice, and genre when people are faced with different writing tasks. Chapter 2 lays more groundwork by describing some of the major stylistic issues to keep in mind as readers engage with the different genres covered in the book. Chapter 3 then introduces readers to the important role reflective writing has in the field of education and familiarizes them with a commonly assigned academic genre: the reading response. Chapter 4 explains the different kinds of research conducted in the field of education and then provides strategies students can apply to find, evaluate, and use sources to write annotated bibliographies and research papers. Chapter 5 explains how to conduct and write effectively about qualitative research—primarily observations and interviews—in the genres of field logs, observation write-ups, profiles, and case studies.

Part II moves into the professional realm by focusing on the writing of education students in graduate/credential programs and as they become practicing teachers. Chapter 6 explores the multifaceted genre of the lesson plan, including the different audiences one might write a lesson plan for and the different purposes the plan might serve. The bulk of the chapter discusses the different elements necessary to create a lesson plan that will facilitate student learning. Chapter 7 describes how education students can articulate their theoretical or philosophical approach to teaching, something they often are asked to do as a culminating assignment for a credential program or in preparation for entering the job market.

Chapters 6 and 7, therefore, are directly related to each other and can be read in either order. As educators, our philosophy of teaching directly informs the way in which we design lessons, just as the way in which we design lessons reflects our teaching philosophies. Using Chapters 6 and 7 in tandem will allow students to see the implications of their lesson plans and how their choices in curriculum design reflect their beliefs as educators.

Chapter 8 provides strategies for writing critical reflections in order to prepare for teaching portfolio assessments, demonstrate teaching effectiveness in annual reviews, and foster ongoing professional growth. Chapter 9 discusses writing to various stakeholders at the teaching site, district, state, and/or national level in order to effect policy or program change. Chapter 10 closes the book by explaining American Psychological Association (APA) documentation, which writers in education need to know in order to accurately and effectively incorporate and cite their sources.

This book addresses the current lack of writing guides for undergraduate and graduate students enrolled in education classes. It also meets the needs of practicing teachers looking to further develop as writers. We hope that the guide reminds educators of two of their responsibilities as teachers: to use writing to improve students' learning conditions and to use their voices to advocate for improved teaching conditions. Because the guide is written for educators at any stage of their career, readers can refer to it again and again as they encounter new or unfamiliar writing tasks.

Acknowledgments

The publication of this guide ends a long process with many stops and starts. While still drafting our proposal, the three of us were struck by a tree branch on the UC Davis campus during a discussion of our writing in education course. The concussions we suffered slowed, and at times stopped, our progress. But even through this severe accident, we persisted with the help and support of our students, colleagues, and families. We learned real-world lessons about the strength of collaboration in scholarly work. This guide is stronger because of the assets each of us brought to the project. While writing, we were constantly informed by the philosophy of the National Writing Project in which teachers' voices always matter and writing is an important professional endeavor.

We particularly want to thank the students from our Writing in Elementary and Secondary Education courses. Your persistent desire to create educational equity for your future students is inspiring. Without some of you graciously allowing us to include your work, this book would not have been possible. In particular, we would like to thank Faith Overhall, Emily Matsuda, Deanna Gallegos, Veronica Ruiz Quinonez, Molly Farmer, Jeremiah Pilkerton, Katrin Jaradeh, Lauren Lesyna, and Michelle Kolhmann. We also would like to thank the other teachers who contributed written work and valuable ideas to this guide: Jessica Shaffer, Kevin Gee, Lee Martin, and Sarah Hochstetler. Last, we thank Melissa Browne, the education librarian at UC Davis, for providing most of the information presented in Chapter 4.

Another big thank you to Emily Spangler, acquisitions editor at Teachers College Press, for supporting our vision for this book; Dakota Caulder, for helping us prepare our rough draft; Laura Horowitz, our thoughtful development editor; and Karl Nyberg, our production editor.

Finally, we thank our families, whose support throughout this process has allowed us to write a book we are proud of. In particular, Katie thanks Rob, Carsen, Ashton, and Owen; Alison thanks Jason, Jonah, and Hannah; and Brenda thanks her husband, Tommy.

Part I

ACADEMIC WRITING

CHAPTER 1

The Educational Landscape
How and Why Educators Write

Educators today are facing a changing educational landscape, one that requires us to be flexible, adaptive, and understanding of the many facets of the discipline of education, including how and why educators write. At the federal level, while the 2001 No Child Left Behind Act is still law, it has been largely replaced by the 2015 Every Student Succeeds Act. Betsy DeVos is our Secretary of Education—an appointment that has caused many educators to worry about the state of public education in America. States need to prepare teachers to teach according to standards and, if they are using the Common Core State Standards, prepare students to be "college and career ready." Meanwhile, we must contend with parents demanding the end to reductive curricula that force teachers to "teach to the test" and the era of accountability that has led to a reduction in funding for programs in music, the arts, and physical education.

To move forward in an educational climate like this, you will need to learn skills to advocate for best teaching practices and the most effective learning conditions. Since teachers write so much on a daily basis, and because they can use their writing to effect positive change for their students and their profession, it is becoming increasingly important to learn strategies for approaching new and different writing situations. In short, you should develop rhetorical awareness in order to examine your writing task and effectively shape your writing for your audience and purpose.

WRITING IN EDUCATION IS RHETORICAL

Whenever you are confronted with a writing task, you need to think about why and how you are writing, to whom, and in what circumstances, in order to shape your writing to convey your message effectively. Bitzer (1968) tried to articulate the concept of rhetorical situation when he wrote about his interest in "the situation which invites the orator's application of [their] method and the creation of discourse" (p. 2). While prior work in rhetoric and composition studies had focused on thinking about audience, speaker, subject, and occasion, they were treated largely as separate entities. Bitzer, however, wanted to know how audience, purpose, speaker, and context work together to create the rhetorical situation. As a result of Bitzer's work, many writing teachers (and college writing centers) have developed their own iterations to help students understand these rhetorical elements. Figure 1.1 is adapted from a visual developed by California State University, Sacramento's (CSUS) Online Writing Lab (2011) that shows the interconnected nature of the four major elements of the rhetorical situation: context, purpose, audience, and voice. Effective communication of your written message depends on noting the reciprocal relationships of the rhetorical elements.

Context

Context refers to the specific circumstances in which you write, which then influence how you write. For example, when writing a critical reflection of your teaching in order to complete the requirements of a teacher credential program, it is useful to consider the context of this rhetorical situation: a high-stakes environment that will determine whether you will earn your credential. As a writer, analyzing the context, or the occasion, of the writing task—whether this means considering your (high-/low-stakes) environment, your physical location, the time period in which you're writing (e.g., early in your career, 5 years into your career), the sensitivity of the topic, how long you have to complete the writing, and so on—can help you make decisions about how to write. Writing doesn't happen in a vacuum; it takes place within certain geographical, historical, and time constraints. Effective writers identify the context prior to writing in order to make decisions about purpose, audience, voice, and genre.

Figure 1.1. Visual Representation of the Rhetorical Situation

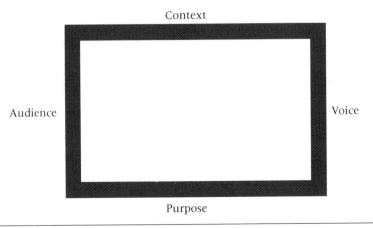

Adapted from material developed by CSUS Online Writing Lab.

Purpose

Any time you read something, you should be able to identify the author's purpose for writing. In other words, you should know *why* someone wrote something. Likewise, anytime you write, you should be able to articulate your purpose, or reason, for writing before you start. The clearer you are about *why* you are writing something, the more likely you will be to make rhetorical decisions during the writing process that will best communicate your message.

Reasons for writing can vary; you may need to argue, explain, educate, inform, or entertain. You may need to accomplish two of these purposes at the same time. A proposal for educational policy change, for example, seeks to inform the reader about an educational topic and argue for a solution. Knowing why you are writing something is critical because it forces you to think about how you should write, in what genre, and to whom. While you are still in school, it is important to move beyond reasons of "to get a good grade" or "to pass a test," and begin thinking about what, specifically, you are trying to accomplish in writing a piece. As you move forward in the field of education, you may find yourself writing to describe an educational setting, analyze a student's learning condition, justify a lesson you've designed, explain your teaching philosophy, or reflect on your teaching practice—to name just a few purposes for writing.

Audience

When you carefully consider the demographics—educational attainment level, gender, age, cultural background, and socioeconomic class—of your audience, you can make more informed decisions about how to approach your writing. The more you, as the writer, reach out to your audience and close any gaps, the more you increase the odds that your message will be delivered effectively. As Flower (2012) points out, in order to "create a momentary common ground between the reader and the writer," you must consider the following: (1) the readers' knowledge about your topic; (2) their attitude toward your topic; and (3) their personal or professional needs (p. 91). Knowledge level refers to what your audience already knows about your topic and what information you will need to provide for readers. Under- or overestimating your readers' familiarity with the subject can cause your message to fall flat. Anticipating your readers' attitudes toward your topic is helpful when determining how best to present evidence and deciding what evidence will be most convincing. Last, you should have a good sense of what your readers will need from you so that you can achieve your purpose. For instance, do they need a certain method of organization or a certain tone?

When you are faced with a writing task in education, first analyze your audience and determine the answers to Flower's (2012) three areas of concern so you can shape your writing to reach your intended audience. Based on your answers, you can make rhetorical decisions across a range of items: choice of topics/content, method of organization, types of evidence to use, use of visuals, and vocabulary/word choice. For example, if you are a practicing teacher who wants to write to your school board to argue for a policy change at your school site, you may discover that the board members have been closely involved in the issue, but that they would likely oppose your ideas based on cost. Hence, you might try to find information that would help build common ground between you and them, perhaps by re-examining their mission or goals statement about the ideal learning conditions for students. When proposing your idea, you might begin with the solution that would be easiest or most cost-effective to implement and then move toward more complicated or costly components of the proposal.

Voice

We all know how important tone of voice can be in an oral conversation. Think, for example, of the difference between a mom's stern whisper to her child: "You have to hold my hand in a parking lot," and her communication of the same information in an upbeat tone. Likewise, voice in a written piece—*how* you write—can be critical. After you have considered the context, purpose, and audience for your piece, you'll want to think about what tone will be most effective for communicating your message. Knowing the context within which you are writing, and to whom you are writing and why, often will determine the tone you need to use. For example, when you write a critical reflection as a teacher, you try not to sound overly critical and harsh about yourself; instead, you want to come across as someone who acknowledges the personal shortcomings in your teaching practice and is inspired to improve.

There are many rhetorical choices you can make to alter your voice: vocabulary (specialized, nonspecialized), types of examples you use to support your points, how you organize your information, rhetorical devices (e.g., analogies, repetition), and formatting. The goal is to use the language your target audience would expect so that you demonstrate you are part of the same discourse community. In writing to your school board, for example, you'll want to use vocabulary that is precise but not too jargon-heavy, as well as provide examples that will be appropriate and convincing for that audience. As a preservice teacher, your voice also reflects who you are, or will be, as an educator; this also is known as your *ethos*. Because we believe that good teachers never stop learning, we encourage you to think about establishing your voice as a well-informed student of education who is also a lifelong learner.

GENRES AS RESPONSES TO RHETORICAL SITUATIONS

Once you have examined the rhetorical situation surrounding your writing task, you can determine the genre, or type, of writing you should use. Carolyn Miller—largely regarded as the founder of rhetorical genre studies in the composition and rhetoric field—defines genre as "a set of shared expectations [or] social understandings in people's heads" (quoted in Rinard & Masiel, 2017, p. 466). Questions you might ask yourself to understand a genre include: "How do people talk about it? How do they respond to it? What do they do with it?" (Rinard & Masiel, 2017, p. 467).

Rather than being static, genres constantly are evolving and responding to new and different rhetorical situations and social contexts. Much of the challenge in writing effectively, then, lies in figuring out what the shared expectations of a genre are. Chances are you already have a good understanding of genres in other fields or areas of interest, such as music, movies, or literature. Dirk (2010), for example, writes about the country music genre, saying it has the following set of shared characteristics:

- Country songs tend to tell stories. They often have characters who are developed throughout the song.
- Country songs often have choruses that are broad enough to apply to a variety of verses.
- Country songs are often depressing; people lose jobs, lovers, and friends.
- Country songs express pride for the country style and way of life.
- Country songs are often political, responding to wars and economic crises, for example. (p. 250)

Close analysis of many country songs helped Dirk generate this list. Likewise, this book will provide you with samples of genres in educational writing so that you can build your knowledge of common characteristics and expectations of them. Remember, though, that genres change, as do characteristics and expectations, so the most valuable skill you can learn from this book is how to analyze rhetorical situations and the genres you encounter, to enable you to adapt your writing as necessary.

As Dirk (2010) also makes clear, genres are more than just forms; they also have a function. They are used to accomplish a goal or bring about some kind of specific response. For example, when you write lesson plans in your teaching career, it is essential that you consider what action is most useful for accomplishing the task (Miller, 1984) or what actions pertaining to the genre will help you complete the task. All genres are used to elicit a reaction or serve some function of social action for the reader. For example, educators use the genre of lesson plans to accomplish the action of student learning.

Devitt (2009), well known in the writing studies field for her work on genre pedagogy, emphasizes the importance of maintaining a "critical genre awareness" and teaching this awareness to our students (p. 337). Devitt (2009) argues that having this awareness leads to greater agency since we are no longer passively participating in the language practices around us; instead, we seek to understand why things are written the way they are to "participate in those genres" (p. 338). This awareness also keeps us mindful that each genre carries with it certain political, economic, or ideological beliefs, so that when we use—or assign—particular genres, we know that we promote certain values. In this way, learning about genres—how they work and how to write them—serves to free and enlighten us. Dean (2008) encourages K–12 teachers to use genre theory in their classrooms and provides detailed instructional suggestions for helping younger students develop an understanding of genre awareness.

Developing genre awareness in the way outlined by these theorists will help you navigate this guide and think through the different genres and rhetorical situations you are likely to encounter in your career. Table 1.1 lists possible contexts, purposes, audiences, voices, and genres you may encounter when writing as an educator.

Table 1.1. Example of Possible Varied Contexts, Purposes, Audiences, Voices, and Genres

Context	Purpose	Audience	Voice	Genre
Lesson in your classroom	To assess a learning target	Students	Student-friendly, appropriate level of vocabulary, accessible	Rubric
Observation of a concerning incident in the classroom	To address a concerning issue for a student	Parents	Professional, warm, empathetic	Email
Observation of how departmental reading lists are decided	To improve student learning conditions	Site supervisor/ principal	Professional, specialized vocabulary, solution-oriented	Presentation
Observation that an existing policy or lack of a policy inhibits student learning	To argue for policy change at the district level	School board/ superintendent	Professional, convincing, well-researched	Proposal

THE ROLE OF REFLECTIVE WRITING IN EDUCATION

In addition to assessing the rhetorical situation when faced with writing in education, it is equally important that you understand how reflecting on your teaching practices, and/or your students' learning conditions, is central to the field of education. Reflective writing, in which you use personal and professional experience to reflect on course concepts and your own development as a teacher, underlies most of the writing you'll do and serves as the bridge connecting the chapters in this guide.

Because reflection is embedded in nearly everything we do as educators, it sets our profession apart from many others. Unlike other professionals, educators spend the majority of their time working alone in their classrooms with their students. What is more, educators and their students often lack a voice when it comes to the decisionmaking processes that affect their teaching and learning conditions. Such decisions typically are made by higher-level administrators or school board members who have varying levels of experience (if any) in the classroom. As a result, these decisionmakers and their policies can be out of touch with what teachers and students need. Often they also are facing other pressures—mostly budgetary—that may prevent them from acting in the best interests of teachers or students.

In this unique professional environment, reflective writing serves many purposes for educators: We can use it to demonstrate our understanding of educational issues, assess our teaching effectiveness, and argue for improved teaching and learning conditions in front of various relevant audiences. We use this kind of writing often in our careers as educators, such as when we write reading responses or observation write-ups in our undergraduate classes (see Chapters 3 and 5), teaching philosophies in our credential programs (see Chapter 7), or critical evaluations when we are practicing teachers (see Chapter 8).

As many educational theorists have noted, reflective writing is a key rhetorical tool teachers employ in their work as intellectuals. Giroux (1985) argues that while contemporary educational reform movements threaten to reduce teachers to "specialized technicians within the school bureaucracy" whose job is to "manag[e] and implemen[t] curricula programs," we can combat this reduction by thinking of ourselves as "reflective practitioners" who combine practice and scholarship with the aim of educating students to be active citizens (pp. 36–38). In our role as intellectuals, we can use reflective writing to improve the teaching and learning environments we find ourselves in. We can use reflective writing in small ways, for example, writing a reading response for a class in which we are asked to respond to a reading that advocates a particular vision for education reform. Or we can use it in more impactful ways once we gain experience in the field, such as writing a proposal for policy change in a school district (see Chapter 9).

Wharton (2012) defines reflective writing in education as writing from personal experience that assesses teaching performance, reflects on lessons learned, and articulates possible future improvements to our teaching. Reflective writing is valuable at all stages in our careers because we are using our experiences working in the classroom and with children to inform our stance on a topic. In other words, by reflecting on our pedagogical experiences, we can facilitate change.

As you progress through your undergraduate and graduate coursework in education, the kinds of reflective writing you'll do will increase in complexity

Table 1.2. Types of Reflective Writing in Education (Increases in Complexity)

Context	Genre	Format/Content	Purpose
Undergraduate education course	Reading response	1–3-page summary of/ response to a required course reading; usually informal writing	Reflect on personal experience and course concepts to respond to an opinion/theory about education
Undergraduate, graduate, or credential education course	Observation write-up, profile, case study	Several pages of formal writing that examine a teacher's practice or a student's learning conditions	Use course concepts and extensive observation or interview data to illuminate/ explain a teacher's practice or a student's learning condition
Credential program course	Lesson plan	Many pages of formal and detailed writing that articulate a plan for meeting learning objectives and justify the teacher's approach	Reflect on pedagogical content knowledge, course concepts, and firsthand experience in the classroom to explain how students will learn and why a particular approach will be successful
Credential program course or practicing teacher	Teaching philosophy	1–3 pages of formal writing that articulate a teacher's theoretical or philosophical approach to teaching	Reflect on how theoretical underpinnings coincide with choices in curriculum design to shape one's beliefs as an educator
Credential program course or practicing teacher	Critical reflection	This can take various forms, but is most likely several pages of detailed and formal writing that evaluates one's teaching	Reflect on one's own teaching practices with the ultimate goal of improving these practices to enhance student learning
Professional career	Proposal	Many pages of formal writing that incorporate extensive research to propose a change to a policy or program	Argue for a solution to a problematic policy, or lack of policy, that will result in improving teaching or learning conditions

(see Table 1.2). Credential students engage in more critical and higher-stakes reflective writing when they are preparing their teaching portfolio assessments at the end of their credential programs. The Education Teaching Performance Assessment (edTPA, 2018) requires credential program students to reflect on their teaching and articulate how they can improve their instruction and/or assessment for future teaching. Similarly, practicing teachers, as part of their evaluation and promotion process, write critical reflections of their teaching that describe pedagogical growth and mastery in their subject area. Also, as Hicks, Whitney, Fredricksen, and Zuidema (2017) note, having the time and space to reflect on their teaching practices in writing can provide the incentive for teachers to consider their work and how they might write for change to a more public, targeted audience.

TYPES OF WRITING IN EDUCATION: HOW THIS GUIDE IS ORGANIZED

This guide is designed to familiarize you with the most common types of writing tasks you will encounter in the field of education (from the least to the most complex) and to equip you with the rhetorical strategies you'll need in order to write successfully for a variety of audiences for a variety of purposes.

Like other social sciences, the field of education is broad, with research in subfields spanning language, literacy and culture, learning and mind sciences, mathematics education, science and agricultural education, and school organization and educational policy, to name a few. The field of education is also interdisciplinary, with research and pedagogy overlapping with other fields such as sociology, psychology, economics, and English. Because of the research-to-practice orientation of the field, this guide is designed to move your thinking and writing about education from an approach based on your personal experiences to one grounded in this substantial research base.

Along with its research focus, the field of education is also a credentialing discipline, meaning that preservice teachers must become familiar with the writing tasks that will be required of them when they begin credential programs and when they start their careers as practicing teachers. Writing in this context requires an understanding of the broad research base, pedagogy, clinical experiences, and the connections among them all. Many of the writing strategies we discuss are based on frameworks from the National Council of Teachers of English and the National Writing Project, two professional organizations recognized for their research on best writing practices across disciplines and grade levels. The writing for credentialing information is based on reviews of state standards and assessment bodies, such as the edTPA.

Figure 1.2 orients you to the book and shows you how we've organized the different types of writing in education.

Figure 1.2. Four Major Categories of Writing in Education

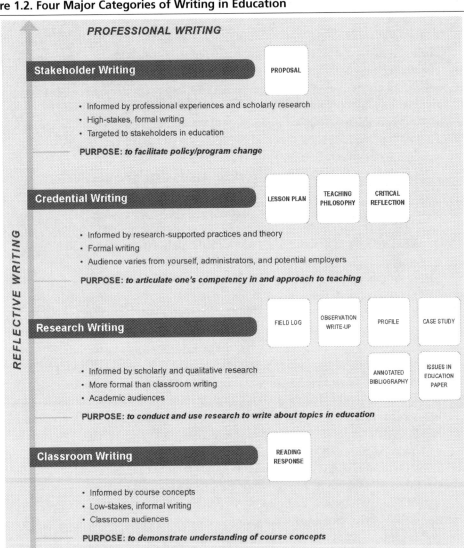

Classroom Writing

This guide defines classroom writing as common writing tasks you encounter in your undergraduate or graduate classes. These tasks include key genres you will build on later as you move closer to professional writing. For example, professors assign reading responses primarily as writing-to-learn exercises so that you can personally reflect on assigned readings and think about how they support or complicate theories you are studying in class. While the reading response tends to be a more informal genre—typically written for professors—it introduces you to the important and foundational concept of reflective writing, even if, at this stage, it is focused more on personal experience. As you move toward more professional writing in education, reflective writing manifests as critical meta-analyses of your teaching practices and students' learning processes.

Reading Responses. Professors of undergraduate and graduate education classes regularly assign reading responses to assess students' understanding of course concepts. Students typically write short responses to a reading, such as a contemporary theory of learning for an educational psychology class. For this type of assignment, the professor expects you to not only summarize the reading or respond to it personally, but also to critique the key ideas in the reading(s) based on what you've learned in class. Professors also may ask you to summarize a reading and then write an educational recommendation based on your understanding. In Chapter 3, you will learn specific strategies for summarizing a text and formulating your response with personal and/or textual evidence.

Research Writing

This guide then explains more demanding and formal academic genres that require you to conduct and use research to write about topics in education. Since the field of education is a social science based on quantitative and qualitative research findings that improve teaching, policy, advocacy, and assessment, education classes often will require you to engage in a scholarly research project where you locate and use sources to support an argument. Learning how to research effectively is a critical skill set that grows in expectation and intensity as you move toward credential/master's coursework. While in an undergraduate course you may be asked to write a more general "issues in education" research paper, graduate students moving closer to becoming practicing teachers may need to communicate their research to a broader audience of professionals in the field and explain why the research matters. Chapters 4 and 5 discuss how to conduct, evaluate, and use different kinds of research in a variety of genres.

Annotated Bibliographies and "Issues in Education" Papers. In Chapter 4, we describe annotated bibliographies as written genres that help to scaffold a larger paper: an "issues in education" research paper. Most academic and professional assignments will require you to first understand a topic based on scholarly sources before you begin writing; an annotated bibliography grounds your writing in the literature of the field and acts as a springboard to more complex writing assignments. Therefore, we discuss how to move from your annotated bibliography to a research paper draft.

Field Logs and Observation Write-Ups. Professors of undergraduate and graduate education classes, especially those with an internship component, often ask their students to create observation write-ups based on experiences in a classroom environment or school community. These assignments require you to describe key details of your experience and reflect on these in a meaningful way that connects to the ideas you are encountering in course readings. Hence, we show you how to keep detailed notes of your observation(s) and choose data that allow you to critically engage with the course concepts.

Profiles. You may be asked to write a profile of an educator in order to learn more about that individual's practices and to highlight important aspects of the teaching profession. More complex in nature because of the possible varied audiences and purposes, a profile assignment typically will ask you to interview K–12 educators about their teaching practices. The interviews can be lengthy, generating a lot of data. Your task, then, is to sift through the data and create a story. The story may be about how a teacher has overcome adversity in order to better teach her students, or it may be about how a teacher is incorporating best practices in his classroom to reach English language learners.

Case Studies. As you move toward more professional writing in education, you may be asked to write a case study. A case study is an in-depth analysis that pulls from multiple qualitative data sources to provide a better understanding of teaching and learning conditions. In a teaching credential or master's program, for example, students conduct action research in their own classrooms and then propose pedagogical action plans to address identified concerns. Beginning teachers also must write case studies as part of induction programs in order to better understand their students.

Credential Writing

Credential students and practicing teachers will need to articulate their competency in teaching. The writing required in credential programs is often more formal and higher-stakes, as you write to obtain a teaching position and demonstrate continued professional growth.

Most major universities have teacher credential programs either included with the bachelor of arts (BA) degree or a post-BA program. These programs can include a combined BA and teaching credential program; a stand-alone, multiple-subject (elementary) or single-subject (secondary) credential program; or a combined teaching credential and master of arts (MA) program. Some writing instruction in these credential courses is driven by certification tools, such as Pearson's edTPA, developed by Stanford University faculty for preservice teachers to "demonstrate readiness to teach through lesson plans designed to support their students' strengths and needs; engage real students in ambitious learning; analyze whether their students are learning, and adjust their instruction to become more effective" (edTPA, 2018). Credential programs that use the edTPA, or a similar assessment tool, require preservice teachers to submit a portfolio of materials attesting to the aforementioned skills once they've completed their student teaching and before they receive a credential certifying them to teach in K–12 public schools.

Lesson Plans. Lesson plans are written in complex rhetorical situations: classroom assignments, professional assessments, and career advancement. Due to this complexity, you will need to carefully examine the teaching environment for which you'll design your lesson plan. Implementing your own content knowledge will allow you to design a lesson plan that will meet relevant standards and the needs of your students. When you design your lesson plan with a clear sense of what you want your students to produce or accomplish, they will be better able to successfully meet these goals. Chapter 6 will lead you through the process of writing each of these elements of your lesson plan.

Teaching Philosophies. K–12 educators need to articulate their theoretical or philosophical approach to teaching, often as an assignment in a credential program or in preparation for entering the job market. The context of a teaching philosophy, therefore, is often a high-stakes environment. You will need to name your core beliefs in education, which should be grounded in specific theoretical influences and research-based practices. You also should be able to articulate how your core beliefs influence your understanding of school communities so that your audience understands what kind of colleague you will be. Articulating both your theoretical and practical understanding of the profession will allow you to present yourself as a reflective and well-informed preservice teacher.

Critical Reflections. In order to become a practicing teacher, you must demonstrate your teaching effectiveness to an assessment body, such as the edTPA. In most cases, this assessment demands that you design and implement lesson plans (as discussed in Chapter 6) that represent your teaching philosophies (as discussed in Chapter 7) and offer commentary on the outcomes of these lessons. Chapter 8 discusses how to write critical reflections, or meta-analyses, of your teaching practices, with the ultimate goal of improving these practices in order to enhance student learning. The chapter also discusses the importance of developing mastery in this genre, as you may write critical reflections throughout your teaching career when participating in regular annual reviews.

Stakeholder Writing

Stakeholder writing uses extensive scholarly research to target decisionmakers in an effort to facilitate policy/program change. Writing in education often requires writing to various stakeholders in federal and state government, school and district administrators, community organizations, and parents or colleagues. While the writing tasks for these audiences vary, all require you to understand the bridge between research and practice, student learning, national trends, and how these connections work toward the public good. Chapter 9 demystifies how to propose program or policy changes based on research and experience, by explaining key rhetorical choices you can make to reach your intended audience.

Proposals. Professors of some advanced undergraduate or graduate courses require their students to write a proposal for a course, policy, or program change. The proposal genre allows for an in-depth and focused approach to researching a problem and articulating a solution. Within this genre, you can respond to current education policy, apply critical thinking, formulate a nuanced opinion supported by research, and advance a plan for improvement to a stakeholder audience.

CONCLUSION

This chapter has provided valuable background information on the rhetorical situation, information that will help you when you face a writing task in the field of education. Remember that genres are fluid and that you should evaluate purpose, audience, context, and voice every time you write. This chapter also has introduced you to the critical role of reflective writing within the field of education.

Before we discuss our first genre, a reading response, we want to acquaint you with some of the key stylistic concerns you should be aware of as you write in education. Chapter 2, then, explains these stylistic issues and provides examples of how you can make decisions to improve your writing.

Style Issues in Writing in Education

In addition to considering the rhetorical situation of writing tasks you will encounter as educators, as outlined in Chapter 1, you will need to pay attention to many stylistic concerns common to writing in the field of education. Because education is such a large and wide-ranging field, this chapter will outline the characteristics of strong and effective writing that educators need to consider. We believe that the characteristics of effective writing in education are not a matter of choice or preference, but rather a means through which educators represent their pedagogical principles, such as respect for students, through specific and deliberate choices in style.

The stylistic issues we discuss come from the 6th edition of the *Publication Manual of the American Psychological Association* (2009), which sets "sound and rigorous standards for scientific communication" with the purpose of advancing scholarship not only in the field of psychology, but also in education and the social sciences more broadly (p. xiii). *APA Style* is a term we use throughout the guide to refer to stylistic, formatting, and citation conventions that are expected of those who are writing in the field of education.

UNDERSTANDING THE HIERARCHY OF RHETORICAL CONCERNS

If you are anything like the students in our writing in education courses, you may not always feel that you are a strong writer. Many of our students start the course with misconceptions about the writing process, writing instruction, or their abilities as writers. Learning more about the hierarchy of rhetorical concerns can give writers insight into what's really important in effective writing. For preservice teachers, this understanding may allow you to revise your assessment of your writing abilities.

As we discussed in Chapter 1, there are many different rhetorical elements to consider when writing effectively in the field of education, which can feel overwhelming at any stage of the writing process. Understanding the hierarchy of these elements can give you insight into which elements to consider at different points of the process. For example, focusing on using correct grammar or mechanics while drafting your text may prevent you from developing your ideas or organizing the text.

Like a lot of other writing teachers, we categorize these rhetorical concerns into two groups: higher-order concerns and lower-order concerns. Higher-order concerns are focused on the content of your text and include:

- Ideas: argument, claim, or thesis
- The rhetorical situation: audience, purpose, context, voice, and genre
- Evidence
- Organization

Lower-order concerns are focused on the sentence-level issues of your text and usually should be addressed *after* your higher-order concerns. Lower-order concerns include:

- Style
- Grammar: parts of speech, syntax, and sentence structure
- Mechanics: punctuation, capitalization, and spelling

As you can see from these lists, grammar and mechanics, while important, are less so than concerns related to the rhetorical situation we discussed in Chapter 1. For example, in the following statement there are clear errors in grammar and mechanics; however, there are also higher-level rhetorical concerns that are more important.

Lara et al. proposes that the lack accessibility to contraceptives and the socio-demographics of the region cause constant mobility that ultimately gives root for higher chances of teen pregnancy.

While there are errors with the conventions of the sentence, such as a missing preposition and incorrect APA Style citation, the writer needs to focus on clarifying a higher-order concern—the meaning of the sentence. The claim of cause and effect that the author is trying to make is not clear to the reader. A revision addressing the higher-level rhetorical concerns and making the claim more explicit to the audience will improve the sentence.

Lara, Decker, and Brindis (2015) proposed that the lack of accessibility to contraceptives as well as the socio-demographics of the region, which relies on the constant mobility of migrant labor, ultimately facilitated higher rates of teen pregnancy.

Additionally, there is a hierarchy of concerns within conventions, specifically within grammar. That is, some grammatical errors are more important than others. Grammatical errors that interfere with the meaning of a sentence are more important than those that do not. Familiarizing yourself with the hierarchy of grammatical errors will help you develop as a writer. For example, errors in word order, word form, and verb tense may prevent your reader from understanding the message of your sentence. Therefore, if you see these patterns of error in your own writing, you need to address these concerns before less impactful ones. Grammatical errors that usually do not prevent your reader from understanding your message can include: incorrectly using singular or collective nouns, choosing incorrect prepositions and articles, and using incorrect spelling.

Understanding the hierarchy of grammatical errors will help you determine which errors are necessary to revise in your own writing. For example, there are several grammatical errors in the following sentence:

> My fifth grade teacher, Mr. Gray, is one of the reasons that I want
> become a teacher because he was so fun in the classroom, with game
> and trivia every day, that it felt like we not really in school, although
> through all our work, we really did learn lot.

Instead of becoming overwhelmed by a sentence like this, consult the hierarchy of errors and address the more important problems, namely, errors that confuse meaning. Employing this knowledge could facilitate a revision such as:

> Mr. Gray, my fifth-grade teacher, is one of the reasons I want to become
> a teacher. He incorporated so many dynamic activities in his lessons,
> like games and trivia, that the classroom became a positive environment
> where the students worked hard and learned a lot.

Understanding the hierarchy of errors also will allow you to prioritize your style concerns when writing in different rhetorical situations within education. When you think of grammar in a traditional sense, you likely think of the rules governing sentence-level conventions. However, rhetorical grammar refers to knowledge you already have. You employ this rhetorical knowledge when you make grammatical choices depending on your audience and purpose. That is, you are not writing to every audience in the same way (Kolln, 2003). For example, if you are not sure that you understand the main concept of a lecture in an education classes and are looking for clarification, you would ask for help in one way from your professor and in a different way from a friend in the class. You might write a formal email to your professor like this:

Dear Professor Johnson,
    Will you be able to meet with me in office hours on Tuesday from 9–9:30? I want to make sure that I understand the concepts covered in today's lecture and would like to discuss them with you one-on-one.

Thank you in advance,
Mike

However, to your friend, you probably would send an informal text like this:

Ahh!!!!! U get lecture today? What am I missing????? 😰

When writing to your professor, you may consciously think about using correct grammar, but when you text a friend, you may not even consider it. In this situation, you are employing rhetorical grammar to effectively communicate the same message to two different audiences.

An awareness of rhetorical grammar in your writing means that you are thinking strategically about the grammatical choices you make in order to meet a specific purpose for a specific audience within a specific context. Considering rhetorical grammar also may include thinking about the most effective genre in which to communicate your message.

AVOIDING BIAS IN YOUR WRITING

Avoiding Deficit Language

Because you will write about (and teach) a broad range of student groups, some of whom may be stereotyped by biased language and labels, you will need to understand that your language choices sometimes may reflect a view of a student's abilities that implies a cultural or cognitive deficit. For example, you might write about an "at-risk student" without considering the negative implications associated with this term. A more appropriate description would be "a struggling reader," as it moves away from a label to describing the actual person. The basic rule here is to call people what they want to be called. Be aware of your own cultural and implicit biases and respect the preferences of the students you're writing about.

The terms many use to label students may perpetuate either positive or negative stereotypes or biases, but both can have negative unintended consequences. Concerning the use of labels in your writing, the Purdue Online Writing Lab (2018a) suggests that "making adjustments in how you use identifiers and other linguistic categories can improve the clarity of your writing and minimize the likelihood of offending your readers."

For example, in the text of No Child Left Behind (NCLB, 2001), students whose first, or primary, language was not English were described as "English deficient." Today, however, we call students learning English "English learners," "bilingual," or "multilingual" in order to stress the additive aspects of learning and knowing multiple languages. Similarly, "developmental," rather than "basic" or "remedial," should be used to describe students enrolled in a course aimed at preparing them for grade-level work.

Even labels that usually are considered positive can be harmful. The term "gifted," for example, can prevent students from seeking out new opportunities and challenges because they may fail and lose their "gifted" label. In a similar vein, teachers may assume that "gifted" students already know the curriculum and ask them to tutor their fellow students, particularly in group activities. The label also obscures the typically uneven development and variation in all students; some may be better in math than in writing, or excel at writing fiction but struggle with a lab report.

In addition to labels that refer to types of learners, APA Style recommends avoiding bias when writing about students' races and/or ethnicities and students' disabilities (APA, 2009). For a complete list of problematic and preferred labels, please refer to the Purdue Online Writing Lab (2018a).

In general, when using labels to describe students in your writing, you want to highlight their strengths and avoid singling out or overgeneralizing about specific groups of students. There are many labels in the field of education, and knowing when, or whether, to use them can be complicated. If you have a question about using a label in your writing, you can consult the students you are writing about to see whether they prefer a particular label, or you can consult the above Purdue Online Writing Lab article or the APA Style Blog (located at blog.apastyle.org/) for discussions about bias-free language and preferred labels.

Avoiding Sexist Language/Using Inclusive Language (Pronouns)

At times it may be important to refer to the gender of students in your writing. For example, if you conduct an observation or study that looks at how boys respond to a certain educational approach in comparison to girls, you would need to specify gender in the results. But otherwise, you should avoid using gendered terminology. As APA Style points out, you should not use "he," "him," "mankind," or the like to refer to both sexes. Likewise, you should not use the pronouns "she," "s/he," or "he or she" to replace "he" in your writing because the awkward construction can distract your reader. Additionally, using "he" or "she" to refer to the general student should be avoided, since this creates an image in the reader's mind of one gender, which may not clearly communicate your point (APA, 2009).

In order to avoid bias that may result from using gendered pronouns, the Purdue Online Writing Lab (2018a) recommends using plural pronouns, such as "they" or "their," dropping the pronoun altogether and rephrasing the sentence, or replacing pronouns with nongendered nouns like "individual."

For more information on addressing gender in your writing, please refer to "APA Guidelines for Non-Sexist Use of Language" (Warren & APA Committee on the Status of Women in the Profession, 1986). You also can consult the book *How to Be Good with Words* by LePan, Buzzard, and Okun (2017). This book covers pronoun usage and vocabulary to use when discussing gender identity, with a "bias-free vocabulary" list. In general, you should call your students what they want to be called, since language equals respect. A good strategy is to ask your students for preferred pronouns on the first day of class and to use those pronouns. Transgender students, in particular, may have specific pronouns they want you to use, and you should respect their decisions.

Establishing a Respectful Tone

Because educators regularly write for multiple, varied audiences, it is important to establish an effective tone for each audience. An effective tone will allow you to achieve your document's purpose, which in education is primarily to facilitate student learning. When you use a respectful tone in your writing, you demonstrate your admiration for learners and the learning process. Establishing a respectful tone is dependent on both your audience and the context of the document.

When writing, or communicating, to your students, you can establish a respectful tone by speaking directly to the students as critical stakeholders in their education rather than talking over them to their parents or your colleagues. You can enact this process in whichever method is appropriate for your teaching environment, but in most situations you can establish a respectful tone by valuing students' input into their learning processes.

Similarly, when you communicate with the parents of your students, it is important to establish a respectful tone. When you choose your language, make sure that you honor the parents' time, commitments, and areas of expertise. Ultimately, parents are experts in their children, and when you respect this source of knowledge, you facilitate student learning.

When you communicate with colleagues, you can establish a respectful tone by honoring the role of learners and the learning process. For example, when conferring with a colleague about a student's progress, refer to the student by name and not by a label; discuss Soon's and Monica's progress, rather than your "ELL kids." Another way to create a respectful tone with colleagues is to avoid criticism of your teaching environment: your students, the school site, administration, or school district. Similarly, you should be aware of establishing a respectful tone in your personal communications, particularly in public spaces such as social media. Writing critical or disrespectful comments in these contexts could have negative effects in the future.

Another important way to establish a respectful tone in your writing is to honor the confidential nature of student information and to keep personal information about your students completely private. You can do this by being aware of the context in which you discuss students (both in writing and in oral conversation) and refraining from sharing personal information with outside audiences or those not connected to your students.

WRITING CONCISELY AND CLEARLY

Achieving Conciseness:
Eliminating Wordiness and Constructing Lean Sentences

Because students worry about word counts for assignments, they often fluff up their sentences to make them longer. While these long sentences make it easier to meet the word requirement, they can confuse readers. To write effectively in education, you will need to do your best to eliminate wordiness and repetition, and work toward paring down sentences to make them leaner and stronger.

Example of a less concise sentence:
From my point of view, the quick write is usually less stressful and because it isn't stressful, it can get students into a mode of thinking. It is also probably safe to say that having a prompt can jog the brain into thinking and getting into the mode of writing a quick write.

Example of a more concise sentence:
Because quick writes are less stressful to compose and often are accompanied by a prompt, students may feel more encouraged to write them.

As you write and edit, try to eliminate phrases and words that don't contribute to the meaning of your sentences. "From my point of view" isn't needed since the reader knows it is the writer's point of view. Additionally, "because it isn't stressful" merely repeats what was said earlier in the sentence. "It is also probably safe to say" is padding that adds nothing to the meaning of the sentence.

A good strategy for paring down your sentences is to look for ways to combine any sentences that are similar or redundant. For example, above we combined the original two sentences into one and managed to keep all of the meaning intact. Eliminating unnecessary words and condensing information into simpler and more direct sentences helps your readers focus on what you are saying.

Another way to avoid wordiness is not to use the phrases "I think" and "I believe" at the start of your sentences unless absolutely necessary. These phrases slip into sentences as part of the process of working out ideas on paper. But since it's assumed that if you write something you think or believe it, these phrases are redundant.

Examples of less concise sentences:

In order to be an inspirational teacher, **I believe** that I will need to gather many different teaching experiences so that I can have a broader understanding of how to reach each student.

I think the process of becoming a good teacher requires time and reflection after numerous encounters with children.

Examples of more concise sentences:

In order to be an inspirational teacher, I will gather different teaching experiences so that I can have a broader understanding of how to reach each student.

The process of becoming a good teacher requires time and reflection after numerous encounters with children.

ACHIEVING CLARITY: USING SPECIFICS INSTEAD OF GENERALITIES

To make your writing clearer, try to move away from using general examples and information; instead, add specific examples, data, and details to your paragraphs. When you use general examples, it is much harder for your reader to grasp what you are saying. Adding the weight of specific, concrete examples helps readers visualize what you are discussing.

A statement that uses generalities:

My choice of education as a career was not made lightly, rather it was the culmination of a process of reflection about what I wanted to do with my life and my education. I thought a lot about the career of a math teacher and realized I enjoyed helping others and sometimes I would help a classmate understand material so they could finish their homework.

A statement that uses specifics:

My decision to become a math teacher was not made lightly. While in high school, I spent hours every day after school helping reluctant students find answers to their math problems. When their faces lit up after applying the right formula and solving the problem, I knew this was the job for me.

Using Active Verbs and Active Voice

When you use strong, specific verbs, you help your reader visualize what you are talking about. When you use weak, general verbs, your reader has to work harder to understand what you are saying. As a general rule, minimize or avoid using "to be," "to do," "to make," and "to have" verbs in your writing and focus on integrating active verbs. Note, for example, the difference between the following two sentences:

> She made a note on the board.
> She scribbled a note on the board.

You can see how changing the verb helps your reader visualize what you are describing. Choose active verbs that immediately let your reader know who is doing what in your sentences. One strategy for addressing this concern is to highlight your weak verbs and replace them with more active verbs.

Active voice refers to making the subject of your sentence clear from the beginning. Usually active voice is preferred over passive voice in writing in education. An exception would be if you want to focus on the recipient of the action rather than the actor. Both examples are included below.

Example of active voice:
Collins conducted her study in a kindergarten classroom.

Example of passive voice:
The study in a kindergarten classroom was conducted by Collins.

In the first example, the writer focuses on Collins. In the second example, the focus is on the location of the study.

Using Effective Transitions and Avoiding the "Naked This"

When we talk about "flow" in writing, what we really mean is that the writing is cohesive—that each sentence leads logically from the previous sentence, and that new information is linked to old information. As the writer, you may know how your ideas connect, but your reader probably won't unless you make the connections explicit. One way to achieve this goal is to use connecting, or transition, words. You can think of transitions as signposts for your reader—indications of what is to come. See Table 2.1 for different types of transitions and when/how to use them.

Another way to achieve cohesion is to avoid the "naked this." The "naked this" is simply the word *this* without a noun after it to show what you're referring to from the previous sentence.

Examples of sentences with a "naked this":
The teacher broke students into groups of three every day. This shows she values groupwork.

Table 2.1. Types of Transitions

Cues that lead the reader forward	Cues that make the reader stop and consider	Cues that tell the reader you are providing examples or summarizing	
Moreover,	But,	For example,	In other words,
Next,	Yet,	For instance,	Because
In addition,	However,	To demonstrate,	Therefore,
Finally,	Although	In fact,	Consequently,
Furthermore,	Meanwhile,	Indeed,	As a result,
Last,	Conversely,	In brief,	In conclusion,
Again,	On the other hand,		
	In contrast,		
	At the same time,		
	Nevertheless,		

This can be done in many ways, such as using Ayers's idea of journaling as a way to help bridge the distance between the subject matter and the students.

Examples of sentences without a "naked this":
The teacher broke students into groups of three every day. **This grouping of students** shows she values collaborative work.

Getting students to identify with the material they're reading can be done in many ways, such as using Ayers's idea of journaling as a way to help bridge the distance between the subject matter and the students.

Avoiding Poetic Language

In your past English classes, you likely read, analyzed, and/or produced creative writing that used figurative language such as metaphors, symbolism, connotation, or repetition. These strategies may not always be appropriate for writing in education. As the Purdue Online Writing Lab (2018b) notes, writers in the social sciences should avoid this kind of literary style, as "such linguistic devices can detract from conveying your information clearly and may come across to readers as forced when it is inappropriately used to explain an issue or your findings." Rather than incorporating literary devices to make your writing more passionate, APA Style prefers pared-down, straightforward, concise sentences.

For example, in a response to a theoretical reading on the inherent complexities of being a teacher, a student wrote:

The author shines light on the many hats an educator wears and why these are important for parents or higher ups in the education system to understand.

In this summary of the author's argument, the student used the literary device "shines light," when a more direct verb, such as "argues that" or "explains that," would have communicated the author's intention more clearly. Additionally, instead of using the symbolic "the many hats an educator wears," the student could have written, "an educator's complex and varied duties or expectations." Overall, education students should avoid using figurative language in their writing and instead use simple and plain language that doesn't risk confusing their readers.

Using Targeted Language/Word Choice

Another way to increase clarity in your writing is to choose your words and/or terms carefully. Within the field of education, commonly used words can take on different meanings depending on how those in the discourse community understand and think about them. Because the words you use to convey your point can have a significant impact on your readers, you should make strategic and precise choices about your words.

An example of imprecise word choice:

For those who may be struggling, I will give the material in such a manner that relates to their experiences.

Here, the reader doesn't know who is struggling and with what. The reader also doesn't know what material will be provided and how it will be provided.

An example of improved, precise word choice:

For those students who are struggling readers, I will provide one-on-one assistance to reinforce their understanding of the lesson concepts.

In this revised version, readers understand that the author is talking about students who are struggling readers. Readers also understand the specific way in which the author will provide help for these students.

One simple way to be sure you include careful word choice in your writing is to eliminate ambiguous pronouns. Doing so will help your readers better understand who and what you are talking about and increase flow between sentences in a paragraph.

An example of sentences including ambiguous pronouns:

American Civil Liberties Union of Northern California (2003) introduces the fact that California only requires HIV/AIDS prevention education and does not require sex education. **It** is an option to teach sex education, also known as family life education. **They** also reveal that many schools use outdated materials and **they** do not actually have a set curriculum for sex education. **It** is self-designed and reflects site-specific priorities.

As you can see, the ambiguous pronouns, which are bolded, make it difficult to follow the meaning of these sentences. Readers are not entirely sure to whom/what the ambiguous pronouns refer. Eliminating these pronouns helps increase the readability of the sentences.

An example of sentences without ambiguous pronouns:
American Civil Liberties Union of Northern California (2003) introduces the fact that California requires only HIV/AIDS prevention education and does not require sex education. **California schools** have the option to teach sex education, also known as family life education. American Civil Liberties Union of Northern California (2003) also reveals that many schools use outdated materials and **they** do not actually have a set curriculum for sex education. **The curriculum** is self-designed and reflects site-specific priorities.

Adding specific words to replace the ambiguous pronouns helps readers understand what the author is saying.

One last way you can revise your sentences to include more specific word choice is to be sure you are choosing "that" or "who" correctly when you are referring to a thing or person previously mentioned in the sentence. If you are talking about people, you should use "who." If you are talking about nonhuman things, you should use "that." This is particularly important when referring to students, who are people and not objects.

An example of incorrect usage of "that" and "who":
Overall, districts **who** successfully changed their start times indicate that delayed start times are effective in promoting students' physical and mental well-being.

An example of correct usage of "that" and "who":
Overall, districts **that** successfully changed their start times indicate that delayed start times are effective in promoting students' physical and mental well-being.

Explaining Acronyms

As you may have already noticed, the field of education is filled with acronyms (abbreviations created from the first letter of a series of words, such as CCSS for Common Core State Standards); therefore, one way to improve the clarity of your documents is to make sure that any acronyms you use are clearly defined. Because the field of education is so vast, acronyms that may seem commonplace to you could be completely unknown to colleagues in other areas. The first time you introduce a term that has an acronym, include the acronym directly after the term, such as "Individuals with Disabilities Education Act (IDEA)." Then, for the rest of the document, use the acronym to refer to the phrase.

Consult your state's department of education website for a list of acronyms commonly used in your state. For example, the California Department of Education's (2018) webpage "Acronyms and Initialisms" includes a list of hundreds of acronyms used by the department.

Using the First Person

Writers use a first-person point of view when they refer to a singular "I" or collective "we" in their texts. No doubt, in many of your classes you've been told to avoid using the first person in your writing. Professors recommend avoiding the first-person point of view for two primary reasons: (1) the first person can state the obvious, and (2) the first person can bolster unsupported evidence. In most of your classes, your written arguments should be supported by scholarly research rather than your thoughts or opinions. In the field of education, however, research often begins with a personal observation. A student, teacher, or researcher notices a trend or phenomenon informally, and then designs a research study to collect more data. In these cases, authors may use the first-person point of view in their writing to provide context for their research.

Example of appropriate use of first-person point of view:
In my observations of the third-grade classroom, I noticed that the male students raised their hands to answer questions more than the female students. This observation led me to research the motivation of children in primary school to raise their hands.

It is also important to note the limitations of using the first person in your writing within the field of education. The first-person point of view provides evidence for a singular argument: your own. You cannot make sweeping claims about education based on this single source of evidence.

Example of inappropriate use of first person:
In the state of Tennessee, male students in the third grade raise their hands more than their female counterparts.

Ultimately, the context of your writing will determine whether it is appropriate to use the first-person point of view. Ask your professors for their preferences regarding the use of first person. Also, there are several genres in education, for example, a teaching philosophy or a critical reflection, that are entirely dependent on the first-person point of view.

EXERCISES

1. Work to get rid of deficit and biased language by revising the following problematic terms into preferred terms. Remember to consider the negative, unintended consequences of using biased language and consult the Purdue Online Writing Lab's "Avoiding Bias" Guidelines if you are unsure about the words you are choosing.

Problematic	Preferred
mentally ill	
crippled	
elderly	
at risk	
minority	
mankind	
the gays	
typical female	
mothering	
articulate Mexican professor	
Orientals	
Hispanic	

2. Revise the following sentences for clarity and conciseness. Remember to consider the following: eliminating wordiness, using specifics instead of generalities, using active voice and active verbs, increasing flow by using transition words, avoiding poetic language, and using targeted word choice.

   - I am not assuming this means that I will be the greatest teacher they ever had, because not only are favorite teachers not always good teachers, but I also do not expect every child to value teachers the same way that they may in retrospect later on in their lives.
   - By communicating this to our supervisor we were able to understand that the child did not have a stable living situation, therefore was having difficulties in school
   - Education in a child's life builds the foundation of how the child will live in the next few years of his or her life. Having the opportunity to educate these children gives a person the responsibility of becoming a core role model in a student's life.

CHAPTER 3

Writing a Reading Response

The reading response is an important precursor to the higher-level reflective writing you will do later in your career as a credential and/or graduate student and practicing teacher. The typical reading response assignments you will encounter as an undergraduate ask you to summarize and think critically about course readings and, in the process, articulate how the ideas in the readings are shaping the kind of educator you want to be. Professors expect you to make sense of the course material by applying your personal experience as a student, a classroom observer, and a future teacher.

EXAMINING THE RHETORICAL SITUATION:
PURPOSE, AUDIENCE, CONTEXT, VOICE, AND GENRE

Most undergraduate education classes require students to summarize and reflect on a required reading at some point in the course. This type of writing is primarily a writing-to-learn exercise, meaning that as students write about course readings and contextualize them within the field of education, they develop a deeper understanding of course concepts. Reading responses provide what Creme (2008) refers to as "safe learning space[s]" where students are encouraged to "forge new relationships with different ways of knowing" and "re-make course ideas, and re-make themselves" (p. 62).

Reading responses also allow professors to assess the degree to which students understand the educational concepts being covered in the class and are thinking about how these concepts are affecting their idea of what kind of educator they want to be. As Bean (2011) points out, writing-to-learn exercises are effective because they provide professors with "valuable insights into [students'] thinking processes and provide clues about how to redesign and sequence instruction" (p. 81). If the writing reveals that the students have a gap in understanding, professors can use that knowledge to guide their teaching. Usually, reading responses are lower-stakes assignments, meaning that they aren't graded too stringently or don't count for too much of the course grade. The focus of a reading response is more on providing students with comments, suggestions, or questions to further engage their thinking.

PREPARING TO WRITE A READING RESPONSE: ENGAGING YOUR ACTIVE READING SKILLS

The National Writing Project—a professional development network of "teachers teaching teachers" committed to improving the teaching of writing in U.S. schools—educates teachers on best practices in writing pedagogy and makes clear the importance of good writing skills (National Writing Project & Nagin, 2006). Reflective writing, the teacher network stresses, asks students to "transform the information from the reading material" into articulate statements that reveal deep thinking (p. 47). Because reading responses require you to first apply active reading skills to the research articles you've been assigned and then relate the research to your development as an educator, we include a chart of active reading strategies to help guide you through the reading process (see Figure 3.1).

The first step in writing a reading response is to use an active reading process when reading the article you'll be responding to. Active readers pay attention to the text, as they know they will have to respond to the content later in their own writing. In contrast, a passive reader simply absorbs content without thinking about it. You may be a passive reader when you're consuming entertainment or sports magazines, because you are reading simply to enjoy the content, not because you'll need to write meaningfully about it later. Being an active reader is an important skill to develop and sustain throughout your career as an educator, especially as you come across new research, respond to student work, and engage in your school community.

At its most basic level, active reading means that you are reading with pen in hand, taking notes in the margins, circling words/concepts you don't know,

---

Figure 3.1. Active Reading Strategies

Active readers look for answers to the following questions:

- Why was this text written (purpose) and whom was it written for (audience)?
- In what context, or in what circumstances, was it written?
- What is the intended message or goal of the piece?
- What overall question is the author trying to answer/address?
- What overarching social/historical/political concepts are critical to understanding this author's paper?
- What is the author's argument?
- Does this piece remind me of anything else I've read or seen?
- What research or information is the author using as support for the stated argument? How valid are these data?
- What other points of view does the author shed light on?
- What assumptions does this author make?
- What conclusions does the author draw?
- What are the implications of this author's findings/argument?

---

and underlining key points. If you are reading a digital version of a text, then you should actively highlight and annotate the document using your computer's annotation functions. Use any system of annotation that forces you to engage with and think about what you're reading while you're reading. At this point in your career as a student, you've likely devised such a system and need only to remember to put it into practice.

The physical and mental act of active reading enables you to delve into an assigned article or book and identify questions you need to ask in order to understand the material presented in the reading. If you don't have a solid understanding of the reading, writing a cogent and well-articulated reading response becomes much more difficult. Reading actively helps you develop a critical approach to teaching when you discuss education theories in your class, with peers, and with professionals. This is important because, as Giroux (1985) points out, "reflective practitioners" are able to think critically and raise questions about their pedagogical choices (p. 38). See Figure 3.2 for an example of effective annotation of part of the case study, "An Inspired Model . . . or a Misguided One? Oprah Winfrey's Dream School for Impoverished South African Girls" (Applegarth et al., 2010). Later in this chapter we will discuss a student response to this reading (see Figure 3.4). Please keep in mind that this is just one example of how you can annotate. We underlined important concepts and used the margins to raise questions, note personal reactions, and make connections to course readings.

WRITING A READING RESPONSE: SUMMARIZING THE READING

The second step in writing a reading response is narrowing down the key points of the source text. Once you have identified these points, you'll need to summarize them accurately, effectively, and briefly for your reader, to lay the groundwork for your response. You can either do this at the outset of a paragraph, or integrate pieces of the summary throughout your response. (We will walk you through you an example of the latter method in Figure 3.4 since it is usually more difficult.) Graff, Birkenstein, and Durst (2014) posit that summarizing is a necessary rhetorical move when you are attempting to join an academic or professional discourse community. Knowing what others in your field are saying about your topic is critical to being able to argue persuasively in their presence. While most reading response assignments call for some amount of summarizing, determining how and when to summarize can be a difficult skill to master. You may have a hard time deciding what information is important or how much of the information you should summarize. You may struggle with making it clear that you are summarizing, and that the opinion expressed is not your own. You may have a hard time transitioning from summary to response. Table 3.1 provides some basic dos and don'ts for summarizing in your reading response.

Figure 3.2. Example of an Effectively Annotated Reading

Selecting Winfrey's 'Daughters'

Winfrey knew that selecting which girls would come to OWLA—and which would be turned away—would be difficult. In its first year, the school was looking for a charter group of 150 girls. There were three main criteria for entry. One, the applicant must be economically disadvantaged—but in a country where 57 percent of the population lived below the poverty line, many girls would meet this qualification.[30] Two, the applicant must show academic potential and three, she must show leadership potential. "I want somebody who already knows that education is empowerment, and who wouldn't have had the chance to fulfill the great possibilities of her life had this not happened. I want to change the trajectory of a child's life," Winfrey has explained.[31]

[handwritten margin notes: "Orah assumes these are the most important qualities to look for." — "good point" — "Interesting! But wouldn't this leave many girls out?"]

In 2006, OWLA sent out 5,500 applications to poor areas in each of South Africa's nine provinces, asking different tribes and communities to nominate girls with exceptional leadership potential. Some 3500 girls applied. Each applicant was asked to write an essay about her dreams for the future and to draw her dream house. Of these, 484 finalists were chosen for interviews and academic testing.

[handwritten margin notes: "wow!" — "I wonder how they decided on this & assessment criteria"]

All finalists spent a weekend at St. John's College in Johannesburg, where they underwent a series of evaluative exercises. The girls took academic tests and, under observation, participated in group problem-solving activities. Every girl was interviewed by the OWLA team and had a surprise final interview with Winfrey. Winfrey told the girls—some stunned to tears—that she would make sure that each graduate of the academy was able to go to the college of her choice, anywhere in the world.

[handwritten margin notes: "Big promise! Assumes they'll be accepted to any college."]

Winfrey would later say that, for herself, this was the most difficult—and the most rewarding—part of the process. The shock of the girls, upon seeing Winfrey in person, was well-documented. According to an account in *Newsweek*, one girl doubted her own eyes. Some of the girls blurted out their observations and questions. "You're so skinny in person!" exclaimed one. "Do you spend $500 to get your eyebrows done?" inquired another. But there were emotional moments, as well. One girl, who had lost her mother to AIDS the day before the interview, was shivering so badly that Winfrey had to find her a blanket. Two sisters had, at a young age, seen their father shoot their mother and then himself. Many of the stories were painful, Winfrey says, and she eventually stopped asking about the girls' backgrounds.[32]

[handwritten margin notes: "Is OWLA still operating?" — "how could this decision impact the selection process"]

[handwritten note above: "final #"]

When the final selection was made, Winfrey invited these 152 girls back, telling them that they were being called for "an important final interview." When they had arrived, she said to them: "I brought you all here today to tell you that you will be a part of the very first class of the Oprah Winfrey Leadership

[handwritten margin notes: "So few girls accepted—but they could be a benefit to a larger community... —Laborge & social mobility concept"]

[30] In 2006, OWLA set the annual household income limit at 65,000 Rand, or approximately $8700.
[31] "Building a Dream," *O, The Oprah Magazine*, Jan. 1, 2006. http://www.oprah.com/entertainment/Building-a-Dream, retrieved Feb. 8, 2010.
[32] "Oprah Goes to School," by Allison Samuels, *Newsweek*, Jan. 8, 2007.

HKS Case Program   7 of 11   Case Number 1930.0

Source: 1930.0, "An Inspired Model...or a Misguided One? Oprah Winfrey's Dream School for Impoverished South African Girls," by Stephen Paterson et al. Harvard Kennedy School Case Program.

Perhaps the most important thing to keep in mind when you are summarizing is that you can't and shouldn't summarize *everything* from the source text. You need to strategically choose one or two major points of the author's argument that you'd like to focus on, since your professor is likely looking more for your response than for a summary. It is also important to remember that what you decide to include in a summary often reflects what you think about teaching or yourself as an educator. As Graff et al. (2014) point out, "a good summary requires balancing what the original author is saying with the

Table 3.1. Dos and Don'ts for Summarizing Source Material

Do	Don't
Accurately represent the author's viewpoint	Skew the author's viewpoint to match your own
Use your own words	Copy or plagiarize words/phrases/sentences from the source text and present them as your own
Use specific signal verbs (e.g., "X argues" or "X concedes") to smoothly lead into what the author says	Leave out signal verbs or overuse vague, overly general signal verbs (e.g., "X says" or "X states")
Focus on one or two of the reading's major points	Focus on minor points the author makes or too many of the author's points
Focus on points that will help you make your argument	Focus on points irrelevant to your argument; provide a list summary
Give an objective account of the author's stance	Present a biased account of the author's stance
Embed voice markers to let your readers know you are summarizing someone else's views	Confuse your readers as to which ideas are yours and which are from your source

writer's own focus" (p. 31). In other words, what you summarize should lead smoothly into your response, so emphasize those points that will best help you set up your argument.

Figure 3.3 provides an example of a reading response assignment designed by Dr. Kevin Gee, an associate professor in the School of Education at University of California, Davis. The assignment for his Edu 120 class, Philosophical and Social Foundations of Education, asks undergraduate students to read and respond to some case studies about innovative or controversial approaches or happenings in education. As you can see from the "General Guidance" section, Gee wants students to move beyond summary toward offering critical commentary on the approaches to or effects of education reform. While some students choose to write an entire paragraph of summary, others integrate sentences of summary with their analysis, as you'll see in Figure 3.4.

WRITING A READING RESPONSE: FORMULATING YOUR RESPONSE

Once you have a solid understanding of the source reading, including which major point(s) you'd like to address, as well as the theories you've been covering in class, you're well on your way to formulating your reading response. Like Dr. Gee, many other education professors will expect you to do one or more of the following in a reading response assignment: (1) agree or disagree with the author's argument; (2) evaluate the success or merit of a program or policy; or (3) analyze how an educational theory complicates or supports a particular approach to education. As shown in Figure 3.3, Dr. Gee wants his

(text continues on p. 39)

Figure 3.3. Reading Response Assignment for Edu 120/UC Davis/Prof. Kevin Gee

Case/Reading Response Prompts, Due Dates & Grading Criteria

Case/Reading	Response Prompt	Due Date
An Inspired Model… or a Misguided One? Oprah Winfrey's Dream School for Impoverished South African Girls	Are you are in support of or in opposition to Oprah's decision to open her Dream Academy for Girls? Explain.	Due Wednesday 4/6 by midnight via SmartSite
The Cleveland School Voucher Program: A Question of Choice (A & B)	Do you think the Cleveland School Voucher Program was successful? Explain.	Due Wednesday 4/13 by midnight via SmartSite
Michelle Rhee's IMPACT on the Washington D.C. Public Schools	How might Noguera have critiqued Rhee's approach to reforming the DCPS? Explain.	Due Wednesday 5/4 by midnight via SmartSite
Atlanta Schools: Measures to Improve Performance	What alternative strategies could have been implemented to avoid an "Atlanta cheating scandal"? Explain.	Due Wednesday 5/18 by midnight via SmartSite
Pratham—Every Child in School and Learning Well	Should Pratham continue to operate? Explain.	Due Wednesday 5/25 by midnight via SmartSite

General Guidance

- Your argument should move beyond points made in the case. Do not summarize the case.
- Also, think about how (and whether) to integrate concepts from the course so far to support your point of view.
- Most importantly, you should display critical thinking.
- Strive to be clear and concise.

Evaluation Criteria

- We will grade each of your responses on a scale from 0 to 3.
- How will we evaluate your responses?
  - » A "3" response provides a clear point of view and, where appropriate, **uses concepts & rationales from the course to defend your point of view.** Your response is clearly written and <u>moves beyond mere summary</u> of ideas in the case and you use logical, original and creative thinking to argue a point of view.
  - » A "2" response does take a critical stance on the case prompt; however, your ideas could be better developed (i.e., your point of view is not as clear or evident as it could be), involve less summary of case content and more thoroughly incorporate concepts from the course. Your writing and expression of ideas could be further developed.
  - » A "1" response presents only a summary of ideas in the case and lacks any clear connection to course concepts. Your response shows deficiencies in writing and/or logic.
  - » A "0" response lacks any point of view and relies on summary only; and/or your response is incomplete, incoherent and off topic.

Figure 3.4. Sample of a Successful Student Reading Response (written by Veronica and annotated by the authors)

Veronica Ruiz Quinonez

Case Response One

Despite criticisms of its high cost, I support Oprah's decision to establish the Leadership Academy for Girls because in addition to helping break subordinate groups' chain of oppression, I believe that its lavish nature is what will act as a means of creating enthused world changers. Although only a small number of students are enrolled in this school, the deep investment that is made in each one of these students is an avenue by which the entire community will be positively influenced. Oprah's decision to establish this academy plays an important role in taking a step towards breaking the cycle that keeps black girls and their communities oppressed.

> In her very first sentence, Veronica clarifies that she understands one of the main criticisms discussed in the case study—the high cost of the school—but states that despite this, she supports Oprah's school.

Oprah's large investment in the few girls that are accepted into her academy serves to produce both a private and public good, meaning that benefits accrue to the individual and the community (Labaree, 1997). When these girls first enter their new school, its extravagance is probably a great shock. Coming from impoverished backgrounds, these girls are likely to have their minds opened at the sight of their dreams becoming a reality. I believe that the 40 million dollars Oprah spent on this academy were not futile. The school's prestige and stature allow girls to visually recognize that living a life outside of poverty is within reach. As a result of getting the opportunity to attend this high-end academy, I imagine that these girls would develop a new sense of self-worth and self-efficacy. In combination with their humble beginnings, this would most definitely lead these students to be motivated to create change in their community. Experiencing the academy's lavishness would cause students to see how different life could be, thus inspiring them to find ways for others to experience the same. This large positive movement would not likely take place if Oprah had allocated her financial resources more conservatively. For instance, if Oprah simply used her money to supplement existing schools, it

> Again, Veronica shows she understands another of the major criticisms presented in the reading—that only a few girls can attend the school—but adds something new to the side of the argument that supports Oprah, by saying that it is exactly the high cost and "deep investment" in the girls that will make the school successful. Furthermore, she roots her position in a course concept that she explains in more detail later—the idea that by deeply investing in a small number of girls, the whole community will be "positively influenced."

> Throughout this part, Veronica stays focused on responding to the issue of the high cost of the school. She bases her response on a course concept (Labaree, 1997) and argues that high investment will help the girls develop the skills and attitudes needed to be change-makers in their communities. In this way, she is agreeing with one of the viewpoints in the case study but adding something new to the discussion.

> Here, Veronica addresses the counterpoint raised in the case study. She demonstrates that she understood this point of view but disagrees with it because investing in the existing schools wouldn't produce the change-makers that Oprah's school will.

would slightly raise students' quality of education, but it may not produce radically motivated students who are determined to create further changes in their community. For this reason, the public and private goods provided by Oprah's academy make her large financial investment worthwhile.

The social issues and oppression that cyclically plague certain populations are often a result of poor education. Overcoming such oppression is difficult because of how people in subordinate groups often lack the resources necessary to break its cycle. For this reason, initiatives like Oprah's Leadership Academy for Girls, are important starting points for overcoming the barriers that keep certain populations in subordinate positions. Although only a small percentage of disadvantaged individuals are able to become students in Oprah's school, I believe that her initiative is valuable because it aids a population that would otherwise be left to fester in its subordinate state. The social mobility goal of education, or the aspiration to achieve a higher standing in society through educational attainment (Labaree, 1997), appears to be the dominant goal that has influenced Oprah's school. Although some may disagree with the idea of a school that primarily focuses on this one goal, I believe that in certain contexts concentrating on social mobility is necessary and beneficial. For instance, the social mobility goal that drives Oprah's Leadership Academy helps to break the cycle of poverty that plagues its students, their families, and even surrounding community members. The fact that one person's ability to climb out of poverty can have a positive influence on others makes Oprah's school invaluable.

> Summarizes a primary concept from the case study.

> Veronica reiterates her point, again drawing on Labaree (1997) and some of the concepts he discusses, i.e., social mobility.

Overall, I see Oprah's school as a very constructive initiative. Although its primary focus is on the social mobility goal, as described by Labaree, I believe that the outcomes of this initiative will also provide benefits to society at large. This academy is obviously not the solution to all of South Africa's social and educational problems, but it serves to create positive change in the community. Because of this, I highly support Oprah's decision to establish this school.

> Veronica's response is a good example of reflective writing in that she not only says she supports Oprah's school but also reflects more broadly on teaching and learning conditions. She supports programs that attempt to make positive change in areas of low socioeconomic status.

students to support their position with evidence from course readings as well as their own personal and professional experience in education.

After completing your assigned reading, you might be wondering how you are supposed to come up with original thoughts on these educational issues and create a well-supported argument in a short response paper. As Graff et al. (2014) stress, moving to the "I say" stage after having passed the "they say" stage of summary writing can be frightening in academia because you may feel like a novice trying to join the conversation of experts in the field (p. 53). But you are just reflecting on the ideas raised by the readings and thinking about how they support or complicate what you have been discussing in class. You also will want to think about how the ideas affect your understanding of education, teaching, learning, and yourself as a future educator. In her article on writing in the social sciences, Ackerman (2014) notes that social scientists study people, and because people are complicated, "any study of human behavior is at best partial, taking into account some elements of what people do and why, but not always explaining those actions definitively" (p. 187). Because the field of education is grounded in an interest in people and how they learn, you may hold many opinions on the topics you encounter and may witness lively conversations about these topics. But, as Ackerman (2014) stresses, an opinion isn't enough for writing in the social sciences; you must test what you think against the breadth of data in the education research you encounter in your coursework.

Graff et al. (2014) discuss three possible strategies for responding to a text and entering the academic conversation: agree, disagree, or a combination of the two. These strategies are useful if you are being asked to agree or disagree with an author's argument.

If you find that you agree with an author's argument, or with an approach to education reform, for example, it's important to remember that you can't simply *just agree*. Doing so doesn't demonstrate critical thinking or original thought on the topic. If you agree, you also must add something to the conversation (Graff et al., 2014). In other words, you must explain why the research or argument matters to you as an aspiring educator, to students, or to the field of education. How does the research make you feel about education or your future role as a teacher? Why does or should it matter? How do the research and your own personal experience support the author's point? To provide this explanation, you might employ any of these strategies:

Rhetorical moves for agreeing:
- Contribute to the author's argument by explaining recent studies that support it that the author doesn't mention
- Point out why agreeing with the author is important in light of today's educational environment
- Point out that the author's argument is largely correct, but could be extended in some way

- Explain that we know a lot about what the author is discussing, but almost nothing about some other, closely related topic
- Offer new reasons to support this interpretation

Whichever angle you choose, when you are agreeing, just remember that you are analyzing the data, weighing the contents against your own experience, and adding to the conversation in some way.

On the other hand, you may disagree with the author. While disagreeing may seem like the easiest way to generate content, it does have hidden challenges in that you must explain *why* you disagree and ground that reason in compelling evidence from course readings or personal or professional experience (Graff et al., 2014). When you are formulating your argument, you may find it helpful to look back at the active reading strategies listed in Figure 3.1 to help you identify some points of disagreement that you may have with an author/text. Or you may find it useful to consider some of these strategies:

Rhetorical moves for disagreeing:
- Point out that the author's argument relies on faulty logic or an incomplete or biased reading of the research
- Identify problematic assumptions the author makes
- Explain how the author does not consider alternative points of view
- Argue that the conclusions the author draws could be different
- Consider how new research complicates the author's argument
- Point out that the author contradicts themself
- Stress that the evidence the author cites actually supports a different (your) viewpoint

As Ackerman (2014) reminds us, given the complexity of the topics covered in the social sciences, you may find yourself wanting to agree and disagree with different components of an author's argument/study. This approach usually results in a more nuanced, and potentially more interesting, response to the text, but it also can be trickier to manage successfully. You'll want to think about what you agree with the author on and where your thinking diverges and why. In order to articulate this in writing, consider how the beliefs or values you hold in regard to education conflict with or complicate those that the author espouses. Some questions to consider are given below.

Considerations for simultaneously agreeing and disagreeing in a response:
- How has your personal experience as a student or teacher caused you to think differently about the topic at hand?
- How does information from the reading make you think differently about a policy, approach, or condition of teaching/learning?

- What aspects of education are important to you?
- What kind of teacher will you be?
- What kind of learning environment do you want to establish in your classroom?
- What kinds of topics/concerns will you advocate for an educator?
- What are you able to accept about the author's argument and where does your thinking diverge and why?
- Does the author's work seem incomplete?
- Is the author's conclusion problematic?
- Is there still more research that needs to be conducted on the topic?
- Is the author's evidence problematic or incomplete?

Answering the questions above also will help you think critically about the kind of educator you want to be, which is an important precursor to the kinds of reflective writing you'll do later in your credential career, when you will be asked to articulate the theoretical or philosophical beliefs that inform your teaching practice (see Chapter 7).

Aside from asking whether you agree or disagree with an author's viewpoint, a reading response assignment also may ask you to evaluate the success of a program or a pedagogical model. Alternatively, it could ask you to explain how an educational change could be implemented or how a particular school of thought would respond to an educational reform initiative. In all, a successful reading response demonstrates that you understood the reading and articulates where you stand on the ideas and why.

A SAMPLE READING RESPONSE

In order to get a sense of what a successful reading response looks like, we will walk you through part of a student's writing sample that we have annotated (see Figure 3.4). The student was responding to Dr. Gee's assignment from Figure 3.3. Dr. Gee has his students read a case study that explains where Oprah Winfrey's vision for what became her Leadership Academy for Girls in South Africa came from, as well as the criticism she faced from journalists, educators, grassroots activist groups, and nonprofit directors (Applegarth et al., 2010). The case study also details the support she received from leaders like Nelson Mandela, educators, and nonprofit directors. Overall, the case study presents both sides of the equation: the potential good of the school and the potential bad. The assignment asks students to respond to the following prompt: "Are you in support of or in opposition to Oprah's decision to open her Dream Academy for Girls?" In this example, the student, Veronica, chose to integrate summary throughout her response rather than front-load it with a paragraph or two of summary.

Dr. Gee assessed Veronica's response with the highest possible score of "3" (see Figure 3.3 for rationale). In her response, Veronica summarizes some of the major points made in the case study about the high cost and lavishness of the school, as well as the fact that only a few girls would be chosen. She responds clearly in support of Oprah's school and uses course concepts to bolster her thinking. Throughout the response, she accurately represents what was included in the case study and demonstrates that she has thought critically about the topic. In so doing, she reflects on the value of education for the community and the possible benefits of different education styles/systems.

EXERCISE

Read the following short article and practice your active reading skills by annotating the text with a system that works for you. Then practice your summary and response writing skills by writing a one-page response to the prompt given below.

> **Response Prompt:** Out of Hattie's "5 big ideas," which was the most surprising for you and why? What implication might this finding have on approaches to school reform? Use concepts from your education courses to help you articulate your response.

5 Big Ideas That Don't Work in Education

There are few household names in education research. Maybe that in itself constitutes a problem. But if there was an Education Researcher Hall of Fame, one member would be a silver-haired, plainspoken Kiwi named John Hattie.

Hattie directs the Melbourne Education Research Institute at the University of Melbourne, Australia. He also directs something called the Science of Learning Research Centre, which works with over 7,000 schools worldwide.

Over the past 28 years he has published a dozen books, mostly on a theory he calls Visible Learning. His life's work boils down to one proposition: To improve schools, draw on the best evidence available.

Obvious? Maybe, but it's rarely honored in reality, Hattie claims. "Senior politicians and government officials clearly want to make a difference," he says. "But they want to do this, that and the other silly thing which has failed everywhere else, and I want to know why." In a new paper, "What Doesn't Work in Education: The Politics of Distraction," published by Pearson Education, Hattie takes on some of the most popular approaches to reform.

Small classes. High standards. More money. These popular and oft-prescribed remedies from both the Right and the Left, he argues, haven't been shown to work as well as alternatives.

Hattie doesn't run his own studies. Nor does he analyze groups of studies on a single variable, a technique called meta-analysis. He goes one step further and synthesizes the findings of many meta-analyses, a kind of meta-meta-analysis.

Over the years, he has scrutinized—and ranked—1,200 different meta-analyses looking at all types of interventions, ranging from increased parental involvement to ADHD medications to longer school days to performance pay for teachers, as well as other factors affecting education, like socioeconomic status. He has examined studies covering a combined 250 million students around the world.

The good news, he says, is that most education reforms tested in published studies show at least some positive effect (this should not be surprising, because studies that show no effect or negative effects are less likely to be published).

If you are the kind of person who finds certain graphs sexy, beholding Hattie's ranking of educational effect sizes will be exhilarating.

The average effect, across all the studies he's analyzed, is 0.4 standard deviations. This average also happens to translate—roughly—to the amount of progress a student can be expected to make in one year of school. Hattie believes that all educational reforms should concentrate on interventions with proven effects that fall above that line.

In his ranking, socioeconomic status has an effect size of 0.57, meaning that a student growing up in poverty may be expected to perform roughly a year and a half behind an otherwise similar student growing up more wealthy.

Putting televisions in the classroom, on the other hand, has an average negative impact of –0.18. Holding students back a grade really does hold students back, with an effect of –0.16.

"The problem is there are a lot of effects that are very small," he says, while others are huge. And yet, he says, "We never have a debate of relativity—why are we spending billions on things that have small effects?"

Technical Challenges

Hattie's grand unified theory is simple—maybe too simple. Critics have taken issue with his approach to research, the precision of some of his calculations, even his grasp of concepts as basic as probability.

"Meta-analysis is relatively new in education, and . . . particularly problematic," says Dylan Wiliam, professor emeritus of educational assessment at the Institute of Education, University of London, and an expert on assessment.

He argues, for example, that averaging together studies done on students of different ages, in different settings, with different kinds of interventions and different measures of outcomes, may produce entirely misleading results.

There's a danger, Wiliam says, of mushing good studies together with bad ones, or comparing apples and oranges.

"In education, meta-analysis presents a number of significant technical difficulties," he explains. "Some of these are unavoidable but Hattie does not mention these."

Others, Wiliam adds, "are avoidable, but Hattie does not avoid them."

"The synthesis approach is not an established method," agrees John O'Neill, director of the Institute of Education at Massey University in New Zealand. O'Neill is a coauthor of a 2009 paper critical of Hattie's work, titled "Invisible Learnings?"

At the same time, he acknowledges, Hattie's work "has had a profound effect on education policy and practice globally."

Many of Hattie's basic observations have been upheld by other researchers. And he and his organization continue to advise and influence governments and school leaders all over the world.

Here are five of the most common policy ideas that, he argues in his new paper, are wrongheaded—and the alternatives Hattie suggests.

1. Achievement standards. "It seems very sensible. You set up minimum standards you want students to reach; you judge schools by how many reach them. But it has a very nasty effect," Hattie tells me. "All those schools who take kids in difficult circumstances are seen as failures, while those who take privileged students and do nothing are seen as successful."

By the same token, it seems to make sense to set achievement standards by grade level, but the further along students get in school, Hattie points out, the more of them are performing either behind or ahead of the schedule that's been set.

The alternative: a focus on growth and progress for each student, no matter where he or she starts.

2. Achievement tests. High-performing schools, and countries, don't necessarily give more standardized tests than low performers. They often give fewer.

The alternative: testing that emphasizes giving teachers immediate, actionable feedback to improve teaching.

3. School choice. Many education reformers tout school choice as a tool for parent empowerment and school improvement through competitive pressure. But Hattie says his research shows that once you account for the economic background of students, private schools offer no significant advantages on average. As for charter schools? "The effect of charter schools, for example, across three meta-analyses based on 246 studies is a minuscule .07," he writes.

The alternative: teacher choice. In the United States, variation *within* schools accounts for 70 percent of the differences in scores on the international PISA exam, while variation *between* schools makes up the rest. Hattie argues that if parents had the right to select the best teacher in a given school, that could truly be empowering. It would also be challenging to implement.

4. Class size. This has been one of Hattie's more controversial claims. In the U.S., groups such as Class Size Matters are dedicated to the proposition that fewer students per teacher is a recipe for success. This, Hattie argues, would come as a surprise to Japan and Korea, two of the highest-performing education systems in the world, with average class sizes of 33. Russia is the outlier in the other direction, a below-average performer with average classes around 18.

The alternative: Hattie says reducing class size *can* have a positive impact. That's if teachers are coached and supported to take advantage of it by actually changing the way they teach—to collaborate, offer personalized feedback and continuously measure their impact for improvement, for example.

5. More money. $40,000 per child, from age 6 through high school graduation. That's the rough threshold for reasonable school performance, according to Hattie: Countries that spend less than $40,000, which are all poor, tend to have much lower reading scores on the international PISA exam, and their performance correlates strongly with the money they spend. But for countries above that threshold, there is almost no relationship between money spent and results earned. For example, Korea and Finland far outscore the U.S. on PISA, while spending $60,000 and $75,000 compared with $105,000.

The alternative: Money's a necessity, but more money is not a panacea, says Hattie. "We spend millions on things that don't matter, and then we get jaundiced."

Hattie's forthcoming book, in September, will present case studies of 15 schools that are implementing some of the ideas that have the strongest evidence behind them. He says many of these boil down to empowering teachers to work collaboratively and continuously improve.

"Around the world there is so much excellence," he says. "Have we got the spine to identify and grow that?"

CHAPTER 4

Writing with Scholarly Sources
Annotated Bibliographies and Research Papers

In Chapter 3 you learned how to write an informal academic genre: a reading response. This chapter focuses on writing two other common academic genres: an annotated bibliography and a research paper on an issue in education. In this chapter, you'll learn how to identify and locate a variety of credible education sources. You'll also learn to summarize, critique, and integrate your sources in order to successfully draft an "issue in education" research paper.

EXAMINING THE RHETORICAL SITUATION: PURPOSE, AUDIENCE, CONTEXT, VOICE, AND GENRE

The rhetorical situations for an annotated bibliography and a research paper on an educational topic are typically academic. You'll write a research paper in the context of an education class, so the audience will be your instructor and possibly your classmates. The assignment usually will require you to conduct library and Internet research on a specific issue in education and use a combination of scholarly sources to explain your chosen topic or to connect your topic to what you have been learning in class. Your thesis statement may answer the question, "What is currently known about this topic?" Or you may make an argument about a controversial issue in education. If your purpose is to argue or persuade, be careful, however, not to make a claim based solely on your opinion. Your argument should come from your sources after you have read, summarized, and critiqued them, not before. Although you will start a research paper with a topic and a research question, wait to form any conclusions about your topic until after you read, and thoroughly understand, your sources. One effective strategy for this step is to write an annotated bibliography, which is described in detail later in this chapter.

WHAT IS EDUCATION RESEARCH?

Although you may have written research papers in the past, research papers that focus specifically on educational issues and that use scholarly education sources may be unfamiliar to you. In education, scholarly sources are so varied that defining what is, and what isn't, a scholarly source can be tricky. Although sources do vary, educators usually agree that published, peer-reviewed, original research is the most credible type of source.

One of the largest education library databases, *Education Source*, contains over 1,700 peer-reviewed journals, illustrating the range of research and pedagogy in the field. The largest educational association in the United States, the American Educational Research Association (AERA), sets the standard for education research and publication. AERA publishes some of the most prestigious education research journals and holds the largest yearly conference focused on research in education. Therefore, education students are expected to participate in this research-oriented field early in their career.

Because education is a social science, research studies drive the knowledge of the field. Unlike in other disciplines, such as English, education researchers design qualitative and quantitative studies in order to answer specific research questions. Their research questions arise from the gaps in previous studies or a lack of research in a specific area. While an English scholar may analyze texts, education researchers may spend time in schools to learn about students, teachers, or programs, and analyze texts from these sources. They also may analyze large data sets to answer questions about varied topics, such as national high school graduation rates. AERA (2018) defines education research this way:

> Education research is the scientific field of study that examines education and learning processes and the human attributes, interactions, organizations, and institutions that shape educational outcomes. Scholarship in the field seeks to describe, understand, and explain how learning takes place throughout a person's life and how formal and informal contexts of education affect all forms of learning. Education research embraces the full spectrum of rigorous methods appropriate to the questions being asked and also drives the development of new tools and methods.

As you can see from this definition, education research is a broad area of study, focusing on *all* aspects of teaching and learning in a variety of educational contexts and time frames. In fact, almost anything related to learning can be framed as an educational issue, from the effect of school gardens on children's nutrition to how studying religious texts at a church, synagogue, or mosque may affect children's literacy outcomes. Table 4.1 lists a range of research studies to show just how varied education research can be. It illustrates how researchers use a variety of methodologies in multiple contexts, ranging from observational studies in English language development classrooms to computerized statistical analyses of early childhood learning based on large national data sets.

Table 4.1. Examples of Education Research

Topic	Context	Purpose	Type of Research/ Methodology	Data Collected and Analyzed
Genre-based writing pedagogy for first-generation Mexican immigrants (Rinard, 2010)	Two high school English language development classes in the California Central Valley	To describe an ELD genre-based writing instruction. To explore how writing might be improved for ELD high school students	• Qualitative • Ethnography	• Observations and interviews • Analysis of students' writing samples
School discipline and teacher race (Lindsay & Hart, 2017)	All schools in North Carolina in 2007–2008 and 2012–2013	To determine the correlation between school discipline and teacher race	• Quantitative statistical analysis • Ordinary least squares • Correlation	• Administrative disciplinary data from elementary, middle, and high schools in North Carolina
Pre-kindergarten math, literacy, and behavioral skills (Bassok & Latham, 2017)	National context. Study uses two large national data sets.	To understand whether early skills differ in math, literacy, and behavior from 1998–2010 based on racial and socioeconomic groups	• Quantitative statistical analysis • Ordinary least squares • Regression analysis	• Two large national data sets (1998, 2010) • Student assessments • Teacher-reported measures • Parent and teacher surveys
Ethnic studies curriculum (Dee & Penner, 2017)	San Francisco Unified School District/9th-grade ethnic studies classes	To determine whether an ethnic studies curriculum improves performance and prevents high school dropouts	• Quantitative statistical analysis • Regression discontinuity	• 1,405 ninth-grade students • 9th-grade attendance • 9th-grade GPA • Credits earned

TYPES OF EDUCATION RESEARCH

In order to identify, summarize, and critique the research sources you find, it's important to know about the types of research education scholars conduct. Although education research varies widely, understanding a few categories of research is helpful when you begin searching for scholarly sources.

Scholars conduct *theoretical* research in order to develop or enhance an educational theory; they conduct *applied* research in order to address practical educational problems; and they conduct *evaluation* research in order to find out whether an educational program is effective. All of these types of research use different *methodologies* for gathering information, depending on the kind of research question and how best to answer that question. The three most common types of research methods are quantitative research, qualitative research, and mixed-methods research (Gay & Airasian, 2003). Practicing teachers also conduct action research, a type of qualitative research.

Quantitative Research

Quantitative research is defined as research that collects and statistically analyzes numerical data. Within education, these data could be large data sets collected by the federal or a state department of education, test scores, survey responses, and questionnaires. Scholars who perform quantitative research usually are completely removed from the participants they are studying. They typically work with data from anonymous research participants in the hundreds, thousands, or even millions. They also use deductive reasoning, a process that starts with a hypothesis and analyzes data to reach a conclusion. Quantitative researchers rely less on context; in fact, when using statistical analysis, they are able to control for contextual features that may confound their findings. Some types of quantitative research are survey research, correlational research, and causal research.

Qualitative Research

Qualitative research in education involves collecting information from local contexts, such as schools, after-school programs, and community centers— any place where scholars can observe teaching and learning. Qualitative researchers immerse themselves in the context they are studying and may spend days, weeks, or even years with one group of participants. The number of participants is usually small, because it is so time-consuming to interview and observe in educational settings.

Qualitative research differs from quantitative research because scholars do not start out with a hypothesis or use deductive reasoning. Instead, they use inductive reasoning by first gathering, analyzing, and categorizing their information before they reach conclusions. The answers to their research questions are based on how local participants view the area under study, not on a predetermined set of criteria. Because qualitative research findings are situational, and are not experimental studies, no single research finding can be generalized to all educational settings. Some types of qualitative research are ethnographies and case studies.

As you will read in Chapter 5, qualitative research for preservice teachers includes observations of classrooms or interviews with teachers, students, parents, administrators, and/or others involved in education. As a preservice or practicing teacher, you may even conduct research within your own classroom. This type of research is called *action research*.

Action Research

According to Hines et al. (2016), "educational action research involves participants conducting inquiry into their own practices in order to improve teaching and learning, practices and programs" (par. 1). When teachers conduct action research, they collect and analyze information such as test scores, graduation rates, enrollment rates, demographics, equity reports, and suspension rates at their school site or school district. They also may collect and analyze student work and interview and observe their own students. In Chapter 5, we provide more information on observing and interviewing. In Chapter 9, we provide detailed information on how to find information on local policies and data.

Mixed-Methods Research

This type of research is what its name implies: a mixture of qualitative and quantitative research. For example, a scholar may send out a survey to hundreds of teachers and then, based on what she finds, interview some of the teachers in order to gather more personal or situational information. Or a scholar may analyze the test results of all 3rd-grade students in Ohio. She may then conduct observations of the teaching practices in selected 3rd-grade classrooms in order to discover specific information about successful teaching practices that may have led to higher scores.

Knowing which type of research study you are reading will enable you to better summarize and critique it—skills we will discuss later in this chapter.

THE SCHOLARLY RESEARCH PROCESS

Like writing, scholarly research is a process involving several steps: choosing a topic, narrowing your topic, formulating a research question, revising your research question, and locating scholarly sources. These steps are recursive; you may return to an earlier step in the process as you discover new, or more relevant, information. In particular, you may find that you will need to revise your research question several times as you locate scholarly sources. Figure 4.1 shows the steps in the process, and we explain each one below.

Choose a Topic in Education

Unless your instructor has assigned you a topic, you should start with an issue you are interested in or are curious about. The best topics come out of course readings, class discussions, or internship experiences; they arise organically based on what you are learning in your education classes. You don't have to have a strong opinion on the topic; in fact, it is better to not take a stand, and instead let what you read in your sources guide your opinion. For example, you may be curious about why some students drop out of high school while others don't. You may wonder what the reasons are and whether there is anything educators can do to prevent dropouts. Or you may wonder how educators use technology in the classroom. What types of technology do they use? Does using technology help students learn? Both of these topics are good choices, but they may be too broad for a short research paper.

Table 4.2 lists some educational issues you may want to explore. Notice that you can explore topics based on specific groups of students, teaching strategies, curriculum, and a variety of content areas. This list includes a range of topics, but don't let it limit you. Just about any topic in education will work for your research paper. Of course, if your instructor has provided a list of issues in your assignment, you should follow her instructions on topic selection.

Narrow Your Research Topic

While the topics listed in Table 4.2 are all important, they are very broad, so you will need to narrow your topic based on your rhetorical situation. What is your purpose in writing this paper? Who will your audience be? In order to narrow your focus, ask yourself some questions:

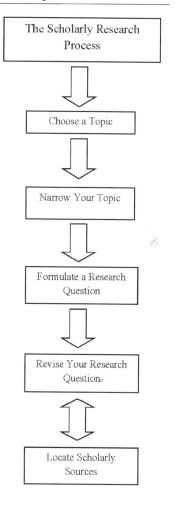

Figure 4.1. Steps in the Scholarly Research Process

Table 4.2. Examples of Topics for the "Issue in Education" Research Paper

Types of Students	Types of Schools	School Practices/ Policies	Teaching Practices	Curriculum	Content Areas
English learners	Charter schools	Disciplinary practices	Teaching with technology	Curriculum standards	Arts education
LGBTQIA students	Online schools	Homework policies	Project-based teaching and learning	Ethnic studies curriculum	Sex education
High school dropouts	Montessori schools	Dress code policies	Culturally relevant pedagogy	History curriculum	Physical education

1. Is there a specific grade level you want to focus on?
2. Is there a specific geographic area you are interested in?
3. Do you want to research teachers, students, programs, or policies?
4. Are you interested in *what* is being taught or *how* something is taught?
5. Which content area most interests you?

Discussing these questions with a classmate, instructor, or librarian will help you to narrow your topic enough to begin crafting a research question. You also may want to spend a few minutes searching online in order to see how others are writing about your chosen issue, but be skeptical as you do. Many people have very strong opinions about education without using scholarly sources to support them. They also may disguise business sources as scholarly sources in order to make their sources appear more credible.

Formulate a Research Question

After narrowing your topic, formulate a question or questions about it in order to focus your search for scholarly sources. Remember that writing a research question is also a process. Your question will become more specific the more research you conduct. In fact, your initial question may change completely as you draft your paper. Don't worry if you start with very vague questions like the following:

1. What types of technology do teachers use?
2. Does using technology in math classes help students learn?

These are great questions to start with, but they are not yet specific enough to help you locate the most relevant sources to answer them.

Revise Your Research Question

One strategy for revising your research question is to specify any broad or vague terms. For example, if you are interested in how people teach with technology, understand that "technology" is a big topic. Do you mean laptops, iPads, Smart Boards, or cell phones? Or are you interested in how teachers incorporate social media into their instruction? Therefore, instead of "technology," a revised research question may use the more specific term "Smart Boards." Instead of "students," another broad term, you may specify "high school students."

Example of a revised research question:

Does the use of Smart Boards in high school math classes help students visualize what they are learning?

After revision, this research question is specific enough to identify keywords to search for in library databases and online. If, however, your revised keywords do not yield the search results you expect, visit a librarian who can help you identify the most current and specific keywords related to your question.

Locate Scholarly Sources

When locating scholarly sources to answer your research question, you'll need to determine whether they are credible.

What is a credible source?

Your high school teachers may have told you to never use Wikipedia as a source, remember? Well, they were right. Why? Because Wikipedia (and other wikis) can be edited by anyone, which makes their information suspect and unreliable. The same is true for many websites, particularly those that don't credit authors for their content. Treat sources without authors with skepticism, and depending on the assignment, think carefully about using them. Usually the most credible websites end in .org, .edu, or .gov. URLs that end in .com are more likely to be commercial, not scholarly, sites.

Google Scholar. When searching for sources, you may be tempted to head for Google Scholar, and for good reason. According to Melissa Browne, an education librarian at the University of California, Davis, Google Scholar is "convenient, straightforward, and includes diverse subject disciplines and is available to students after they graduate." However, she wouldn't recommend it as a replacement for library databases, for several reasons:

- Google is not transparent about what's included and how often content is updated, so it's hard to know exactly what you are searching.
- Google is great for keyword searching, but it lacks other search functionalities that are useful for education research—for example, leveraging subject terms included in database thesauri, limiting results to peer-reviewed journals, and restricting searches by education level.
- For students learning about education research, Google Scholar doesn't really help them understand the structure of scholarly information within the discipline in the same way a subject-focused tool like a database does.

While you may start your search with Google Scholar, once you have a specific research question, it's best to search targeted library databases and websites to find the information you need. Doing so will shorten your search time considerably and lead to an in-depth understanding of how scholarly sources are categorized in education.

Peer Review. The most credible sources are those that have been peer-reviewed, which simply means that experts have read and validated the work before it was published. The best peer review consists of "blind" reviews, meaning that the reviewers don't know the names of the writers so that personal bias is reduced. Usually, for a paper to be published in a respected education journal, at least two experts have performed blind reviews, and the author has revised the piece based on any suggestions from the reviewers. Not all articles are accepted for publication, even after going through the peer-review process, so those that are published are of the highest quality. When searching most online library databases, you can filter your sources to retrieve only peer-reviewed sources.

Table 4.3 provides a list of library databases to consider in a search for peer-reviewed research studies. Notice that because education research can be interdisciplinary, you may want to search for studies in sociology and psychology in addition to education. Not all libraries subscribe to all databases, so it's a good idea to check with your librarian if you have questions about finding specific sources.

Additional Scholarly Sources

Other sources in education can vary from a blog post, to an article in an online magazine (such as *Education Week),* to a literature review published in a scholarly journal. Some of these sources are research-based (they cite research to support their claims). Others are opinion-based and may or may not be credible depending on whether the person writing is an expert in education and whether the article has been peer-reviewed. These types of sources often are divided into sources written for the general public, sources written for practitioners, and sources written for education researchers. As you can see in Table 4.4, these sources can be located in library databases to meet the needs of different audiences.

Gray Literature

Some of your searches may turn up sources that don't fit neatly into any of the categories we have discussed so far. In education, sources that fit this description are called *gray literature* and can include the materials discussed below.

Table 4.3. Databases of Published Original Research

Search this database	In order to find published research studies on . . .
Education Source	All aspects of education
ERIC (Educational Resources Information)	All aspects of education
Sociological Abstracts	Studies from the sociology of education
PsycInfo	Studies from education psychology

Table 4.4. Additional Scholarly Sources

Search this database	In order to find . . .	For this audience
CQ Researcher	Summary articles and arguments about all topics in education	Undergraduates in education
Access World News	Newspaper articles about all education topics	The general public
Oxford Bibliographies	Annotated bibliographies on all education topics	Novice researchers
Educational Leadership	Articles about current topics in teaching practice	Preservice and practicing teachers

Conference Papers and Presentations. Sometimes a study or topic is so new that information about it has never been published. Often, you'll first hear about these studies at local and national conferences, such as the AERA conference. Although these sources can be very useful, particularly for new issues in education, they are usually not peer-reviewed, so use them with caution.

Policy Briefs. Scholars write policy briefs in order to inform federal or state legislative bodies about an issue in education. Based on research, these briefs usually present a specific plan of action the writers want elected officials to take. For example, in a policy brief titled *What Do We Know About the Effects of School-Based Law Enforcement on School Safety?*, the WestEd Justice & Prevention Research Center (2018) defines "school-based law enforcement and summarizes some of the relevant research about its effects on students and schools." This policy brief may then be used by state legislatures or school officials to determine school safety strategies. Research-based sources such as this one are more credible than research-based white papers produced by commercial groups.

White Papers. White papers, like policy briefs, are research-based reports written by government agencies and other groups in order to argue for a solution to a specific problem. More persuasive in purpose than policy briefs, white papers also are used by businesses, corporations, and others as marketing tools. For example, in a white paper produced by Smart Technologies titled "Interactive Whiteboards and Learning: A Review of Classroom Case Studies and Research Literature" (2004), the authors argue that Smart Boards improve student learning. But a closer look at this white paper reveals that the research the authors reviewed was conducted by SMARTer Kids™ Research and was sponsored by the SMARTer Kids Foundation. Therefore, even though this white paper's title suggests a review of scholarly research, the source is suspicious. Did the authors review any research that may have shown that Smart Boards are ineffective? When using a white paper as a scholarly source, be sure to look into who commissioned, and paid for, the research and report. White papers may or may not be credible sources depending on who is writing it and for what purpose.

Policies. You can find education policies at the federal, state, and local levels. Race to the Top, for example, is a federal policy, and you can find information about it on the federal Department of Education website. For state policies, look at each state's department of education website, and for local policies, the Gamut portal is the most helpful for finding district policies. If you want to find policies for individual school districts and schools, look at the school's dashboard. See Table 4.5 for a list of helpful websites.

Curricular Standards. As you will learn in Chapter 6, just like policies, curricular standards can vary from state to state. If you are interested in the Common Core standards, for example, the website corestandards.org is a good place to start. Because the Common Core doesn't cover every content area, you may need to also look at a state's department of education website for more information about the standards that guide areas not covered, such as arts education. Some states have not adopted any of the Common Core standards. For these states, it's best to rely only on the state's department of education website.

See Table 4.5 for a useful guide for finding statistical, demographic, testing, and curricular information.

WRITING AN ANNOTATED BIBLIOGRAPHY

Now that you have chosen a topic, narrowed your research question, and found scholarly sources, it's time to start reading and writing about your sources. Although taking notes while you read is always useful, the most effective way to deeply understand what you read is to write an annotated bibliography.

An annotated bibliography is a collection of sources focused on one topic. Each source is "annotated," summarized and critiqued, in order to answer a research question or to provide information on the topic in a condensed format. Education writers, researchers, and practitioners often read annotated

Table 4.5. Websites to Find Statistical, Demographic, Testing, and Curricular Information

Search this website	In order to find . . .
National Center for Education Statistics: nces.ed.gov/	Federal education statistics and demographics
U.S. Department of Education: ed.gov/	Federal education information
States' departments of education websites. For example, Wyoming: edu.wyoming.gov/	State education information
corestandards.org/	The Common Core standards
csba.org/ProductsAndServices/AllServices/Gamut.aspx	School policies
School and district dashboards. For example, for California: caschooldashboard.org/#/Home	Information about individual schools

bibliographies in order to learn about the most current thinking on a topic. Writers use annotated bibliographies as a way to manage their sources. Once you've written an annotated bibliography, you have a manageable, summarized reference list and may not need to return to the original sources while drafting your paper.

If you are writing an annotated bibliography in an academic class, your purpose for writing is to understand and analyze what you have read in order to effectively integrate your sources as you write your "issue in education" research paper. Although your audience is your instructor and classmates, the most important audience for your annotated bibliography is *you*, because you are reading, summarizing, and critiquing your sources to make your drafting easier. Figure 4.2 shows the format for each source in an annotated bibliography. The number of sources you choose to include will vary depending on your assignment. Although writing an annotated bibliography may seem tedious and unnecessary, every year our students tell us it was the most beneficial writing assignment they completed in our courses. Like the research process, writing an annotated bibliography involves several important steps.

Critically Read Your Sources

In Chapter 3 you learned how to read actively and how to annotate and summarize what you read. All of what you learned in Chapter 3 applies to reading and summarizing your sources in order to write an annotated bibliography. However, your *purpose* for reading changes when you read to write an annotated bibliography and then a research paper, rather than a reading response. When writing a reading response, you usually are responding to just one text.

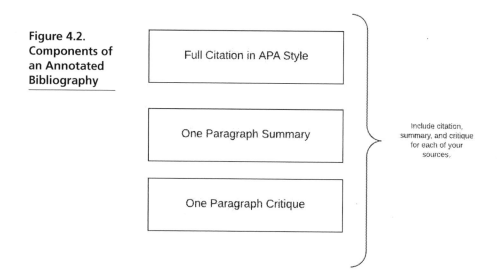

Figure 4.2. Components of an Annotated Bibliography

Full Citation in APA Style

One Paragraph Summary

One Paragraph Critique

Include citation, summary, and critique for each of your sources.

When reading to write a research paper, you should be thinking about which sources are appropriate for different sections of your paper. Will you use a source for background information about your topic? To discuss research findings? To argue for why more research is needed on your topic? To represent the scholarly conversation on your topic? These questions help guide your critical reading of each source.

As you are reading each source, you'll need to determine a way to organize the most important information. Some writers, for example, take notes on what they read. Another useful strategy for reading and summarizing your sources is to use a graphic organizer. Graphic organizers are charts that help you to compare, contrast, and organize information. The graphic organizer in Table 4.6 will help you strategically read your sources. You can use the one we provide here, and adapt it to your needs, or you can create a graphic organizer that is unique to your research.

Summarize Your Sources

Once you've answered the questions in the graphic organizer, you are ready to summarize each source in one paragraph by simply turning your answers into full paragraphs. A summary is a concise paragraph in your own words of another, longer document, usually an article or a report. See Table 3.1 in Chapter 3 to review the characteristics of a good summary.

A sample summary of an original research study on school nutrition is shown in Figure 4.3. You can see that education student Michelle simply turned her answers from her graphic organizer into a cohesive paragraph.

Table 4.6. Graphic Organizer for the Annotated Bibliography

Purpose	Methodology	Findings/Results	Discussion
For research articles:			
What were the researchers trying to find out? Did the researchers have a research question?	Was the study qualitative or quantitative (or mixed methods)? What did the researchers do and with whom? How long was the study?	What did the researchers learn from the study?	What are the implications of the study? Who might care about the results of this study? Does the writer recommend any future research or acknowledge any limitations to the study?
For other articles:			
What is the writer's purpose? Who is the audience?	What types of evidence is the writer(s) using?	What are the main points of this article? What should you, the reader, take away from it?	Why is this an important source for your argument? How will you use it in your paper?

Critique Your Sources

After you have completed the graphic organizer and summarized your sources, the next step is to critique each source based on what you learned about credible sources earlier in this chapter. Before you write your critique, you should have already evaluated your sources, not just taken the information they present at face value. Even if you have chosen credible scholarly sources, you need to think carefully about each source's limitations for the purpose of your paper and your argument. When writing a critique, put in paragraph form the most important limitations to the study or article, and then write how you might want to use this source in your paper, or what evidence you will use from the source to support your claims. In order to write an effective critique, ask yourself the following questions and then respond to the ones most relevant to your topic, audience, and purpose.

Questions for critiquing a source:
- Does the source come from an institute, foundation, or corporation that has a political or economic agenda?
- Are the authors experts in the topic they are writing about? How do you know?
- Do the authors write accurately and fairly about the topic, or do they seem to be biased?
- If the source is a research study, do the authors address the limitations of the study?
- Does the study state conclusions that the study's data don't support?
- Does the study generalize, beyond the research questions, the contexts and population that actually were studied?
- How might you use this source in your paper? What evidence will you draw from it? Which argument will the evidence support?
- How might you organize your paper using these sources? Which sources will work best for the introduction, for example?

In addition to determining a source's credibility and relevance to your topic, you should write a critique because, depending on the purpose of your research paper, you will need to discuss your sources with a critical eye. You will have more credibility as a writer if you write about your sources in a fair and accurate way, even if some aspects of your sources don't neatly support your argument or narrative.

Figure 4.3 also includes Michelle's critique of the study she summarized. In her critique, Michelle rightly points out that although the study is credible, it has limitations. She also writes about how she will use this source to answer her research question: Is there a need for elementary schools to implement nutrition education in order to encourage students to eat a healthy diet?

Figure 4.3. A Sample Student Annotated Bibliography Entry (written by Michelle and annotated by the authors)

Citation

Andersen, L., Myers, L., O'Malley, K., Mundorf, A. R., Harris, D. M., & Johnson, C. C. (2015). Adolescent student use of school-based salad bars. *Journal of School Health, 85*(10), 722–727. doi:10.1111/josh.12302

> Michelle includes the full APA reference

Summary

This study explains that factors such as nutrition education and access to the right foods all contribute to healthier eating, and therefore, lower rates of obesity within school-aged children. The purpose of this study was to analyze the use of school salad bars and factors that are related to the level of usage. The mixed-method study was conducted in 23 New Orleans schools (of all ages), with a salad bar installed in each (installed from a previous study). Students used the salad bars and then took a 60-question survey. Researchers learned that non-African American students were more than twice as likely to eat from the salad bar, and students who chose healthy food preferences on the survey were also twice as likely to eat from the salad bar. Implications for the study include the need for more nutrition education, since those who showed a healthy food preference ate at the salad bar more. Another implication is the need for more elementary schools to add salad bars into their lunch programs in order to give students more healthy options.

> In the first sentence of the summary, Michelle articulates what kind of source she is summarizing.

> Michelle provides an overview of the entire article.

> Michelle states the purpose of the study.

> Here, she explains the methodology used in the study.

> She highlights the study's findings.

> Michelle considers the possible implications of the study.

Critique

Though this study is a peer-reviewed, credible source, it does have limitations. One limitation is that the data were self-reported by the students. This detail means the researchers could not confirm what the students actually ate, leaving the information vulnerable to bias. The researchers suggest that in future studies, actual consumption should be monitored. Though this article focuses on adolescents, an age group not included in my paper, it establishes the idea that nutrition education could be integrated into elementary schools as well. In the introduction, the authors state that other studies have proved that nutrition education along with easier access to healthy food can increase a student's intake of fruits and vegetables. This article will provide evidence for my argument on the need for more nutrition education in elementary schools.

> Michelle opens her critique by noting that the study has limitations.

> Michelle acknowledges that the study is not focused on elementary schools, the group in her research question.

> She notes that the article could still be helpful to her paper, even though it is focused on adolescents.

> Lastly, she states that the evidence from the study will be useful to support her argument.

Move from Bibliography to Draft

Now that you have written an annotated bibliography, you next need to think about where in your "issue in education" paper you will use each source, how each source will support your main points, and what the overall organization of your paper will be. Think of this step as the "bridge" between reading your sources and drafting your research paper. You want to avoid a list-like structure in your paper, meaning you want to avoid simply writing about your sources in chronological order, or in the same order as you list them in your annotated bibliography, summarizing each as you go. If you use this type of organization, why not simply ask your reader to read your annotated bibliography? What makes your research paper unique is how you decide to classify and write about your sources. To do this, first look over your annotated bibliography and think about any possible categories or themes that emerge from the sources you've chosen. Questions to ask yourself include:

- Do I see any trends, patterns, or themes in my sources? For example, can I classify my sources based on research methodologies, findings, or problems?
- Do I notice a debate emerging about this topic/issue?

Think about the emerging themes as headings you will use for the body of your paper and write an informal outline before you begin drafting. What kind of organizational structure makes the most sense based on your sources? Will you organize your paper based on a problem and proposed solutions? Will you highlight an existing debate? Or are you simply providing a current scholarly snapshot of your topic? After you have thought about the organization of your paper and written an informal outline, it is time to start drafting your research paper. Keep in mind that like all other aspects of this process, your categories and headings may change as you draft. But don't worry; since you have already done much of the hard work, drafting your paper will be much easier.

DRAFTING AN "ISSUES IN EDUCATION" PAPER

Because of all your preparation, writing your "issue in education" paper should be fairly straightforward.

But before you begin, ask yourself these questions:

- Who is the audience for my paper?
- What is the purpose of my paper? Am I simply explaining a topic, or am I making an argument?

- How much background information do I need to provide?
- What choices do I need to make based on the audience and purpose?

If you are unsure how to begin, analyzing a sample paper can help. When analyzing a sample paper, keep in mind the questions above and the fact that no two research papers are exactly the same. Each paper will vary depending on the assignment, length requirements, number of required sources, and on whether you can include personal experience to support your claims. See Figure 4.4 for a sample "issues in education" research paper from an educational psychology course. We discuss it in more detail later in this chapter.

Write the Introduction

When writing the introduction for your "issues in education" research paper, you'll need to start with general statements about your topic, ones that provide context for the specifics you'll discuss later. When deciding how general you'll need to be, think about your audience. Most of the time, even if your audience is other educators, you'll still need to provide some important information in your introduction. For example, in order to introduce your topic to readers, you'll need to consider what they may already know or not know about your topic. If they are not immersed in the ongoing conversation about your topic, you'll need to provide some details such as statistics, history, or demographic information.

An introduction is also a good place to define specialized terms that your audience may not be familiar with. In some cases, you also may choose to create your own definitions, either from existing literature or based on your own research. In addition, you may choose to state why this topic is important, who is interested in this topic, and your purpose for writing about it. As you write your introduction, move from general statements to more specific ones; narrow the focus of your paper.

Write the Body of the Research Paper

If you have already completed an annotated bibliography, the body of your paper will be much easier to write. Because you have critically read your sources and summarized them in your own words, it will be easier for you to avoid what we call "patchwriting," paraphrasing sentences that are too close to the original source. When you patchwrite, you literally patch together quotes and paraphrases from your sources, rather than write a paper from your point of view and use sources only to support *your* ideas. Patchwriting also can lead to plagiarism, and you definitely want to avoid plagiarizing your sources in an academic class.

In the body of the paper, you will use your sources to support your main points and to explain any sources in more detail. You also may use your sources to illustrate a debate surrounding your topic, or the information education audiences still need to learn about your topic. The use of headings and subheadings throughout the body will make your ideas clearer and more accessible to your readers. Keep in mind that the number of sections, paragraphs, words, quotes, and sources you include will depend entirely on the assignment and on your rhetorical choices.

Write the Conclusion

The conclusion of a research paper is usually brief, but is an important part of your paper. The conclusion makes your paper feel finished for the reader and may sum up your main points or arguments. It is also a place to discuss any limitations to the sources you used, any critiques of the research you included, or what education scholars may consider about the future of your topic. Is there a need for future research on this topic? If so, what do you suggest? In short, the conclusion is a look back, and a look forward to the future of scholarly work on your topic.

Present the References

The reference list should be included on a separate page at the end of your paper. The references should be in APA Style and in alphabetical order by the authors' last names (for more details on APA Style, see Chapter 10). You should include only the references you used in your paper, not all the sources that you may have read and annotated, but left out of your final draft. And if you wrote an annotated bibliography, you don't need to include your summaries and critiques in the reference list; include just the full citations in APA Style.

Figure 4.4 is a complete "issue in education" paper written by Jay for an upper-division educational psychology course. The assignment required students to choose a personally relevant topic and then use scholarly sources to apply theories from the field of psychology to teaching and learning. Jay chose the topic of music education and music pedagogy in particular. As a musician, Jay had been teaching music and was able to include his experience in the paper as the assignment required.

Throughout this chapter, you have learned how to find and use scholarly sources. In Chapter 5, you will learn how to collect and use other important types of evidence in education: observations and interviews.

(text continues on p. 68)

Figure 4.4. Sample "Issues in Education" Paper (written by Jay and annotated by the authors)

The Sounds of Learning:
Educational Psychology Meets Music Pedagogy

Introduction

Music, no matter its form, is one of the most difficult, yet most rewarding, subjects to study. The ability to play an instrument, understand the concepts of keys and chords, or use the technology associated with recording and packaging music are all important areas for students to learn. However, before people can establish themselves as 'rock gods' or industry legends, they must begin from the bottom; they must become students of music and learn how their field operates. Without appropriate instruction, students will never advance beyond their beginner knowledge and may become frustrated, even quit, when they are unable to learn at a satisfying pace.

Therefore, in order for students to excel in music, they need teachers who are familiar with instructional methods and who can make their knowledge accessible to students. Because instructors were once learners themselves, they may incorporate educational methods based on how they were taught into their own teaching, in hopes to pass on to students the joy that comes from learning music. Though using the methods they learned by may be useful, by explicitly adopting and applying theories from educational psychology to teach music, instructors can more effectively benefit all students.

Education Psychology Theories and Music Pedagogy

Instructors implement a variety of theoretical approaches in music education to encourage students' learning, but theories from educational psychology are particularly relevant. In particular, Lev Vygotsky's Sociocultural Theory and B. F. Skinner's theory of Operant Conditioning could be applied to music teaching. By using these two theories, music pedagogy can be tailored to fit all students' objectives in learning music, whether their focus is on playing an instrument, learning how to use recording technology, or simply understanding how notes fit together.

The Need for Theory-Based Instruction in Music

While music instructors are often educated individuals who have a high level of competency in the subjects they teach, they are not without faults. Some music instructors have little understanding of effective educational methods and how to apply them in the classroom. Parkes and Wexler (2012) assert that instructors at

> The title clearly states what the paper will be about.

> Jay begins his introduction with general background information about music.

> Here he begins to narrow his topic to the importance of music education.

> He further narrows his introduction to the main focus of his paper: the importance of good instruction in music education, instruction that applies theories from education psychology.

> Jay ends his introduction with his argument, or thesis statement.

> The use of headings in the body of the paper helps guide the reader.

> Jay introduces the two educational theorists he will discuss in more detail later in his paper.

> In this section Jay states the need for teachers to understand and apply theories to their practice. He relates this need to his own experience learning music.

> Jay uses a source in APA Style to support his argument that teachers need professional development in order to teach music based on known methods.

either the college or university level "commonly lack formal systematic education in the pedagogical aspects of teaching in the applied studio" (p. 46). In other words, music instructors may lack the knowledge or credentials to teach, to apply what they know effectively in the classroom to benefit the students.

While this assertion may be true in some respects, it is definitely not true in all, as many instructors have formed their own understandings of music and draw upon both their understandings and personal experiences in learning when teaching (Wiggins, 2007, p. 36). As a musician, for instance, the first experience I had was learning an instrument. Though daunting at first, the instrument became easier to navigate through meaningful practice and skill acquisition, skills I now pass on to my students. However, the question remains: how might the theories in educational psychology help one learn music?

> This citation provides a qualified counterargument to the earlier assertion that teachers are not educated in methods.

Lev Vygotsky and Music Pedagogy

One answer lies within the sociocultural theories of Lev Vygotsky, the zone of proximal development and scaffolding. Vygotsky believed that people could "achieve higher levels of competence when supported by a more knowledgeable person (the teacher) in a new activity" (Parkes & Wexler, 2012, p. 46). This concept is best applied in teaching music after the student has begun the basics, but has not yet acquired a high-level skill set. While at this crucial stage of development, students must learn how to properly use the equipment present in their chosen field. Through scaffolding, an instructor can assist students in attaining a greater understanding of their equipment more quickly, by first introducing them to the myriad of tools that are at their disposal, and advising them on how to use each tool in effective ways.

> Jay goes into detail about Lev Vygotsky's theories and how they can be applied as effective pedagogical strategies.

> This source defines the zone of proximal development.

Vygotsky's theory of scaffolding is also useful when a student is first interested in learning how to play an instrument. Scaffolding refers to the "range of tasks that children cannot yet perform independently, but *can* perform [with guidance] from others" (Ormrod, 2008, p. 332). With this concept in mind, Vygotsky believed that learning, and later, development, came from performing tasks that required the help of a more-advanced peer or instructor. Children were the focus of Vygotsky's study; thus those learning an instrument can also be considered "children," as (1) they are malleable and easily influenced due to their lack of authority in music and (2) they must learn from the very basics, similar to how children must when they engage in unfamiliar tasks. In their study, Parkes and Wexler (2012) found that students followed a path of development that reflected Vygotsky's observations. Through the help of an interlocutor with a higher affinity for the task, students were found to "transcend [their]

> Another source is used to define a term.

> Here Jay uses a research source to support his argument that Vygotsky's theories are effective for learning.

> Jay puts the changes he has made to the original quote in brackets.

Figure 4.4. Sample "Issues in Education" Paper (written by Jay and annotated by the authors)
(continued)

limitations" and "[operate] on a higher level as a result of [that] support" (p. 46). Thus, as these individuals learn and develop their capabilities, they evolve into full-fledged adults musically, and are capable of giving help to other 'children' of music.

In application, Vygotsky's theories have the greatest influence on the initial stages of learning music. Instructors realize and understand that most students begin with no knowledge of how to play an instrument, and thus create an inviting, flexible learning environment in which mistakes can, and are expected to, be made. As the learner grows in both ability and desire, the instructor will attempt to aid the learner by introducing compositions or practice exercises that are just outside the learner's skill level. In doing so, the instructor is presenting a task that, according to Vygotsky, would promote cognitive development, as the task is something the learner cannot do on his or her own.

> Jay then discusses how Vygotsky's theories can be applied to teaching music.

Through careful instruction, practice, and daily application, students would learn how to navigate the exercise or composition, and thus develop a new skill set, increasing their "level of potential development . . . the upper limit of tasks that he or she can perform with the assistance of a more competent individual" (Ormrod, 2008, p. 332). I have found that this method is of particular importance to facilitating, not only student development, but student interest as well. Learning is a choice, meaning that students are often faced with the difficult decision to give up or continue their studies. In my experience as a teacher, scaffolding aids the student as well as the instructor. For the student, having someone who is more apt at the skill or practice is both a relief and a challenge. An instructor provides friendly competition for the students, challenging them to reach the instructor's level of mastery at a particular skill. In addition, the instructor also relieves the student from the pressure to "get it right from the beginning," allowing the student freedom to make mistakes and learn from them, as opposed to more callous environments, where mistakes often lead to frustration and feelings of inadequacy.

> Another quotation is used from Ormrod (2008) to argue for applying Vygotsky's theory to music education.

> Jay includes personal experience as evidence to support the use of scaffolding.

For the instructor, scaffolding is a chance to revisit techniques that may have fallen out of his or her daily exercises. Moreover, the instructor can benefit from scaffolding by diversifying his pedagogic knowledge, applying different methods across students, and collecting data to find which methods facilitate the highest levels of student determination. In doing so, the instructor can then tailor each individual lesson to accommodate each individual student, further promoting the chances of student success.

B. F. Skinner and Music Pedagogy

Another theory that may enhance music pedagogy is B. F. Skinner's theory of Operant Conditioning, the "controlling or predicting of human behavior (or its frequency)" (Boyanton, 2010, p. 51). Though this theory is not applied explicitly, teachers may use it to guide students through the wealth of knowledge available to them, focusing on key aspects to help them gain a better understanding of the material in the field of music. Skinner believed that consequences, as opposed to stimuli, had a greater influence on behavioral change (Boyanton, 2010, p. 51). In his experiment, Skinner employed a rat as his subject of study. When placed into a box with a small lever, the rat, after pressing the lever and being rewarded with food, pressed the lever more frequently, thus confirming Skinner's hypothesis. With this confirmation, Skinner established a variety of consequences to influence this "operant behavior," one of which he coined as "fading". According to Carlson and Mayer (1971), fading is the "gradual withdrawal of guidelines, prompts, or stimulus support" (p. 194). This withdrawal requires the individual to act on his or her own, without guidance or other means of support, whether by an interlocutor or otherwise.

> Jay introduces another educational theory from B. F. Skinner. Notice that he separates his discussion of Vygotsky and Skinner into separate sections.

> Another source is used to define a term.

> Jay uses the same source to continue to discuss Skinner.

> Jay integrates a summary from his annotated bibliography to provide more details about Skinner's research.

> Jay integrates other relevant scholars to more fully define Skinner's term of "fading."

This theory can also be applied to music pedagogy. As learners become more and more skillful, acquiring knowledge of how to navigate their field or instrument, they reach a point at which they may know more than their instructors. Thus, instructors who are no longer necessary to their pupils fade from the students' learning experience, requiring students to change their behavior to seek a new instructor to continue improving their musical skills. As an instructor, I have also used this method, specifically after my students have surpassed me in either ability or conceptual knowledge. While I make myself readily available to my students, both current and past, when I find a particular student beginning to excel beyond the scope of my knowledge, I recess, or fade, from my role as their educator. In doing so, I again make it my student's responsibility to find an instructor should they desire to continue learning.

> Jay again makes this discussion personal as required by the assignment.

Conclusion

Music pedagogy is no stranger to the theories of educational psychology. Theories from educational psychology influence music pedagogy and its educators, be they professors of large institutions or seniors in college like me. Because they are typically the first interaction students have with a competent individual in their chosen field of music, instructors should be educated, not only in their subject of study or teaching, but also in how to use effective pedagogies in order to foster both student success and gratification. By effectively educating students through the adoption and explicit instruction of theories presented in educational psychology,

> The first part of Jay's conclusion summarizes the arguments he has made in his paper.

Figure 4.4. Sample "Issues in Education" Paper (written by Jay and annotated by the authors)
(continued)

instructors are ensuring that their students will learn, and thus develop in any aspect of music. But music educators still need to continue to explore how other theories may inform their teaching. More information on how theories from educational psychology could be applied to different age groups would be particularly useful. If equipped with an informed method of learning, motivated students may even advance beyond their instructors and become educated instructors themselves.

> Jay discusses what music educators may still need to know more about.

> Throughout this research paper, Jay integrates the educational psychology theories he is learning in class, how those theories can be applied to teaching music, and his own experiences as a music student and teacher.

References

Boyanton, D. (2010). Behaviorism and its effect upon learning in the schools. In G. S. Goodman (Ed.), *Educational psychology reader: The art and science of how people learn* (pp. 49–65). New York, NY: Peter Lang.

Carlson, J., & Mayer, G. (1971). Fading: A behavioral procedure to increase independent behavior. *The School Counselor, 18*(3), 193–197.

Ormrod, J. E. (2008). Developmental perspectives on cognition. In J. E. Ormrod, *Human learning* (5th ed., pp. 308–349). New York, NY: Pearson.

Parkes, K., & Wexler, M. (2012). The nature of applied music teaching expertise: Common elements observed in the lessons of three applied teachers. *Bulletin of the Council for Research in Music Education* (193), 45–62.

Wiggins, J. (2007). Authentic practice and process in music teacher education. *Music Educators Journal, 93*(3), 36–42.

> Jay's reference list in APA format. Notice that he uses a variety of credible scholarly sources.

EXERCISES

1. Discuss the definition of education research from the American Educational Research Association on page 47. In pairs or in a small group, brainstorm some possible examples of education research.
2. Using the graphic organizer in Table 4.6, find two different kinds of sources and fill in the chart. What similarities and differences do you notice between the two sources?
3. Discuss the sample paper in Figure 4.4. How might your paper be similar to and different from the sample based on your rhetorical situation? How might you improve the sample paper?

CHAPTER 5

Writing with Qualitative Data
Field Logs, Observation Write-Ups, Profiles, and Case Studies

As you learned in Chapter 4, qualitative research involves spending time in classrooms or other settings "in the field" in order to learn about a topic from a participant perspective. When advanced undergraduates and pre-service teachers conduct qualitative research in education, they typically observe educational settings, interview educational stakeholders, and reflect on the research process. If they are practicing teachers, they may conduct action research—described later in this chapter—in order to collect information about their own classroom and school community. Learning to conduct qualitative research and to write about qualitative data are important parts of writing in education.

In this chapter, we will explain how to write four genres that use the qualitative data you collect: a field log, an observation write-up, an educator profile, and a case study. The content is organized so that each genre builds on the next, from least difficult to most difficult. Each of these genres, like all the genres we discuss in this guide, has its own rhetorical situation depending on where you are in your career trajectory.

EXAMINING THE RHETORICAL SITUATION: PURPOSE, AUDIENCE, CONTEXT, VOICE, AND GENRE

The rhetorical purpose for each genre in this chapter depends on whether you are writing for an undergraduate class or for a teaching credential or master's program. In your undergraduate education classes, your instructor may require you to observe a school setting and then write about it. These types of observation write-up assignments are designed to give you experience with teachers and students. If you've never spent much time in classrooms or with children, it's valuable to learn whether you enjoy the experience in order to determine whether you want a teaching career. If you later decide to pursue a teaching credential, these academic assignments prepare you for the professional writing you will complete in a master's program or on assessments such as the edTPA. As you become a practicing teacher, reflecting on what you learn from collecting and writing about qualitative data also allows you to begin identifying what you value in education, often called your "teacher identity." Would you teach like the teacher you've observed? How would you work with a range of students based on what you've observed? The primary purpose of the genres in this chapter, then, is to enable you to accurately record what you see and hear during your fieldwork, take the factual data you collect, and write cohesive narratives using your data as evidence.

Your audience for these assignments also varies depending on context. If you are an undergraduate in an education class, for example, a field log, an observation write-up, and an educator profile are academic assignments, making your audience your instructor, your classmates, and yourself. But you also may complete these assignments in a master's or credential program, making your audience a professional one consisting of teacher supervisors and education professors who are evaluating your ability to work in professional settings. You also may decide to engage with larger audiences such as the general public. For example, you may choose to publish a teacher profile in a local newspaper or blog; in this case, your audience would be people in the local community, particularly people who care about neighborhood schools. Think of these assignments as the bridge, or as a process, that moves you from an academic context with academic audiences to a professional context that allows you to engage with the general public. See Table 5.1 for an overview of each genre's rhetorical situation.

WRITING A FIELD LOG

A step in the process from academic to professional writing in education is to distinguish between facts, interpretations, and reflections. You start learning this distinction through writing an observation field log, a genre that helps you distinguish between observed facts and the interpretation of those facts. After completing a field log, you may complete an observation write-up or, if you are in a master's program, a case study, so your experience makes sense to an outside audience, either academic or professional.

What Is a Field Log?

Many education professors ask students to maintain a running record of their experiences "in the field," that is, in the classroom or other field environments. These assignments may require you to observe a single child or teacher, a classroom, or an activity at a public place where children are present, and record your observations in a field log. Although no qualitative researcher is ever truly objective, writing a field log forces you to be as objective as possible about

Table 5.1. Genres That Use Qualitative Data: Rhetorical Situations

Genre	Audience	Purpose	Context	Type of Discourse	Voice
Field log	Classroom audiences or yourself	To record observations, interpretations, and reflections	Undergraduate or graduate class	Academic	Informal
Observation write-up	Classroom audience	To make your observations clear to an outside audience	Undergraduate class edTPA	Academic	Formal
Educator profile	Classroom audience or the general public	To create a meaningful narrative about an educator	Undergraduate class Public forum	Academic and professional	Anecdotal/ formal
Case study	Classroom audience, academic committee	To meaningfully analyze a single case	Credential program or graduate class	Academic and professional	Formal

what you are seeing, by requiring you to separate your descriptions, interpretations, and reflections. And if you are observing people you know, this separation becomes even more important to prevent you from making assumptions based on your prior knowledge.

A field log is not complicated; it can be as simple as a piece of notebook paper divided into columns. You also may choose to create a log in a Word document, but think about whether typing on a laptop during your observations will distract the people you are observing. You can, and should, adapt the log format to fit your needs based on your exact assignment. One way to write a log is to create a document with three columns titled "Observation Descriptions," "Interpretations," and "Reflections." Table 5.2 provides an example of how to format a field log and some of the observations you may want to include, depending on your purpose for using it.

Why Write a Field Log?

Writing a field log lays the groundwork for other academic and professional assignments. Learning to observe, interpret, and reflect on what you see helps you to understand teachers, students, and your community—knowledge you will apply later to your own teaching practices. In addition, keeping a log gives you a record you can refer to when you begin to write. Although we may think we can remember details from an observation, our memories are not that accurate. You may remember the overall experience, but the small details inevitably will slip away unless you write them down as they are happening.

Table 5.2. Sample Field Log Format

Observation Descriptions	Interpretations	Reflections
The school/class environment	Did you observe approaches, activities, and/or instruction that align with course concepts/discussion/reading?	What did you notice about the class environment? Teacher? Students?
The people present (teachers, students, paraeducators, specialists)		
The progression of time between different activities		What did you notice about the instructional activities/pace?
The instructional activities (warm-up, class discussion, small-group work, assessment)	Did you observe any patterns of activity, behavior, or dialogue?	What questions about teaching/learning did the observation experience invite?
How much time the teacher spends on each component of the lesson	How do the patterns align with theory or research?	How does the observation experience influence the kind of teacher you want to be?
What the students do and say		

A field log is also an important way to scaffold the observation write-up and case study, genres that use qualitative observational data as evidence.

Writing Field Log Descriptions

Good field log descriptions specifically describe what you observe, rather than summarize. For example, in Professor Lee Martin's education course, he explains to his students how he expects them to describe their observations (Martin, 2017). He writes, "'The child was dirty' becomes 'his feet were bare and muddy. The knees of the overalls were caked with grass and dried mud. His hair was mussed and streaked with mud over his ears.'" These details show what you objectively see. You may choose to later interpret these details as "dirty" in your observation write-up, but you want to be as objective as possible in your log. Keep in mind that there are many different perspectives on what constitutes "dirty."

Similarly, rather than using subjective words like *punishing, sharing, polite,* or *misbehaving* to describe people's actions or language, write what people actually do and say. For example, instead of writing, "The boy was jealous of his classmate's toy, and when she wouldn't share, he became angry and stomped away," in your description column, write, "The boy sat and watched his classmate for a minute from 5–6 feet away. He approached her and said, 'mine.' She clutched her toy bear more tightly and turned away. He turned away and left, feet stomping, eyes squinted." You may then choose to interpret the boy's behavior based on human development research and write in your interpretation column, "The boy was angry and sulking, typical of behavior at his age." Keeping the observation details separate from the interpretations helps to minimize assumptions in your notes.

Avoiding Labels and Stereotypes in Your Observation Descriptions. When writing observation descriptions, avoid generalities and labels that may invoke stereotypes. Avoiding stereotypes is particularly important when describing student behavior. Labels such as "troublemaker," "learning-disabled," or "at-risk" are loaded with cultural assumptions and lead to stereotypical interpretations. For example, consider this description:

> The child looked toward the window when the teacher was talking. He then looked down and opened a book on his desk and began thumbing through it. The teacher asked him to "put down the book" and said, "please pay attention." He put the book down for 3 minutes and then picked it up again.

Was this child "acting out" or "a curious reader"? Keep in mind that what might be misbehavior to one person could be curiosity or boredom to another. Writing specific details about what you see and hear in your observations will allow you to avoid judgments based on a single event. Later, particularly if you are writing a case study, you can look for patterns based on numerous observations and put these details into context.

Writing Field Log Interpretations

After writing your descriptions in the first column of your field log, you may interpret your observations based on patterns of activity, dialogue, and any other visual information, such as body language, in the next column. Interpretations arise from education theories such as human development, psychology, sociology, and second-language acquisition, and they are grounded in factual evidence. Interpretations are not personal; they are focused on making your observations meaningful to an outside audience in education. For example, if you are observing a classroom of multilingual students, you may hear students helping one another by translating the teacher's instructions. Or you may observe a student explaining a book to a student at a lower reading level. Both of these examples may evoke Vygotsky's (2012) zone of proximal development (ZPD), the concept that students can do more with guidance than they can alone. You would then record the exact details of what you heard and saw, and interpret the activity as peer tutoring using the ZPD. When writing interpretations, avoid generalizing about any group from your specific details. For example, you wouldn't assume that *all* multilingual students need translations or have lower reading levels simply because you saw one or two examples of peer assistance. Instead, analyze, explain, and interpret your specific observations based on the educational theories you are reading about and analyzing in your classes.

Writing Field Log Reflections

Unlike interpretations, reflections are personal; they are focused on *your* learning, writing, and observing processes. Reflections will vary depending on the assignment requirements, but they may include questions that the observation raises for you (in terms of course concepts and teaching), or how the observation experience influences your understanding of teaching and learning, or how these observations may help you develop your teacher identity. For example, you may be observing a teacher who makes students laugh and wonder whether a teacher with a sense of humor helps students learn. You also may wonder whether a sense of humor is important to your developing teacher identity, and how you might incorporate it when you become a practicing teacher. Or you simply may wonder whether the teacher's humor is an example of purposely using humor in pedagogy. You also can use your reflections to challenge your own biases and stereotypes or to question your assumptions. Think of writing reflections as a running dialogue between yourself and what you are observing and learning.

Table 5.3 is an excerpt from a field log written by Angela, a preservice teacher, after observing a 9th-grade, college-prep English class on identifying figurative language in a Pablo Neruda poem and a Shakespearean sonnet. Notice that in the log the student separates her observations, interpretations, and reflections, and also includes a column on "Notes for Later."

USING A FIELD LOG TO COMPOSE AN OBSERVATION WRITE-UP

When your instructor assigns an observation, they may ask you simply to turn in an expanded version of your field log. More frequently, however, your instructor will ask you to write up the observation in a meaningful way, using your field log as a guide. This observation write-up assignment leads to some questions you'll need to consider:

- Which of my descriptions should I include and why?
- Which theories or course concepts should I integrate?
- If I use my interpretations, will they be grounded in contextual details?
- How will I organize my write up?

The answers to these questions will vary depending on the assignment and research questions you are answering. Keep in mind that you may not use everything you have recorded in your field log. Instead of summarizing all your field log observations, use the following ideas to choose the data to include in your observation write-up:

Table 5.3. Sample Field Log (written by Angela)

Observation Descriptions	Interpretations	Reflections	Notes for Later
9:00 The teacher walks through the classroom handing out instructions for the listening comprehension activity. As he walks among the desks, he smiles at students and asks two of them by name how they are.	This teacher is friendly.	I wonder why he chose handouts instead of writing the instructions on the board.	I want to ask the teacher about this specific choice.
9:05 The teacher plays a recording of Pablo Neruda's sonnet. All of the students are alert at their desks except two. These two students have their heads on their desks with their eyes open.	All of the students are listening to the sonnet recording. This activity is building on what students already know (Piaget).	All the students seem focused on the activity, which surprises me. I wonder what the teacher did during the last class to prepare. When I teach, I want to be sure each lesson builds on the next.	Be sure to ask about it later.
The teacher asks students to raise their hands if they want to hear the sonnet again: "how many of you want to hear it again?" 20 of the 24 students raise their hands.	By asking students to raise their hands, he is using formative assessment. He is checking in to see if the students are listening.	I wonder why four students didn't raise their hands. Two of the students who didn't raise their hands were the ones the teacher referred to by name earlier. I wonder if he is paying special attention to them.	Ask him later about the two students.

- Select the parts of the field log to use based on the purpose of the assignment and the main points you want to make about the observation. Different purposes might include: to practice observing in the field; to connect course concepts and theories to your observational data; or to consider how your observation is influencing your teacher identity.
- Ground your observations in educational theories or pedagogical best practices. If your data support it, you can challenge the theories as well.
- Use your interpretations sparingly and only after you have a pattern of data to suggest an evidence-based conclusion.
- Avoid overgeneralizing based on one observation. One observation is just a small snapshot of students and teachers based on a limited amount of time and in only one context.
- Organize your observation write-up based on your audience and purpose. You may choose to organize your write-up chronologically or thematically based on course concepts.

Figure 5.1 shows how Angela used the field log in Table 5.3 to complete her observation write-up of the high school English teacher. The assignment required her to observe a single lesson and focus primarily on the teacher. Her purpose was to frame the write-up with the educational theories she was learning about in class. Although she may have written reflections about her experiences in her field log, she leaves them out of this observation write-up because she is writing for an outside audience. Notice that she chooses to organize the write-up chronologically because she was observing a lesson from start to finish and needed to describe each step. Where appropriate, she incorporates specific details from her log to create a cohesive observation narrative. She also includes reminders from the "Notes for Later" column. She can follow up later with these questions and observations, but noting them during the observation will help her remember to do so.

WRITING AN EDUCATOR PROFILE

An educator profile requires you to use qualitative data to write a cohesive narrative for an outside audience. The assignment requires you to use information from an interview, another kind of qualitative data. An educator profile is more complex than an observation write-up because it requires you to first write interview questions and then talk with someone you may not know. Just as a field log scaffolds an observation write-up, an interview scaffolds an educator profile, because before you can write the profile, you must collect data by interviewing an educator. For a profile assignment, you usually interview an educator—a teacher, principal, or school psychologist, for example—in order to help you understand a profession in education to see whether you would like to choose a similar career. Because the educator profile amplifies the voice of an educator, this writing task also can facilitate change in education if you choose to write for an audience such as the local school community. The more that educators are highlighted, the more the public understands the professional and intellectual contributions they make to our communities and to society.

Steps in Successful Interviews

Interviewing always takes longer than you think it will because the process can be filled with false starts and setbacks. You may request an interview with someone but never receive a reply. You may set up a day and time for an interview, only to have the person cancel or reschedule. You also need time to research the person, school, and subject matter before the interview. Finally, you need to write interview questions (an interview protocol) and revise

Figure 5.1. Sample Observation Write-Up (written by Angela and annotated by the authors)

The lesson begins with a self-assessment of the learning objectives since the basic idea of constructivism as defined by Jean Piaget is that the knowledge students already have assimilates or accommodates new learning (Powell & Kalina, 2009). The teacher leads a whole-class discussion of a listening comprehension activity, which takes place on the third day of this learning event. Before he starts the activity, he hands out instructions to set up the activity and plays Pablo Neruda's sonnet (the first on the handout) aloud twice. He assigns different rows of students the task of identifying repetition, simile, alliteration, and hyperbole. With eight rows, two rows of students were actively listening for each poetic device. For example, both the first row to my right and the fifth row were assigned repetition, and after delivering instructions, he played the sonnet aloud once and made a formative assessment by a show of hands, asking students who need to hear the sonnet a second time. 20 of the 24 students raised their hands. He then reminded students to be listening for their device or, if they identified it, listen for another one. His directions allow some students to contribute to the whole-class discussion for devices not originally assigned to them. He then plays Neruda's sonnet a second time, and he leads instruction by gesturing towards the rows with repetition and calling on a student in one row, who identified "I love you" as an example of repetition. The teacher then projects the text of the sonnet on the screen, and students write their analyses of one of the poetic devices. To provide support for this analysis, the teacher has written on the board the sentence frame, also on the handout, and a list of strong verbs that students can use to write their analyses. The teacher then modeled one example with simile after students had written their analysis, and then called on students to share. They then moved onto the second sonnet, "Sonnet 147" by Shakespeare. Social constructivism, Lev Vygotsky's (2012) take on constructivism that incorporates social learning, is apparent in the instructional design of this learning segment.

> The writer frames the observation with a learning theory.

> After framing the narrative in a theory, the writer organizes the write-up chronologically.

> She orients the reader as to when this observation takes place.

> Specific details from the field log.

> An interpretation of the activity using course concepts on assessment.

> More specific details from the field log.

> An interpretation based on detailed observational data.

> Use of course concepts.

> Ends with an educational theory in order to interpret the entire observation.

them after getting feedback. If you aren't comfortable talking with people you don't know, you also may want to practice the interview with a friend. Long before your deadline, you'll need to start thinking about the following steps for successfully conducting an interview.

Choose Your Interview Subject Wisely. When thinking about whom to interview, you may be tempted to choose someone you know or someone close by. But instead of choosing the easiest person, choose the person who will best answer the questions you have. Don't worry about reaching out to someone you don't know. Often people are flattered by interview requests and welcome the idea of speaking about their expertise. You also should think about the interview as a way to network and meet people who may later help you when you begin your teaching career. In short, choose an authentic interview subject, not a convenient one. Think about what you want to accomplish from this interview. What are your goals? Generate a list of your ideal interview subjects. If you can't interview your first choice, it's a good idea to have a couple of other choices in mind.

Make Contact. After you have chosen several possible interview subjects, you need to ask them for an interview. It's always best to ask people for favors in person, particularly if you have never met. However, it's not always possible to meet in person, particularly if the person lives far away. The most important thing to consider when contacting people for interviews is to respect their time. They will be doing you a favor, so thank them up front. If you are contacting them through email, first explain why you are conducting the interview. Is it for a class assignment? If yes, explain the class and the assignment so they know the context of your questions. We suggest providing the following information in your email:

- Who you are
- Why you are conducting the interview
- Why you selected this person to interview
- What types of questions you will be asking
- How long the interview will take
- Where and when the interview will take place
- Whether you will record the interview
- The audience for the interview (who will be reading it)
- Whether the information will remain confidential
- Whether the person can remain anonymous
- Whether you will publish the profile outside of the classroom

Figure 5.2 provides an email template you can adapt to your needs.

Choose the Interview Format. After you have chosen an interview subject and received a reply, you will need to choose which format to use. Face-to-face interviews are best, but not always possible. Another choice is to use Skype or Zoom; both formats allow you to record the interview and see the person's facial expressions during the conversation. A last resort would be to email the list of questions and ask the teacher to respond in writing. Although email

Figure 5.2. Interview Request Template

To: lgutierrez@schooldistrict.edu
From: jrodrieguez@washington.edu
Subject: Request for Interview

Dear Mr. Gutierrez,

My name is Julia Rodriguez and I am a student in Dr. Murphy's Education 100 class at Washington University. For one of my class assignments I need to interview a high school math teacher, and Dr. Murphy suggested that I contact you because you use project-based learning in your class.

I would like to ask you a few questions about your pedagogy, focusing specifically on how you use project-based learning to teach math to English learners. I will need only one hour of your time, and I'm happy to meet you in your classroom at a time that is convenient for you. I would also like to record the interview, if you agree. Since this is for a class assignment, only my professor and I will read your responses.

Thank you in advance for your time.

Best,
Julia Rodriguez

---

interviews are helpful in one way—they provide already-typed transcripts—they do not allow you to easily ask follow-up questions or to see facial expressions and body language.

Write an Interview Protocol. Regardless of the format you choose, you'll need to prepare by writing an interview protocol, a final list of interview questions. Although it may be tempting to simply "wing it" in an interview, having a prepared list of questions will keep you on track and help you avoid appearing nervous. Having an interview protocol also helps you redirect the person you are interviewing if they get off track. Your protocol can be based on a teacher profile assignment or, if you are conducting action research, on your qualitative research questions.

Types of Interview Questions. When writing your questions, it's useful to write a variety of types to get the information you need. When writing each question, consider the goal/purpose for each question. Why are you asking this type of question? What information do you hope to gather? For example, Steiner Kvale (2008) suggests starting the interview with open-ended *introducing* questions that begin with phrases such as, "Can you tell me about . . . ?" or "Do you remember an occasion when . . . ?" Questions like these help you and your subject ease into a deeper, more specific discussion in which you can ask prepared *follow-up* questions to get more detailed information. In order to elicit more detailed information, you also can ask *probing* questions, such as, "Could you say something more about that?" "Can you give a more detailed description of what happened?" "Do you have further examples of this?" Don't be afraid to ask *direct* questions as the interview proceeds, especially if you don't think you are getting the information you need to answer your research questions. Questions such as, "Have you ever received money for good grades?" or "When you mention competition, do you mean a sportsmanlike or a destructive competition?" are easier for your subject to answer once they feel comfortable with you. You can end the interview with an opportunity for your subject to share additional information you may not have asked about. For example, asking, "Is there anything else you'd like to say?" or "Would you like to ask me any questions?" signals the end of the interview and provides time to ease out of the interview rather than abruptly ending it. Finally, don't forget to thank your participant for their time and expertise; both are valuable to your work.

Your interview questions should be detailed and focused on the purpose of your interview. You don't need to include Kvale's (2008) question types, but understanding that questions can fulfill different purposes will allow you to better prepare for any interview situation.

Table 5.4 is a template you can adapt to focus your interview questions on the audience and purpose of your specific profile assignment.

Table 5.4. Interview Protocol Template

Person being interviewed:
Interview purpose:
Profile audience:
Audience's needs:
Provide interview context for interview subject (e.g., assignment, no publication without permission, offer a pseudonym, recording permission, etc.):
Questions before beginning?
Interview questions
1. Question—goal
2. Question—goal
3. Question—goal
4. Question—goal
5. Question—goal
6. Question—goal
7. Question—goal
8. Question—goal
9. Question—goal
10. Question—goal
Questions before closing?
Plan for follow-up (sending draft of assignment, etc.).

Table 5.5. Interview Protocol Sample

Question	Question Type
Could you start off by telling me a bit about yourself (personal life, educational background, etc.)?	Introducing question
Which grade levels have you taught and why?	Introducing question
What does your current educational work involve?	Follow-up question
To what extent do you know what is going on with your students outside of the classroom?	Structuring question (changes to the focus of the interview)
Do you mean that you know what your students do in their spare time?	Interpreting question
How does information help you differentiate your instruction?	Follow-up question
How do you make sure each student gets the level of attention they need (meaning, spreading out your time and identifying who needs what)?	Follow-up question
Can you say more about how you manage your time to meet each student's needs? Can you give me an example?	Probing question
How do you specifically reach students who don't want to engage?	Specifying question
Have any books or articles informed your teaching?	Structuring question
What advice would you give new teachers about getting a full picture of their students in order to differentiate instruction?	Structuring question
Do you have any questions for me?	Direct question

Table 5.5 is an interview protocol for a science teacher. The purpose of the interview was to understand how teachers form holistic views of their students and how they apply the knowledge of their individual students to differentiate their instruction. The student conducting the interview had interned in this teacher's class, so she was able to write the interview protocol using some of Kvale's (2008) question types. Because she had observed his teaching, she was better able to ask targeted questions about his pedagogy. The interview based on this protocol took approximately 1 hour to conduct.

Conducting an Interview

After arranging an interview and writing your interview protocol, you are all set to conduct your interview. We recommend recording the interview using available technology on a smartphone. But always ask for permission ahead of time. We also recommend taking detailed notes during the interview. It is important to remember that while all the strategies we have given you in this chapter help you prepare, when interviewing, you need to be patient and listen rather than talk. Be in the moment and respond based on what the subject has said, not based on what you are thinking about. Be flexible and move away from your protocol if necessary, but direct your subject back to the questions gently if needed. Also, don't judge or make assumptions about what your subject believes or thinks. Always remember that you are there to learn about, and from, the subject.

Transcribing an Interview

If you have recorded an interview, you may want to transcribe it in order to write your profile or case study. An interview transcription allows you to read the interview in order to find relevant quotes or discover patterns or themes. You may not have to transcribe the full interview, depending on your purpose. If you are a graduate student working on a case study, it may make sense to transcribe the entire interview, but in most undergraduate classes, simply listening repeatedly to the interview and taking notes on the relevant information are often enough.

Selecting Usable Data from an Interview to Write a Profile

Like an observation write-up, an educator profile requires you to be selective about which qualitative data you will use. In fact, one of the problems with qualitative research is that you may feel overwhelmed by data and have to learn how to narrow and select which data are most important. You can't, and shouldn't, write about everything, so choose the details you think are most important to your specific audience. Consider the following questions:

- What story about education are you trying to tell?
- What do you want your reader to learn?

Also, when reviewing your interview transcripts, notes, or recording, keep the following in mind:

- Choose relevant quotes that highlight the story you want to tell and that will be interesting to your audience.
- Avoid stereotypes without factual data even if they come from your interview subject.
- Distinguish between opinion and fact.
- Find specific details that will help your reader picture the educational setting.
- Consider whether the interview data lend themselves to any other organizational structure: Cause and effect? Chronological order? Reverse chronological order?

An educator profile is not simply a summary of the interview; if it were, your reader could just read your interview transcript. You want to highlight what makes this educator special or different, so choose an organizational method based on those characteristics.

If you plan on trying to publish your profile, choose the publications you want to target before you write. You will need to submit a profile based on the publication's audience and space requirements. For example, Figure 5.3 is a teacher profile published in *The Davis Enterprise*, a local newspaper for the city of Davis, California (Jaradeh, 2015). Davis is a university town with a strong science focus. *Enterprise* readers take pride in their public schools and value the teachers who focus on college preparation. Because space was limited, Katrin, the author, had to distill a lengthy interview into the most important aspects of the teacher's pedagogy: a holistic approach to teaching science.

Figure 5.3. Sample Educator Profile (written by Katrin and annotated by the authors)

Teacher's Holistic Approach Works

"I like to consider the child in a holistic way by learning what motivates them and increases their curiosity," says Kenneth McKim, a science teacher at Harper Junior High School.

> The profile begins with a quote from the teacher to highlight the thesis of the piece: a holistic approach.

> The reader knows who the teacher is right away.

I had the pleasure of interning in McKim's classroom this spring and watched him put that philosophy into action. Classroom visitors can easily see how dedicated McKim is to the students, and how comprehensive his approach is when addressing struggling students. The community of Davis is fortunate to have such an understanding science teacher who prepares students for their bright future.

> Katrin speaks directly to the audience while highlighting the exceptional work teachers do.

McKim strongly believes that "if a student is not ready to learn that day, leave them be and allow them to become ready to learn." He knows that not every student is alike, and that some need extra help to excel in the sciences. Furthermore, his main goals are to educate the students and prepare them for college.

> Katrin integrates the most important quotes, but doesn't overwhelm the reader with them.

As a fourth-year biology student at UC Davis, I was very impressed with the complexity level of the labs students completed in McKim's class. For example, the students took part in DNA isolation labs using equipment such as micropipeters and epindorffs. These students are fortunate to have a teacher who can properly prepare them for college and various post-baccalaureate tests.

> Here Katrin makes her ethos clear. She is a biology undergraduate so she is a good judge of McKim's class.

Many people often forget the importance of writing in science, but McKim has found many ways to incorporate it into his lesson plans. His philosophy of holism corresponds to his varied teaching style to accommodate the diverse population of students.

> Another mention of the main point in order to keep the reader on track.

For starters, after students complete an experiment, they are asked to write a full lab report that includes data and analysis.

> Katrin highlights McKim's writing focus because it is something that makes him stand out.

Figure 5.3. Sample Educator Profile (written by Katrin and annotated by the authors)
  (continued)

This type of writing is important to learn in such a low-stakes environment because it is a crucial skill in college.

Furthermore, students are asked to write reflections to test questions in order to find a pattern for their mistakes. It is important to teach students to reflect on their work and find out their weaknesses in order to grow. This is not only a useful skill for his classroom, but for their entire educational career.

McKim's love for science is apparent not only through his teaching style, but also his classroom environment. Walking into his classroom is like walking into a museum. There are big globes from different eras hanging from the ceiling, different organic molecules on the walls, various periodic tables, and live animal tanks.

> Katrin uses specific details from her field log.

McKim facilitates a creative and safe learning environment where students respect each other. In our busy world, it is refreshing to step into a classroom where the teacher takes time to get to know each student and his or her learning style.

> Katrin returns to the opening paragraph about McKim's holistic approach.

—Katrin Jaradeh will graduate from UC Davis this month with a biological sciences degree. She interned this spring in Kenneth McKim's science classes at Harper Junior High School.

Source: *The Davis Enterprise,* June 9, 2015, reproduced by permission.

WRITING A CASE STUDY

As you move from your undergraduate writing assignments into your credential or master's program, you may be asked to conduct qualitative research in order to write a case study. The term "case study" refers to both the research methodology and the final written genre. As we mentioned in Chapter 4, a case study is one type of educational qualitative research that requires you to be in the field collecting observational and interview data. As the name suggests, case studies "identify a single social unit—a person, a group, a place or activity, or some combination of those units" (Dyson & Genishi, 2005, p. 3). Case study research prioritizes context and argues that meaning develops from the particulars, and that educational sites reveal complex social activities and relationships (Dyson & Genishi, 2005). The case study is a genre that requires you to apply all that you have learned in this chapter about field observations, interviews, and selectively choosing data to write about. Because a case study requires you to synthesize scholarly sources and multiple types of qualitative data, it is the most difficult genre covered in this chapter.

When conducting case study research, you should begin with a research question (see Chapter 4) and systematically collect data in order to answer your question, always keeping in mind that your research question may change according to your data. In fact, in order to decide what your case will be, you first need to know what you are trying to find out. For example, if you want to understand English learners from a student perspective, it makes sense to choose a student learning English, instead of the student's teacher, as your "case." In this instance, although the case study research would involve interviewing teachers and observing the child in the classroom, your primary focus would be the student. In addition to observational and interview data, you may need to collect information from students' cumulative folders or permanent records, test scores, demographic data about the local school community, and any other information you can gather.

Although there are many books on case study research (see Dyson & Genishi, 2005; Swanborn, 2010; Yin, 2003), and just as many different approaches to case study research, we focus on the type of case study you most likely will write for a teaching credential or a master's program. Like the other assignments in this chapter, a case study requires a similar rhetorical move: writing a cohesive narrative using qualitative data as evidence.

Analyzing a Sample Case Study

The Qualitative Data. Because most case studies can be 20 pages or more, here we analyze excerpts from a case study so that you can see how one preservice teacher used qualitative data to create her case study narrative. The excerpts are from a case study by Emily Matsuda, a preservice teacher in California's Central Valley. The case study centers on Pamela, a student who previously was considered an English learner, but who has now been re-designated as English proficient. Pamela, the "case" of this study, speaks Hmong as a primary language but is considered fluent in English. Before writing her case study, Emily conducted extensive qualitative research in order to contribute to the existing knowledge on the language usage and abilities of re-designated English learners. The data she collected included:

- *Observations of the student's mainstream classes.* Emily observed five different teachers on two separate days.
- *Interviews.* Emily interviewed the student and three of her teachers: her past English language development teacher, her English teacher, and her French teacher.
- *The student's cumulative folder.* The folder included the student's California English language development test scores, a kindergarten language assessment, and information about the student's language background.

- *The district's course management system.* The system includes tools that allow for parent/teacher communication, classroom assignments and announcements, and student grades.

Because she explored Pamela's past and present language ability, and observed her in many different contexts, Emily was able to use these data to paint a full picture of Pamela. Interviewing Pamela also allowed Emily to include the student's perspective, rather than relying solely on Pamela's teachers' views. Emily chose to organize her case study based on the types of qualitative data she collected: observations, interviews, and student information. Although her organizational strategy worked well, you may choose to organize your case study by themes or course concepts. We suggest asking your instructor or committee members which organizational structure they prefer. You also might ask whether they have any samples from former students that you could use as a guide. As with all samples we analyze in this guide, keep in mind that you can organize your writing according to *your* specific rhetorical situation.

Emily's case study includes a few outside scholarly sources, but she doesn't include a literature review or a theoretical framework to frame her discussions. If Emily were to pursue a doctorate in education, she would be required to include extensive references and choose a theoretical framework to help make sense of her data. But, for our purposes, we analyze Emily's case study based on how she has applied the skills and concepts we have discussed in this chapter.

Writing About Observational Data. Just as you may have done for observation write-ups in the past, when conducting observations for a case study be sure to use a field log and then selectively write about the observations to shed light on your case. When Emily observed Pamela's mainstream teachers, she focused on how they approached teaching English learners because Pamela is a re-designated English learner. Figure 5.4 is an excerpt of Emily's observation write-up in her case study.

Figure 5.4. Case Study Excerpt of a Teacher Observation (written by Emily and annotated by the authors)

Attending Pamela's classes allowed me to observe five of her teachers on two separate days. Pamela does not have an English language development (ELD) teacher; all her teachers teach in mainstream classroom settings. Mr. Dunbar and Mrs. Nguyen clearly scaffolded instruction for their students, while Mr. Bennett, Mr. Galvin, and Ms. Wilson focused on delivering content. Overall, Pamela is an attentive, obedient, and quiet student who completed her work; she does not engage with peers or teachers unless directly

| Specific background information about the observations in order to orient the reader. |

| Interpretations of Pamela based on factual observations. |

approached. Her participation did not vary throughout the classes. She spoke very little throughout the day, walking alone to classes. Her isolation was social, linguistic, and academic in nature. She had few opportunities to give verbal output and collaborate with peers who speak her target language of English.

Mr. Dunbar scores high across the Observation Protocol for Academic Literacies (OPAL) rubric for scaffolding instruction. He gave students material, verbal, and visual supports in order to speak beginning French. Mr. Dunbar occasionally repeated and clarified directions in English and spoke using shorter and less complex sentences. These specially designed academic instruction in English (SDAIE) strategies promoted quality interactions among the students because the input simplification allowed students to comprehend Mr. Dunbar's directions and complete their task. Mr. Dunbar also checked frequently for understanding. He began class with student–teacher interaction in which conversations were modeled, and then students transitioned into peer-to-peer interaction with the same concepts. During both of these activities, Mr. Dunbar specifically called on or checked in with Pamela; he was the only teacher to speak one-on-one with her. Pamela seemed prepared for the class since she only must produce words and very short sentences. Pamela was also able to connect this subject to her life, interviewing her older sister to compare their traits and qualities. French provides Pamela with the most scaffolding since language teachers use strategies to support all their students as language learners.

> Detailed examples of scaffolding.

> Focus on how the teacher communicated with Pamela.

Pamela's other teachers had learning environments, lessons, and styles that were less EL-friendly. Scoring low on the OPAL rubric, Mr. Bennett did check for comprehension to review for an upcoming test. However, the review entailed no student-to-student interaction, no meaningful connections, and no visualized key terms and main ideas. The classroom environment, which only displayed sports memorabilia, could have supported ELs with a word wall. Mr. Bennett's modeling of problem-solving was not a SDAIE strategy because he gave students answers and explained specific problems rather than main concepts. Despite her low performance on a recent test, Pamela never participated when Mr. Bennett asked students to volunteer problems they wanted to review. Pamela likely would not ask for help in this environment even if she was actually confused.

> Emily remains focused on how the teacher observations relate to Pamela, a re-designated English learner.

> Here Emily is contrasting Mr. Dunbar's observation with Mr. Bennett's.

Figure 5.5. Case Study Excerpt of Teacher Interview Information (written by Emily and annotated by the authors)

One of Pamela's mainstreamed classes is English 9P with Mrs. Nguyen. Mrs. Nguyen identifies Pamela's greatest need in her writing. Pamela has difficulty expressing comprehension, although at this point it is unclear whether that difficulty arises from lack of linguistic "tools" to express herself, like vocabulary, or lack of understanding. The best way to determine the difference is to have a discussion with Pamela and have her verbalize her comprehension skills. Mrs. Nguyen stresses a concern she has in meeting Pamela's needs: Mrs. Nguyen may not have enough time to work with Pamela on her writing—her greatest area of need in literacy—and Pamela may slip "under the radar" because she is well-behaved, produces work, and studies. Consequently, evidence of her struggling may not be as glaring as for other students. Mrs. Nguyen and I both question how the needs of Hmong students may differ from those of other EL students. Teachers need to remember to give more attention, Mrs. Nguyen suggests, and to consider how students like Pamela fare with complex reading tasks like *Romeo and Juliet*, an upcoming unit in the spring semester. For now, Mrs. Nguyen will encourage Pamela to make it a norm to receive extra writing help, whether with us or through the peer tutor program on campus.

> The interview write-ups all focus on Pamela and avoid including extraneous information.

> Emily includes relevant words and phrases from the interview and avoids including long quotes.

However, Mr. Bennett, like Mrs. Nguyen, has noticed that Pamela needs extra time to produce the language. His theory behind this difficulty again relates to vocabulary: Pamela needs extra time because she processes between languages—from Hmong to English to French, or Hmong to French, or English to French—while she pulls from her vocabulary store in Hmong or English, neither of which may be that expansive.

> Emily effectively compares how different instructors assess Pamela's language skills.

Writing About Interview Data. After Emily interviewed Pamela's English teacher, she again wrote only about the sections of the interview that focused on Pamela, even though she may have talked with the teacher about many other issues. In the excerpt in Figure 5.5, you can see that she used quotes from the interview sparingly, including only relevant key terms and phrases in quotation marks.

Emily interviewed three of Pamela's teachers in order to get a picture of Pamela from several perspectives. When writing about multiple interviews, look for how you can compare and contrast the information. As in the observation section, Emily remains focused on the parts of the interview that related to Pamela, particularly her language abilities.

Figure 5.6. Case Study Excerpt of Pamela's Interview (written by Emily and annotated by the authors)

When I asked Pamela about her home literacy, I discovered that she uses Hmong more often at home but does occasionally use English. Conversely, she sometimes uses Hmong with friends at school. Thus, her language use is blended in both her home and school environments. Her parents speak only Hmong, but her nine siblings, most of whom are older, also speak English, so Pamela uses English to communicate with her siblings at home when she needs help with homework. In other cases, Pamela uses Hmong at home, though she states that she never had formal schooling in her primary language. Instead, the Hmong that she knows was learned mainly from her siblings, as well as her parents. When asked about her language preferences, Pamela hesitated. She finds that she feels more comfortable using a certain language depending on the modality—speaking, writing, listening, and reading, all of which are tested through the California English Language Development Test (CELDT). Specifically, Pamela prefers to speak in Hmong but to write in English, and she believes herself to be a fluent reader in English, and in my opinion, a fluent listener. She describes writing in Hmong as "difficult." Her challenge with writing in English makes sense because she has less experience writing in Hmong from which she can transfer knowledge and skills.

> When reading this excerpt, you can see the types of interview questions Emily asked.

> Use of specific details.

> Provides context for the reader about how language abilities are tested in California.

> Emily uses the exact terms Pamela uses to describe herself.

Interviewing Pamela. After writing about her observations and interviews with Pamela's teachers, Emily sought information from Pamela because she is the focus of the case study. All of the data collection for the case study provided context, and this interview illustrates how Pamela views her own language use compared with how Pamela's teachers view her language abilities. Because Pamela is the "case" of the study, no research would be complete without interviewing her; qualitative research values and prioritizes the voices of those under study. Figure 5.6 shows an excerpt from Emily's case study description of her interview with Pamela.

Writing About Additional Student Information. In order to get a fuller picture of Pamela's language abilities, Emily also looked at the information contained in her cumulative folder—the folder that contains a student's educational information starting in kindergarten, or when a student first enters U.S. schools. By reviewing these data, Emily could start to see whether any patterns or relationships existed between what she saw during her observation and Pamela's past. Because students' folders contain sensitive and private student information, you may not always be given permission to access them.

Figure 5.7. Case Study Excerpt About Additional Student Information (written by Emily and annotated by the authors)

Pamela's school folder goes beyond basic information like CELDT scores, language background, and transcripts because of the documents it includes. Most documents are from Pamela's initial primary language assessments in 2008 as a kindergartner: a Primary Language Diagnostic rated Pamela as fluent in Hmong, an Oral Primary Language Assessment transcribed an interview with Pamela, and a Home Language Survey completed by Pamela's mother declared Hmong as the first language Pamela spoke and the most frequently used language at home, by parents, and by other adults around Pamela. These documents offer data more qualitative and subjective in nature that are notably absent since 2008. In the case of the Oral Primary Language Assessment from 2008, the interviewer insightfully commented on Pamela's demeanor around unfamiliar people: "[Pamela] seemed shy. I have a feeling that if she was more comfortable with me (knew me) she would have responded more." This reticence to speak seems to have carried over from kindergarten to English 9P, though the five-year-old Pamela did speak in complete and colorful sentences in Hmong. In fact, from all my transcriptions, I hypothesize that Pamela may be more of an active conversationalist in Hmong than in English.

> Emily explains why the additional information is useful.

> Detailed descriptions of the information.

> Emily's interpretation of the data.

> Emily connects the past information to the present.

> Emily hypothesizes about Pamela's language usage based on all of her data.

In all qualitative research studies, you need permission from your participants to observe, interview, and collect additional classroom artifacts such as student work. Figure 5.7 provides an example of a case study addressing this additional information.

CONDUCTING ACTION RESEARCH

Although Emily's case study taught her much about one student and one school context, at the time she wrote it she was not yet a practicing teacher with her own classroom and students. If she had been, she might have chosen instead to conduct action research, a type of education research in which you are the focus of the research process. Like case studies, action research requires you to observe, interview, and collect additional student and school data, but with your own students and school community. The primary reason to conduct action research is to explore how to deepen your own pedagogical knowledge or to solve a problem within your school. Because you are systematically investigating your own practice, you are what is called a "participant researcher," meaning that you are actively part of what you are studying.

Action research is also far more reflective than other forms of research. While reflection is part of any research process, in action research, reflecting on your students, your practice, and your school is central to your study. And, like all research, action research requires you to read and cite scholarly sources, create research questions, and collect and analyze data, with the final product perhaps being published in a teacher-centered journal such as *Action Research*. You can think of writing about your action research as the professional application of everything you have learned in your undergraduate education classes and your teaching credential or master's program.

Although we won't go into more detail about action research in this book, to find out more you can read one of the many guides available, such as Efrat and Ravid's *Action Research in Education: A Practical Guide* (2013). Conducting action research is the next step in your professional development and can lead to you speaking as an expert in order to make change in your practices, students, and community.

EXERCISES

1. Find a place outside the classroom and spend approximately 15 minutes writing a field log about one group of people. How does it feel to observe? What types of observations are you able to record? What are the challenges to observing human behavior? Come back to class and discuss your observation process in pairs or groups.

2. In pairs, write an interview protocol about any topic for your classmate using Kvale's (2008) question categories. Then, using the protocol, interview each other. What did you learn about the interview process? Share your reflections with the class.

3. In small groups, discuss the sample case study excerpts in Figures 5.4, 5.5, 5.6, and 5.7. What is effective about them? What could be improved?

Part II

PROFESSIONAL WRITING

CHAPTER 6

Writing Lesson Plans

In Chapter 5, you learned how to conduct observations and interviews of students and teachers. In this chapter, we'll discuss how to put that knowledge into practice to develop lesson plans that are designed to meet the needs of students in your specific teaching environment. After using your observation and interview techniques to learn who your students are, and to understand the teaching and learning conditions at your school site, you will be able to design a curriculum that effectively facilitates student learning.

EXAMINING THE RHETORICAL SITUATION: PURPOSE, AUDIENCE, CONTEXT, VOICE, AND GENRE

Lesson plans are a common genre for teachers to write. Because of their frequent use in the educational context, lesson plans have a rich rhetorical situation. The purpose for writing your lesson plans may vary depending on where you are in your teaching career. The purpose for writing lesson plans in your methods courses is to demonstrate your pedagogical content knowledge. The purpose for writing a lesson plan in your credential or master's program as part of your teaching practicum is to determine your efficacy in your placement. In your teaching portfolio assessment (like the edTPA), the purpose of your lesson plan is to determine your competency as an educator. When you write lesson plans for a substitute teacher, the purpose is to ensure that pedagogically sound activities take place in your classroom during your absence. The purpose of your lesson plan in your annual review is to reflect your professional growth to your school administrator. And while all of these purposes are critical in your development as a teacher, ultimately the most important purpose of your lesson plans is to facilitate your students' learning.

The audiences for your lesson plans may be as varied as the purposes for writing them. In your education courses, your audience may be your professor or your cooperating teacher. As a classroom teacher, you will write lesson plans for yourself. However, if you are submitting lesson plans as part of an evaluation of your teaching, your audience could be an administrator or evaluator. As a practicing teacher, you may share (or distribute) your lesson plans with colleagues or the parents of your students. A more frequent audience for your lesson plans may be a substitute teacher. Drafting your lesson plans with specific audiences in mind will allow you to achieve these different purposes.

The voice that you'll use in your lesson plan will be dependent on your audience for the document. When you write lesson plans for yourself, your voice will be informal and personal. Your word choice will have to make sense only to you, and you'll be able to use slang or abbreviations. When you write lesson plans for a substitute teacher, you can still use an informal tone, but you'll want to make sure that your word choice is clear and direct. Using a friendly and informative voice, use language that is free from ambiguities. With specific word choice, which provides contextual information about your classroom environment, your substitute will be able to achieve the learning outcomes for the lesson plan.

However, when you write lesson plans for assessment or evaluation purposes, the tone will need to be significantly more formal. When your audience is a professor, a cooperating teacher, an outside assessor, or an administrator, you will need to use a professional and informed tone. Your word choice should reflect your knowledge in the field of education; therefore, you may want to include specialized words or jargon from the field of education. The stance you take in your lesson plans will depend on their purpose. Because your stance in a lesson plan reflects your teacher identity, consider how you want to present yourself to the audience for your plan and use your voice accordingly. See Table 6.1 for a visual representation of the rhetorical situations surrounding lesson plans.

The format of a lesson plan varies widely and depends on the plan's purpose and audience. While there are certain stable characteristics that most lesson plans share, teachers regularly develop their own format for the lesson plan genre. There are many credible Internet sources for lesson plans, such as readwritethink.org or pbs.org/teachers. A search through one of these websites will demonstrate the wide range of elements within plans. Teachers are collaborative in their design of curriculum and assessment and encourage the sharing of ideas. If you choose to include in your plans the ideas or materials of other teachers, be sure to make the correct attributions and to properly cite the materials (see Chapter 10 for more information about citing sources). One thing to keep in mind if you choose to include the work or ideas of other teachers is that they will not know the context in which you teach (or plan to teach). Consider the rhetorical situation of your lesson plan and choose the form of the genre that will be appropriate for your lesson's purpose and your students. This means that you most likely will have to modify, sometimes significantly, the content or approach of lesson plans you find online to meet the specific needs of your particular students.

The format of the lesson plan will depend on the rhetorical situation. If you are writing lesson plans in order to complete an assessment of your teaching for a professor, administrator, or credentialing board, the format often is dictated by the assessors. It is your responsibility to follow the requirements of

Table 6.1. Rhetorical Situations of Lesson Plans

Purpose	Audience	Context	Voice
To demonstrate pedagogical content matter	Education professor	Education methods course	Professional tone, specific word choice, clear stance as a novice teacher
To determine your efficacy in your placement	Teaching practicum site supervisor and cooperating teacher	Credential or master's program	Professional tone, specific word choice, stance based on your experiences in the classroom
To determine your competency as an educator	Teaching portfolio assessment evaluators (practicing or retired classroom teachers)	Teaching portfolio assessment (such as the edTPA)	Professional tone that is confident and articulate, specialized word choice and jargon, stance based on personal experience and research-based practices
To address standards and/or framework for your grade level or discipline	Yourself; additionally, collaborating teachers and parents of students	Daily curriculum of your teaching environment	Informal, personal, word choice that can be abbreviated or slang, stance based on local classroom community
To ensure pedagogically sound activities occur in your classroom	Substitute teacher	Your absence from the classroom	Informal, friendly, word choice that is clear and specific, stance based on local classroom community
To reflect your professional growth	Your school administrator	Your annual review	Professional tone, specific word choice, stance based on your experiences in your specific classroom

the format as set by the audience. When you are the sole audience of your lesson plans, they may become personal and informal in both format and tone, as they are meant to be read only by yourself. If you review other teachers' lesson plans, you as a reader will note how different they may look, sound, or even feel. Some teachers are influenced by the way in which they were taught to write lesson plans, while others produce plans based on the resources they have available to them.

With such varied audiences and potentially varied purposes, before you begin drafting your lesson plans, it is important to consider every aspect of the rhetorical situation of lesson plans. Use the graphic organizer in Table 6.2 as a reflection tool.

KNOWING YOUR TEACHING ENVIRONMENT IN ORDER TO WRITE AN EFFECTIVE LESSON PLAN

Once you have carefully examined the rhetorical situation surrounding your lesson plan, it is necessary to investigate the teaching environment in which

Table 6.2. Lesson Plan Rhetorical Situation Graphic Organizer

What is the **purpose** of this lesson plan? What are your reasons for writing this lesson plan, in addition to student learning?
Who is the **audience** for this lesson plan, beyond you as the teacher? Is there more than one audience? What do you want them to see or notice in your lesson plan?
What is the **context** surrounding your lesson plan? What are the circumstances surrounding your lesson plan?
What **voice** do you want to establish in your lesson plan? How can your word choice and tone articulate the objectives of the lesson and achieve the document's purpose?
What is the specific format of the lesson plan **genre** you are required to use? What elements must be included in your lesson plan? Is there flexibility in the genre?

you plan to give your lesson. What are the circumstances surrounding student learning in your classroom? In order to answer this question, it is imperative that you use your data collection skills (as discussed in Chapters 4 and 5) to collect the necessary information to shape the construction of effective lesson plans. This information may include the content or standards required in your lesson, as well as the abilities and interests of your students. A great place to begin thinking about how you will effectively write your lesson plan is to consider *how* you will teach the content to your students.

Applying Pedagogical Content Knowledge to Your Lesson Plan

A teacher's ability to convert her own knowledge of a topic (or content knowledge) into successful pedagogical practices is called the teacher's pedagogical content knowledge, "which goes beyond knowledge of subject matter per se to the dimension of subject matter knowledge *for teaching*" (Shulman, 1986, p. 9, emphasis in original). Shulman (1986) defines pedagogical content knowledge as a teacher's understanding of "the most useful forms of representation of those ideas [of the lesson], the most powerful analogies, illustrations, examples, explanations, and demonstrations" (p. 9). In other words, pedagogical content knowledge means that you not only understand a concept but also have the tools to teach it to your students.

Often, your pedagogical content knowledge will help you scaffold your lesson. Scaffolding is the process of organizing your lesson into "chunks" and "providing [your students] a tool or structure, with each chunk" (Alber, 2011). Effective scaffolding is informed by your pedagogical content knowledge, as this knowledge "also includes an understanding of what makes the learning of specific topics easy or difficult: the conceptions and preconceptions that students of different ages and backgrounds bring with them to the learning of those most frequently taught topics and lessons" (Shulman, 1986, p. 9). Thus, your pedagogical content knowledge will allow you to anticipate the areas of your lesson plan that students may find challenging or easy. Scaffolding in an effective lesson plan may include introducing the content (in an appropriate mode of instruction), modeling the skills and knowledge required by the learning outcomes, and offering students the chance to practice the skills in a low-stakes environment before their summative assessment. See "Plan for Instruction" in the sample lesson plan in Figure 6.2 for a model of effective scaffolding.

Understanding the Standards in Your Teaching Environment

In order to successfully incorporate standards into your lesson plan, you first must determine how they are used at your school site or for the task you have been assigned. Some districts are more flexible than others in how they mandate incorporating standards into the curriculum, but effective teachers need to know which grade-level standards and major content concepts are required to be included in their lesson plans. In your education courses, you may have been introduced to the political history surrounding state curricular standards in this country. However, you may not fully understand the political, social, or economic histories surrounding the standards, or why some of your professors or cooperating teachers may hold strong, and sometimes opposing, positions on standards design, use, or implementation in your state. Writing lesson plans is a great opportunity to learn more about the standards your state has adopted.

At the time of this book's publication, 41 states, the District of Columbia, and four U.S. territories have adopted a local version of the Common Core State Standards (CCSS Initiative, 2018). And while a small number of states have not adopted the CCSS, this does not mean that they do not have state curricular standards. As we discussed in Chapter 4, you can locate your state's standards through your state department of education's website and, once you've located the text of these standards, isolate the standards for your grade level or discipline.

Your state also may have adopted, or may be considering adopting, discipline-specific standards, such as the Next Generation Science Standards. Some states have also adopted curricular frameworks to ensure that classes in the disciplines across the state are covering similar content in their courses. For example, in 2016 the state of California adopted the *History-Social Science Framework for California Public Schools Kindergarten Through Grade 12* (California State Department of Education [CDE], 2017). In this framework, required content areas are outlined and curricular outcomes are framed through questions. For example, the framework for 8th grade includes a section on "the development of American constitutional democracy," and contains three questions:

- "Why was there an American Revolution?"
- "How did the American Revolution develop the concept of natural rights?"
- "What are the legacies of the American Revolution?" (CDE, 2017)

In this example, the framework gives 8th-grade history teachers a specific topic from which to develop their lesson plans. Therefore, it is necessary to learn as much as you can about the standards and frameworks in your state or discipline before you draft your lesson plans, so you'll know exactly where to focus the content.

Thinking about state standards as a support system rather than as the actual content of your lesson may be a useful way to incorporate them into your lesson. When discussing the writing standards, Murphy and Smith (2015) promote this lens through which to view the Common Core State Standards: "The CCSS are not a curriculum. They provide a flexible kind of road map for teaching writing and identifying ultimate destinations, but they do not require a particular route for getting there" (p. 132). The content of your lesson plan is the route you have designed for student learning, and as you draft your plan, make sure that this route includes destinations that are required by the state standards for your grade level and discipline.

Navigating Vertically Aligned Standards

As you review the CCSS from kindergarten to grade 12, you'll note that the language and goals of the several sections of standards may sound similar across grade levels. That is, the main principles of some of the standards remain consistent, while the level of complexity increases as students advance through the grade levels. This approach to developing standards is referred to as vertical alignment, a term you may have heard in your education courses. An awareness of the vertical alignment of the standards addressed in your lesson plan can give you a clear understanding of how the standards in your lesson differ from similar standards in the grades below and above your own. This awareness will allow you to articulate how your lesson plans are meeting the grade-level needs of your students. Table 6.3 demonstrates how the complexity of one standard in the CCSS English Language Arts Standards in Speaking and Listening increases across grade levels.

Writing Lesson Plans for Specific Students

After you've reviewed how standards are used in your teaching environment, it is necessary to learn more about the students for whom you will be writing your lesson plans. A great place to find information about your students is your district's website. Your district will have valuable information on your

Table 6.3. Vertically Aligned Speaking and Listening Standard

Grade Level	Language of Standard
Kindergarten	CCSS.ELA-LITERACY.SL.K.4 "Describe familiar people, places, things, and events and, with prompting and support, provide additional detail" (National Governors Association Center for Best Practices & Council of Chief State School Officers, 2010f)
Grade 3	CCSS.ELA-LITERACY.SL.3.4 "Report on a topic or text, tell a story, or recount an experience with appropriate facts and relevant, descriptive details, speaking at an understandable pace" (National Governors Association Center for Best Practices & Council of Chief State School Officers, 2010b)
Grade 6	CCSS.ELA-LITERACY.SL.6.4 "Present claims and findings, sequencing ideas logically and using pertinent descriptions, facts, and details to accentuate main ideas or themes; use appropriate eye contact, adequate volume, and clear pronunciation" (National Governors Association Center for Best Practices & Council of Chief State School Officers, 2010c)
Grade 9–10	CCSS.ELA-LITERACY.SL.9-10.4 "Present information, findings, and supporting evidence clearly, concisely, and logically such that listeners can follow the line of reasoning and the organization, development, substance, and style are appropriate to purpose, audience, and task" (National Governors Association Center for Best Practices & Council of Chief State School Officers, 2010d)
Grade 11–12	CCSS.ELA-LITERACY.SL.11-12.4 "Present information, findings, and supporting evidence, conveying a clear and distinct perspective, such that listeners can follow the line of reasoning, alternative or opposing perspectives are addressed, and the organization, development, substance, and style are appropriate to purpose, audience, and a range of formal and informal tasks" (National Governors Association Center for Best Practices & Council of Chief State School Officers, 2010e)

school site's student populations, test scores, and the number of children who qualify for free and reduced lunch, as well as other useful sources of data. Your state may also have a Dashboard, which may include even more specific sources of data about your student population. See, for example, the State of Texas Dashboard at texasschoolaccountabilitydashboard.org/.

What will the students you are planning for be able, and excited, to learn? Base student interest and ability on data collected in your observations or in your scholarly research. If you have not spent a significant amount of time in a classroom setting, use this opportunity to apply the skills you learned in Chapter 5 to collect further data on student interest and ability: Interview a teacher, speak to parents, review the standards in your state, or look for representative student work. For example, CCSS *Appendix C: Samples of Student*

Writing includes samples of students' writing from grades K–12, which may help you conceptualize the spectrum of students' writing and critical-thinking abilities (National Governors Association Center for Best Practices & Council of Chief State School Officers, 2010a). Similarly, consult the education research that you've read in your coursework to ensure that the content of your lesson and the modes of instruction reflect the best practices in the field of education, or your discipline, as determined through research.

A final consideration in learning more about your teaching environment is to consider whether all of your students will have opportunities to achieve success in the plan. Offering various opportunities for success in your lesson is called differentiated instruction, which may allow you to acknowledge who your students are as learners and offer them targeted opportunities for success (see, for example, Subban, 2005, for more information about differentiated instruction). However, differentiated instruction may also conceal as much as it can reveal about your students in that it can use categories to make generalizations about large groups of student learners. The most effective way to combat overgeneralizing about your students is to familiarize yourself with who they are as learners by maintaining an open dialogue with them and respecting them.

DESIGNING A LESSON PLAN

Write your lesson plan with the larger picture of your plan in mind. Carefully consider how the elements of your lesson will work together to meet the stated purpose(s) of the plan. Figure 6.1 outlines the close relationship of several key elements included in lesson plans. Because of the interconnected

Figure 6.1. Interconnected Relationship of Lesson Plan Components

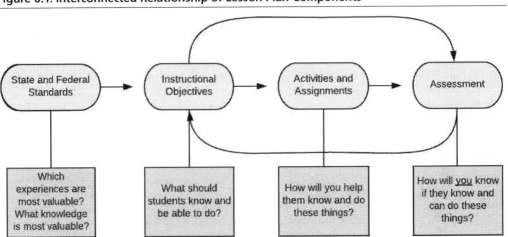

relationship between these elements, it is important that you do not write any elements of your plan in isolation. Instead, consider how the elements work together to facilitate student learning.

Now that you have considered the rhetorical situation of your lesson plan, the teaching environment in which you will be implementing your plan, and how the elements of your plan are related to one another, it is time to start drafting your plan. Table 6.4 outlines possible components to include in your lesson.

Table 6.4. Possible Lesson Plan Components

Teacher, course and/or grade level, date	Include any identifying information that will give context for your lesson.
Topic, content, or title	Indicate the content and allude to the primary objectives.
Lesson overview	Summarize your lesson, including lesson goals and methods of instruction.
Rationale	Justify the choices for your curriculum design, including placement of lesson in unit or annual plan.
Standards addressed	Select specific standards that are appropriate and/or necessary for your student population.
Learning targets	Articulate, in student-friendly, first-person language, what students will be able to do by the end of the lesson.
Learning objectives	Identify what students will be able to do by the end of the lesson.
Preparation	Determine what steps must be completed by the beginning of instruction.
Materials, including mentor texts	Include a list of all materials necessary for the instruction of the lesson.
Formative assessment	Determine your students' previous knowledge about the content of the lesson with a low-stakes assessment.
Instructional sequence/Plan for instruction	Create a detailed plan for instruction, including anticipated time spent on each activity.
Differentiated instruction	Articulate the specific needs of the learners in this lesson. Determine how to accommodate the lesson for a variety of abilities.
Summative assessment	Measure your students' understanding of learning objectives and lesson content.
Accommodations for students	Consider what types of accommodations you will make for students with specialized needs, students with parental consent to opt out of the lesson, etc.
Assessment of objectives	Review the initial learning objectives for the lesson, determine a metric by which objectives can be measured, and administer assessment.
Reflection	Review the success and shortcomings of the lesson. Isolate areas for improvements.

Sample Lesson Plan from a Preservice Teacher

Figure 6.2 shows a sample lesson plan to help you design your own lessons. Faith completed this plan as an assignment for her high school writing methods course (English 297: The Teaching of Writing) in her credential program at Illinois State University. Faith is planning to teach in the Chicago Public Schools and has designed a lesson plan on using precise language to facilitate cultural inclusivity in her students' writing. Faith's English 297 professor, Dr. Sarah Hochstetler, notes that Faith's lesson plan is "excellent in its attention to liberating and culturally sustaining pedagogy" for her intended audience of 9th- and 10th-grade students. In fact, Dr. Hochstetler shared that Faith's lesson plan on inclusive language was also instructive to and appreciated by her peers.

We will refer to this lesson plan throughout the remainder of this chapter.

(text continues on p. 109)

Figure 6.2. Sample Lesson Plan (written by Faith and annotated by the authors)

Teacher: Ms. Faith Overall
Grade Level: 9–10
Date: 4 April, 2018
Lesson Title: "Well That Just Ain't Fair!": Inclusivity and Fair Language in Essay Writing
Text(s): N/A

Lesson Overview	This intervention lesson teaches students how to incorporate language that is fair and inclusive into their writing. The lesson shows examples of controversial language and provides the appropriate replacements. Students will then be able to identify words/phrases that are unsettling or exclusionary. Additionally, we will discuss, in person, the impact unfair/fair, exclusionary/inclusive has on rhetoric and credibility.
Lesson Rationale	Students have been asked to complete their first ever research paper. The general topic of their research paper is "Issues of Social Justice," and while students have been able to identify multiple areas of interest, they themselves have been struggling to use fair or inclusive language in describing the topics of their choice. Topics include: • Ability • Socioeconomic status

Annotations:

Faith has articulated a clear and descriptive title for her lesson plan that gives her audience insight to her lesson topic.

This lesson focuses on developing a writing skill that is reflective of contemporary issues and the larger thematic unit of social justice.

In the lesson overview, Faith highlights the thematic focus of social justice with concrete elements of argumentation.

Lesson Rationale (continued)	• Racial/Ethnic representation • Gender • Sexuality The purpose of this lesson is to encourage students to talk about the things they care about while demonstrating social consciousness. This focus on language use will express to students how use of unfair language is also harmful to the parties they speak of. In *Inside Out: Strategies for Teaching Writing*, Kirby and Crovitz (2012) explain that ". . . your role as a responder may be more to function as a critic, arguing fine points of diction, asking for a more consistent point of view, and challenging the writer to rework the piece" (p. 176). The purpose of this lesson isn't to scold or "nit-pick," but is instead intended to redirect students and promote language that is all-encompassing. As stated in the NCTE Position Statement "Professional Knowledge for the Teaching of Writing," "the ultimate goal is not to leave students where they are, however, but to move them toward greater flexibility, so that they can write not just for their own intimates but for wider audiences."
Common Core State Standards/ ELA	CCSS.ELA-LITERACY.W.9-10.2.D Use precise language and domain-specific vocabulary to manage the complexity of the topic. CCSS.ELA-LITERACY.W.9-10.1.D Establish and maintain a formal style and objective tone while attending to the norms and conventions of the discipline in which they are writing.
Student-Friendly "I Can" Language	• I can identify instances of unfair and exclusionary language. • I can apply knowledge of unfair and exclusionary language to make appropriate revisions. • I can apply my knowledge of writing to adequately demonstrate my thoughts on the topic. • I can determine the effects of fair language on my essay topic.

Margin annotations:

This lesson allows students to choose their topics within the thematic unit. Student choice in this lesson may facilitate the discussion of sensitive topics.

The focus on unfair language is designed to apply to writing skills, but can also improve socioemotional skills.

Faith has grounded her lesson plan in educational theories discussed in her English/language arts methods course.

Faith has considered possible resistance to her lesson, and also developed a research-based response to this potential resistance.

While Faith's lesson plan may potentially address additional standards, she has carefully chosen two standards from CCSS in which to ground her lesson.

Faith's lesson targets are clear, manageable, and student-centered.

Figure 6.2. Sample Lesson Plan (written by Faith and annotated by the authors) (continued)

Learning Objectives	Student will be able to: • Judge common threads of unfair language • Correct use of unfair language • Demonstrate knowledge of fair language usage in their own writing		Faith has included some student accountability for fair language in the students' final project.
Informal and Formal Formative Assessments			While Faith's learning objectives do not include a criterion from which to measure success, she makes a clear effort to write clear objectives that are not open to interpretation.
Informal Assessment	*List Assessments and Types:* Quick write: Students will be given 3-4 minutes at the end of class to write 3-4 sentences on their research paper topic. This quick write will be submitted to the instructor as an exit slip and returned to them the following day to incorporate.	*Assessment Feedback:* Students will earn a completion grade (✓+,✓-), denoting not only the completion of the task, but whether or not they have implemented the new language. Written feedback will explain whether or not the 3-4 sentences are appropriate.	Faith's lesson includes both informal and formal assessments. Faith's informal assessment metric is directly related to the lesson outcomes.
Formal Assessment	Revised research papers will display fair language usage. Students will be expected to submit proof of changes.	Because this is an intervention lesson, criteria regarding fair language use would be added to the rubric. This component would be rated between 1-5 like the others. Feedback will acknowledge the original point of concern, recognize the improvement, and explain how it has benefited the paper.	The formal assessment in this lesson is authentic in that Faith's students will revise their research papers to enact the inclusive language choices covered in the lesson. Faith will formally assess the outcomes of this lesson in the rubric for the research paper that is the culminating assignment for the larger unit plan. Faith makes plans to assess via two measures: on a numeric scale and with summative narrative feedback.
Plan for Instruction	**Beginning:** On the board, student-friendly objectives and "I can" language is written. Also on the board would be name, date, class, and grade level. On the projector would be the title slide of the presentation.		Faith outlines the necessary preparation to take place before the lesson.

Plan for Instruction (continued) • Opening Focus • Objectives • Teacher Input • Modeling • Shared Demo • Guided Practice • Independent Practice • Closure (Gradual Release of Responsibility— all phases of release may not occur in one 50-minute lesson)	**Opening Focus:** Class will begin with a community check-in. Students will be asked to share one word to sum up how they are feeling and say them aloud, beginning with students on the left side of the classroom. Students should preface their descriptions with one of the following categories: (1) Physically (2) Emotionally (3) Spiritually (4) Mentally Ex: "Mentally Exhausted." Affirm or encourage the class depending on majority response. **(5 minutes)** Lesson will begin with the context of the lesson, and dialogue would "set the stage." Students have been in the process of completing their first research paper. While writing on the general topic of "Issues of Social Justice," students themselves have been using unjust or unfair language in their writing. Let students know that they are not the first class to have used unfair language, and the lesson will later include distribution of sample student writing. There will also be an appointment clock activity. **(5 minutes)** Distribution of materials should also occur at this time.	The lesson plan has a clear and logical sequence that includes the specific amount of time necessary.
		The opening activity of a "community check-in" mirrors the inclusivity highlighted in the content of the lesson.
		In the timing of this lesson, Faith has included shorter periods of time for independent and pair activities and longer increments of time for whole-group activities, all of which fill a 50-minute class period.
The lesson highlighted here is part of a larger unit and is designed to scaffold the students' language use in their research papers.		In her "Opening Focus," Faith's students will share their feelings about the topic of the lesson, unfair/ exclusionary language, through a community check-in before Faith shows the students a Google Slides presentation during the "Teacher Input" section of the lesson. After this presentation, Faith's students complete a worksheet to practice identifying this type of language, before they work independently to review sample paragraphs (with unfair/exclusionary language) and revise their paragraphs to remove this bias. Faith effectively scaffolds the content of her lesson by sequencing the activities in a specific order that allows her students to transition from learning about unfair/ exclusionary language to eliminating this language by the end of her lesson.
Faith's lesson includes various modes of instruction, including an informative lecture.	**Teacher Input:** Walk through Google Slides lecture. Students should be called on to help read the content of the presentation. Slides will include definitions of unfair/exclusionary language, will identify the area of concern, will point students in the right direction, and will explain the effects such concerns have on student rhetoric and credibility. Throughout the Slides presentation, students should be filling in their worksheets. (**15 minutes**) At this point, students should have received the sample writing from prior students. During this "Appointment Clock" students will have the opportunity to read the sample and assess the "damage" by recollection of Slides presentation. Prompt students to focus on what is "wrong" with the language. (**5 minutes**)	
		Faith offers her students the opportunity to assess unfair language in sample student essays in a controlled manner.

Figure 6.2. Sample Lesson Plan (written by Faith and annotated by the authors) (continued)

Plan for Instruction (continued) • Opening Focus • Objectives • Teacher Input • Modeling • Shared Demo • Guided Practice • Independent Practice • Closure (Gradual Release of Responsibility—all phases of release may not occur in one 50-minute lesson)	**Model:** "That Ain't Fair" Worksheet explanation and walk through. Begin by explaining the purpose and layout of the worksheet. The purpose is to highlight common misuses of language, and to move students in the right direction. The layout of the worksheet moves from "acceptable" to "example" to "unacceptable." On the document camera, model the worksheet by completing the first example as a class. Call on students to help identify areas of concern and how to improve them. Worksheet is not linear, as each category will have the example(s) left as blank boxes. Allow students time to complete this portion of the lesson. (**10 minutes**) **Independent Practice:** Applying this new knowledge of fair and unfair language, students must use the sample paragraphs and rewrite them appropriately. (**5 minutes**) **Ending Quick Write:** For the purpose of this lesson, the sample topic students have received will be the same as their hypothetical research papers. At this time, ask students to continue the conversation on the given topic and write the next 3-4 sentences of the paragraph, as those fresh lines can and will be included in their revised papers. (**5 minutes**)	Faith models both the process of isolating this type of language, and possible revisions for moving the language from "unacceptable" to "acceptable" before students complete their independent practice. The skills Faith's students are developing in the independent practice section of this lesson plan will prepare them to write their research papers, which serve as the summative assessment of this lesson. Students complete their own independent practice. Students close the lesson by generating potential text for their research papers.
Materials & Equipment Technology (Teacher and Students)	*Students:* • Copy of research papers • Technology/Notebook • Pen/Pencil *Teacher:* • Whiteboard • Projector • Computer • Appointment Clock directions • Unfair Language Worksheet • Sample paragraphs	Lesson plan includes a detailed list of materials for both the instructor and the students. Faith designed two handouts to distribute to her students as separate documents.

Questions: Sometimes it's hard to "think on your feet" to ask effective levels and types of questions to generate discussion and/or scaffold through a lesson; script them ahead of time.

> Faith has included several targeted questions designed to facilitate class discussion, if necessary.

1. What do I mean by unfair/exclusionary language?
2. What do I mean by fair/inclusive?
3. Who can help us name synonyms for the word "fair"?

Selecting State Curricular Standards

On your first reading of the relevant standards for your lesson, you may feel that every single standard in the area relates to your lesson plan. While this may be the case, strong lesson plans highlight a few specific standards. Before selecting anchor standards for your lesson plan, consult the rhetorical situation surrounding it and follow any associated requirements for using standards in the lesson plan. Figure 6.2 includes two ELA CCSS, one on word choice and the other on tone, that directly target the objectives of the lesson on incorporating inclusive language in formal research papers.

Articulating Clear Learning Objectives

Once you have determined the standards or content framework for your lesson, it is necessary to conceptualize exactly *what* you'd like your students to learn and *how* your students will be able to demonstrate that they've learned the concepts covered in your lesson plan. Note in Figure 6.2 that the anchor standards of the lesson articulate how students will "use precise language" (National Governors Association Center for Best Practices & Council of Chief State School Officers, 2010h) and "establish" a specific tone (National Governors Association Center for Best Practices & Council of Chief State School Officers, 2010g), while the objectives for the lesson state that by the end of the lesson, students will be able to "judge" unfair language, "correct" use of unfair language, and "demonstrate" knowledge of unfair language in their own writing. In the objectives outlined in Figure 6.2, Faith has clearly established what she wants her students to be able to do by the end of the lesson. Well-articulated objectives not only will allow you to more effectively assess your students in the content covered in the lesson, but also may help you more critically reflect on the success of the lesson in your own reflection on or rationale for the plan. The more effectively written your objectives are, the better prepared you'll be to assess the success of the lesson.

Winegarden (n.d.) argues that effective objectives are clear and understandable by students. She states: "A good objective communicates your intent well and leaves little room for interpretation" (Winegarden, n.d.). In order to articulate the intent for what your students will be able to do at the end of the lesson, draft objectives that complete the following sentence: "At the end of

Table 6.5. Specific Verbs for Writing Learning Objectives

to solve	to list	to revise	to illustrate
to define	to write	to edit	to draft
to describe	to draw	to choose	to build
to argue	to research	to evaluate	
to compare/contrast	to name	to respond	

this lesson my student will be able to . . ." Thus, most lesson objectives begin with verbs in their unconjugated or infinitive form. In Table 6.5 you can find a list of specific verbs teachers may use when writing learning objectives.

Writing objectives with more specific verbs that are open to fewer interpretations will provide your students with a clearer understanding of what is expected of them by the end of the lesson. Clear objectives will give students more opportunities to successfully achieve the desired outcomes and will facilitate the assessment process.

Keep the audience for your lesson plan in mind as you draft your objectives. Administrators and assessors need to understand your expectations for your students, and your students also will need to understand these key elements in order for the lesson plan to be successful. Share the goals and objectives of a lesson with your students (and parents) in whatever mode is appropriate (on the board, as part of the assignment, in your course management system, etc.). Note that the objectives in Figure 6.2 are written both as "learning objectives," for an audience of administrators or assessors, and also in "student-friendly 'I can' language," for an audience of students.

Designing Instructional Activities and Authentic/Creative Assignments

Design your course materials and corresponding teaching sequence so that they will both address standards and meet the learning objectives. Wiggins and McTighe (2005) call this approach to curricular design "backward design," in which educators first "identify desired results," then "determine acceptable evidence," and finally, "plan learning experiences and instruction" (pp. 17–18). Backward design, or "results-focused design," as opposed to "content-focused design," prioritizes student performance over specific content (Wiggins & McTighe, 2005, p. 15), and, for many, is a more targeted approach to designing lesson plans. Thus, instead of writing your lesson plan with a focus on what content or which standards to cover, you can use backward design to focus on achieving your stated learning objectives through assignments and activities.

Backward design requires that you think about what format your students' assignments will need to take in order to meet the learning objectives. Ask yourself, "What do I want to read or grade?" When we review assignment ideas with our preservice teachers, we regularly ask them, "Do you want to read or assess 35 (or 200) of these assignments?" Starting with the end in mind may facilitate the assessment process (which we'll discuss in a later section) and also may prevent plagiarism. This approach will require that you design your assignments with creativity, specificity, and flexibility.

Constructing assignments creatively means that you'll write assignments designed to get your students to think critically about the content of your lesson, rather than to just recall information from the content of the lesson. Creative assignments move beyond traditional assignments, such as standard research reports or multiple-choice exams, and instead draw from students' own interests or pre-existing knowledge. For example, your assignment can ask your students to adopt and argue a position different than their own or to construct a physical representation of the lesson's content.

A wealth of resources are available for teachers to support the design of creative assignments. Incorporating creative writing assignments into your lesson plan is one way to do this. For example, see Tom Romano's texts on multigenre writing (1995, 2000, 2013) or the list of possible written genres to assign students in Figure 3.4 of Murphy and Smith's *Uncommonly Good Ideas* (2015). Table 6.6 presents more ideas for designing effective and creative assignments. Creative assignments offer your students a variety of options, or you can ask them to create their own. Students may choose options that best meet their learning styles or their individual learning needs. Therefore, creative lesson plans may offer your students the greatest number of opportunities for success.

As you can see from the assignment suggestions in Table 6.6, creative assignments can offer students deeper connection with the content of your lesson. A popular method for constructing assignments that fosters greater student connection with content is project-based learning (PBL), which "allows students to learn by doing and applying ideas. Students engage in real-world activities that are similar to the activities that adult professionals engage in"

Table 6.6. Elements of Effective Assignments

Clear Assignment Requirements	Opportunities for Sharing or Publishing Assignment	Assignment Based on Student Interest or Pre-Existing Knowledge
Clear connection between assignment requirements and lesson outcomes	Assignments that solve real problems students have observed	Assignments that include multiple components or take place over an extended period of time, such as portfolios
Real-world context for assignments	Real audiences for assignments	Assignments that include various formats or genres
Sequences of assignments that are closely related to one another	Assignments that are well scaffolded	Assignments that employ a variety of data or sources

(Krajcik & Blumenfeld, 2005, p. 317). PBL's emphasis on assignments with real-world applications is designed to increase student engagement with their own learning, as students develop authentic skills they can transfer to college and careers. Designing these types of authentic assignments in your lesson plans may also help you construct authentic assessment for the assignments. (This information will be described in detail in a later section of this chapter on "Designing Assessments to Meet Learning Objectives.")

Sequencing Your Lesson

Effective sequencing first requires that you evaluate your students' pre-existing knowledge of the content of the lesson. An informal formative assessment activity can introduce your students to concepts, processes, and ideas, as well as determine your students' pre-existing knowledge of a topic. These introductory assignments, sometimes called "warm-up" or "try it on" activities (Murphy & Smith, 2015), can introduce students to lesson concepts (through definitions or instructional activities), give them space to test their thinking on the concepts, and offer them a place to ask you questions about areas of the lesson that may be unclear. These activities include class discussions, journals, freewrites, reading logs, postings, early drafts of assignments, marginal notes, thinking pieces, or exit slips. Once you have determined your students' knowledge based on your lesson's content and answered any of your students' concerns about the lesson, you can introduce the lesson concepts. The "Plan for Instruction" in Figure 6.2 contains an example of a sequence of clearly linked assignments. As you review the sample plan, consider how the teacher uses her students' pre-existing knowledge in her opening activity.

There are various modes of instruction that you can include in your lesson plan, including, for example, lectures or presentations, classroom discussions or problem-solving activities, group or individual projects, and inquiry-based learning. In your methods courses, you will learn about the philosophy and practices associated with different modes of instruction. The important thing to keep in mind while writing your own lesson plan is that different modes of instruction privilege different pedagogical elements, like the roles of teacher and student; therefore, choose the mode, or modes, that are most appropriate for you and your students, and those most likely to facilitate your students' success in the lesson.

What mode of instruction will best meet the needs of your students as learners? Which modes of instruction are developmentally appropriate for your students? Will you assign reading or writing assignments to your students? Will you require your students to solve a specific problem set? Will you create presentations or show videos in your lesson? We recommend that you choose several modes of instruction or several different types of activities within your lesson plan. Oral lectures given in conjunction with visual presentations and physical manipulatives may resonate with students more than an oral presentation given in isolation.

As you sequence your lesson, we also recommend that you consider the essential characteristics of the learners themselves (e.g., English language learners, students with IEPs, gifted students, etc.). When you write your plans, attempt to vary the activity or mode every 20 minutes or so in order to reach as many students as you can. You also should be prepared for students who complete tasks in a shorter or longer period of time, such as advanced students who may complete tasks at a faster rate. Although you may not always be able to address the individual need of every learner in your class within a lesson, write your instructional activities with clear goals that are developmentally appropriate for the age of your students and are within their zone of proximal development (Vygotsky, 1978). Working within the ZPD, which is defined as what your students can do with your guidance but cannot do without your support (Vygotsky, 1978), will give your students the support that will allow them to find success in your lesson plan.

After sharing the content of the course with your students, it is important that you offer your students the opportunity to practice or investigate the content of the course in low-stakes tasks, either individually or in groups. You can facilitate your students' practice with the content of the lesson by modeling the activity for your students. Your lesson plan should include a detailed description of how you will facilitate your students' low-stakes practice with the content or skill highlighted in the lesson. Carefully outline the modeling process in your plan so that your audience will have a clear understanding of how your students will master the skills they are practicing. See Figure 6.2 for an example of a whole-group modeling process within a lesson plan.

Another way to model the content of your lesson for your students is to provide them with samples of the assignment (either from past students or samples that you create yourself) and to include copies of these *mentor texts* in your lesson plan. A mentor text can serve as a sample for your students if your lesson includes a writing task and also as instructional material for your lesson, as your students can read and re-read a mentor text at any point in your lesson in order to learn specific concepts. Be sure to check the availability of mentor texts in your teaching environment (such as the adopted curriculum in your district) and the credibility of additional mentor texts before including them in your lesson plan.

Effectively Pacing Your Lesson

While it is important to write assignments that are specific enough for your students to successfully complete the tasks, it is also important to make sure that your assignments (and corresponding activities) include some flexibility. Creating lesson plans that do not allow for some movement (in the focus of the lesson or the time allocated to each activity, etc.) may prevent you from facilitating real student learning. Allowing for flexibility in an assignment or activity might mean that you incorporate student input into your curriculum design. It also may make it more likely you'll meet the needs of your students by giving your students the space necessary to engage with their learning.

Flexibility in lesson plan design also requires that you pay careful attention to the timing and pace of your lesson. As beginning teachers, it can be difficult to gauge the amount of time it will take for your students to complete a task, but even expert teachers may incorrectly judge the amount of time to allot to a set of activities or assignments in a lesson plan. While we encourage our students to implement a new activity every 20 minutes in their lesson plans, we also know that sometimes what a teacher thinks will take 20 minutes may take as few as 10 or as many as 40 minutes for students to complete. Pacing also should be based on the age of your students. Think about your students' abilities and consider how long they can focus on a lesson. Because of the variation in student ability, we recommend over-planning in your lessons.

Staying flexible in your lesson plan design and implementation also can directly reflect your teaching philosophy and/or priorities, as your flexibility can demonstrate your respect for your students. For example, you may have a student or parent who requests an alternative assignment based on personal beliefs, such as religion. When you are confronted with such a request, consider how you can both respect your student's beliefs and adhere to the standards and other requirements in your teaching environment.

Writing Rationales for Your Lesson Plans

In order to create a truly rewarding learning experience for your students, it is imperative that you take a moment to reflect on your lesson plan design choices and develop a rationale for your lesson plans. While you are writing your activities and assignments, consider why you are making specific choices in your lesson plan. In a rationale, a teacher offers the audience for the lesson plan (an administrator, parents) a justification for the teacher's pedagogical choices. The rationale explains why students in a specific grade or discipline should learn the content of the lesson plan beyond the fact that the standards require this content. See the section "Lesson Rationale" in Figure 6.2 for an example.

While you draft your lesson plans (or after you have completed them), reflect on why you have chosen to develop this lesson on this content. Consider why it is important that your students learn this information at all. As teachers, we know that our students will be required to demonstrate competency in many fundamental subjects through standardized tests, but beyond this requirement, *why* do you think the information in your lesson plans is relevant or valuable to your students? How will it benefit them in the future, either as students or as members of a larger organization or society? How does the lesson fit into a unit plan developed by your department? More important, a rationale includes a discussion about how or where the lesson fits into the larger curricular unit or yearlong plan.

Next, consider the method of instruction to use in your lesson plans to deliver the intended content. Why have you chosen this method of instruction? How does this method best meet the unique needs of your students? Why are the content and method of instruction in your lesson plan a valuable use of both your and your students' time? By considering the answers to these questions, you will be better prepared to fulfill the multiple purposes of your lesson plans. Most teachers start thinking about these things at the beginning of the lesson plan writing process. However, teachers can continue to revise the rationale even after they teach the lesson. If you write your rationale at the end of the lesson plan (or after you have given your lesson), you also may want to reflect on the outcomes of the lesson plan using the reflection skills we will discuss in Chapter 8.

Designing Assessments to Meet Learning Objectives

After your students complete the assignments and activities in your lesson plan, it is necessary to evaluate your students' performances. Assessment plays an integral role in the interconnected elements of a lesson plan, as shown in Table 6.4. Your assessment must determine whether the objectives for the lesson plan have been met. Thus, when you design assessment metrics for the assignments and activities in your lesson plan, you want to make sure that they are strategically aligned with the standards, objectives, and procedures established in the lesson plan.

In this section, we encourage you to think beyond one-dimensional modes of assessment, such as a multiple-choice exam, and instead incorporate more dynamic, or authentic, assessment into your lesson plan. Authentic assessment incorporates the context of your lesson plan and places value on student learning rather than student performance. A great place to learn more about designing authentic assessment measures is the Authentic Assessment Toolbox from the National Education Association. Assembled by a retired teacher, "the Authentic Assessment Toolbox is a resource to help K–12 teachers, especially new teachers, create authentic tasks, rubrics, and standards for measuring and improving student learning" (Nast, n.d.).

Before designing an assessment metric, consider how your students will be able to demonstrate success in the lesson. Is it simply by completing the task? Is it by correctly recalling information? Is it by appropriately putting knowledge into practice? Once you determine the criteria for success in your lesson, you'll be able to determine a metric to represent those criteria. Then, refine how you will be determining student success in the lesson plan. Will you be looking at the students' assignment as a whole, or are you interested in evaluating more specific elements within the assignment? Are you interested in assessing student knowledge throughout the lesson (formative assessment), or do you want to assess your students at the close of your lesson plan (summative assessment)? Regardless of the format your assessment metric may take, it is your responsibility as an educator to make expectations for assignments and criteria for evaluation clear and understandable for all of your students so that they are all afforded opportunities for success.

Formative Assessments. Formative assessments are typically informal, or low-stakes, assignments in which student work is evaluated via a simple metric, which constitutes a small percentage of the students' final grade. Low-stakes assessments typically employ a basic metric for assessment, such as a check mark scale—check plus (✓+), check (✓), and check minus (✓-)—or a holistic evaluation of the quality or completeness of student work. When you assess student learning throughout your lesson plan, the results of your assessment may influence the pace and the content for the rest of the lesson plan. Including formative assessment at the beginning of your lesson plan can determine your students' pre-existing knowledge of the subject of your lesson. Many of the opening activities described in the "Sequencing Your Lesson" section of the chapter can function as early formative assessment techniques.

In Figure 6.2, Faith opens her lesson with a student "check-in" that moves into a whole-class discussion, which functions as formative assessment in this lesson. Faith also includes an informal formative assessment in which students are evaluated via a check-mark scale based on the completeness of the task and ability to incorporate the skills introduced in the classroom instruction.

When metrics are offered throughout the lesson or at the close of one activity, you can determine your students' comprehension of the lesson's content. Class discussions, informal blog responses, or low-stakes quizzes can help you determine what your students know about a topic. Anonymous short quizzes given throughout the lesson or exit slips included at the end of a class are additional methods of simple formative assessment.

Summative Assessments. Summative assessments evaluate the final assignment or activity within your lesson plan. As you begin to design the summative assessment metric for your lesson, consider which elements you will be assessing in your students' work and how the assessment criteria align with the standards and learning objectives of your lesson. Will you be assessing the students' processes for completing the assignment, the final product, or both?

When designing authentic summative assessment tools, it is also necessary to consider your students' learning context. Summative assessments must be relevant and appropriate for your students and also may have to adhere to local and national requirements. Depending on the context of your lesson plan, you may have required or assigned metrics for student success from your district or school, for example. Once you are aware of any required assessment criteria, you can incorporate these requirements into your own assessment tools for your lesson plan.

Summative assessments are often formal, or high-stakes, assignments. A student's performance on high-stakes assignments may have significant or long-term effects. A formal summative assessment in your lesson plan may represent a large percentage of a student's grade, while the outcome of high-stakes, standardized assessments can determine a student's academic ranking or placement into specific programs. Because of these potential outcomes, high-stakes assignments in your lesson plan require detailed and complex summative assessment metrics. A detailed assessment metric will carefully articulate to your students the criteria for success and may offer them more opportunities to succeed. A detailed summative assessment metric also may create a more didactic experience for your students, from which they can more specifically isolate personal areas for improvement. A popular metric for formal summative assessment is a rubric.

Rubrics. Many school districts rely on rubrics as their primary metric for assessment. And while rubrics are not without their critics (see, for example, Wilson, 2006), they are a mode of assessment that allows teachers to articulate specific criteria for assessment. Rubrics also can be tailored to meet the specific needs of an assignment because the size or scope of the criteria included in the rubric can be adjusted easily. Most rubrics include descriptions of the desired criteria and a scale of assessment measuring the outcome of these criteria.

Holistic rubrics, for example, assess the entirety of the assignment, and their scoring criteria can employ general or detailed descriptions of the holistic evaluation criteria (Ferris & Hedgcock, 2014). Some educators may associate holistic rubrics with standardized assessments, primarily because holistic rubrics facilitate the evaluation of a large number of assignments in a relatively short period of time. On the other hand, analytic scoring rubrics assess targeted elements of an assignment and include a grading or value scale related to the descriptions of each criterion outlined in the rubric. Because analytic rubrics can offer greater detail than holistic rubrics, analytic rubrics can align more readily with specific standards or genre features.

Table 6.7 is an example of a 2nd-grade narrative writing rubric designed by the Delaware Department of Education (2017). The rubric includes three criteria for assessment—organization/purpose, evidence/elaboration, and language/conventions—all of which are clearly aligned with the Grade 2 Common Core State Standards. It also includes four levels of evaluation: below grade level (1); approaching grade level (2); on grade level (3); and above grade level (4). Each level of assessment includes a clear description that is based on the language and goals of the CCSS for this writing text type. The

(text continues on p. 120)

Table 6.7. Sample 2nd-Grade Narrative Writing Rubric

	Score of 4—Above Grade Level	Score of 3—On Grade Level	Score of 2—Approaching Grade Level	Score of 1—Below Grade Level
Organization/Purpose 2 × ___ = ___	The writing— • establishes a situation and introduces a narrator and/or characters (3W3a) • organizes an event sequence that unfolds naturally (3W3a) • uses temporal words and phrases to signal event order (3W3c) • skillfully provides a sense of closure (3W3d) • produces writing appropriate to task and purpose, with guidance from adults (3W4)	The writing— • appropriately sequences events (2W3) • uses temporal words to signal event order (2W3) • provides a sense of closure (2W3)	The writing— • attempts to recount a short sequence of events • attempts to use temporal words to signal event order • attempts to provide a sense of closure	The writing— • makes little or no attempt to recount a short sequence of events • makes little or no attempt to use temporal words to signal event order • makes little or no attempt to provide a sense of closure
Evidence/ Elaboration 2 × ___ = ___	The writing— • develops real or imagined experiences or events using descriptive details and clear event sequence (3W3) • uses dialogue and/or descriptions of actions, thoughts, and feelings to develop experiences and events or show the response of characters to situations (3W3b) • uses information from experiences or print and digital sources, when appropriate (3W8)	The writing— • recounts a well-elaborated event or short sequence of events (2W3) • includes details to describe actions, thoughts, and feelings (2W3) • uses information from experiences or provided resources, when appropriate (2W8)	The writing— • attempts to recount a well-elaborated event or short sequence of events (2W3) • attempts to include details to describe actions, thoughts, and feelings • attempts to use information from experiences or provided resources, when appropriate	The writing— • makes little or no attempt to recount a well-elaborated event or short sequence of events • makes little or no attempt to include details to describe actions, thoughts, and feelings • makes little or no attempt to use information from experiences or provided resources, when appropriate

Language/Conventions

$1 \times$ ___ = ___

The writing—
- demonstrates a command of grade-level appropriate standard English grammar, usage, and conventions (3L1-2)*
- has errors that do not interfere with understanding (3L1-2)*

The writing—
- demonstrates a command of grade-level appropriate standard English grammar, usage, and conventions (2L1-2)*
- has errors that do not interfere with understanding (2L1-2)*

The writing—
- attempts to demonstrate a command of grade-level appropriate standard English grammar, usage, and conventions
- has errors that may interfere with understanding

The writing—
- makes little or no attempt to demonstrate a command of grade-level appropriate standard English grammar, usage, and conventions
- has errors that interfere with understanding

CONVENTIONS CHART, GRADE 2

Spelling	Capitalization	Punctuation	Grammar Usage	Sentence Completion
• Generalize learned spelling patterns when writing words (e.g., cage—badge; boy—boil). (2L2d) • Correctly spell words at grade level and below	• Capitalize (2L2a) • holidays • product names • geographic names	• Use commas • in greetings and closings of letters (2L2b) • Use an apostrophe • to form contractions in frequently occurring possessives (2L2c)	Nouns: • Use collective nouns (e.g., group). (2L1a) • Form and use frequently occurring irregular plural nouns (e.g., feet, children, teeth, mice, fish). (2L1b) Verbs: • Correctly use the past tense of frequently occurring irregular verbs (e.g., sat, hid, told) (2L1d) Adjectives: • Use adjectives and adverbs, and choose between them depending on what is to be modified (2L1e) Pronouns: • Use reflexive pronouns (e.g., myself, ourselves) (2L1c)	• Produce, expand, and rearrange complete simple and compound sentences (e.g., The boy watched the movie; The little boy watched the movie; The action movie was watched by the little boy) (2L

* as appropriate for grade level

Adapted from the *Smarter Balanced—Conventions Chart—April, 2014*. Students are expected to demonstrate grade-level skills in conventions as specified in the CCSS as well as those specified for earlier grades.

rubric also includes a conventions chart to elaborate grade-level expectations for grammar, usage, and conventions.

It may be more effective for you to design your own rubric for your lesson plan. You can do this by creating a simple table in a Word document that includes the assignment's desired criterion, a grading or value scale, and a description of the criterion at each value point. For guided assistance in creating a rubric, you may want to consider using a web-based rubric-generating software product, like RubiStar. Such a tool can help you manage the criterion and grading values of your rubric and produce a visually appealing rubric for your students.

Alternative Forms of Assessment. Although many school districts and standardized tests currently rely on rubrics as their primary mode of assessment, they are not the only way to evaluate student learning in your lesson plan. As we've noted elsewhere in this section, rubrics can become inauthentic if they are not clearly aligned with the standards and objectives for your lesson. As you design your lesson plan, you may choose to include alternative assessments, if you have this flexibility in your teaching environment. Educational theorist William Ayers (2010) advocated for alternatives to the standardized test as a mode of assessment, noting:

> Alternatives to standardized tests can be thought of as the three p's: projects, portfolios, and performance. These are attempts to keep assessment authentic, that is, to assess students in the real context of their lives. Authentic assessment strategies move away from tests that stand as surrogates for the real world and assume that the real world matters. (p. 129)

For Ayers, projects, portfolios, and performance reflect a more authentic mode of assessment because they reflect modes that our students may be evaluated by in other areas of their lives.

Thus, instead of taking an exam or writing a research report to recall information about the history and design of the Brooklyn Bridge, students, as a summative project, can build a replica of the bridge to put the design principles into practice.

Portfolio assessment, which is a common metric in writing and fine arts courses, can be implemented in any course where students produce multiple assignments. Students self-select materials to include in their portfolios, often based on guidelines from their teacher, and include multiple drafts of the same assignment to demonstrate their growth over time. Students also write a reflective cover letter to their teacher, as the reader of the portfolio, to guide the teacher's reading of the documents.

Performance can be utilized as an assessment metric in any lesson in which students are responsible for recalling specific information. For example,

10th-grade biology students can stage a dramatic performance to demonstrate the process of mitosis and meiosis for their classmates. Incorporating "the three p's" (Ayers, 2010) into your lesson plan takes creativity on your part as the teacher but ultimately will benefit your students' learning through more authentic assessment.

Reflection. Regardless of the metric of assessment you employ in your lesson plans at the conclusion of the lesson, it is important that both you and your students reflect on the outcomes of the lesson. You can build student reflection into your assignments through cover sheets or reflective letters. In these types of reflective texts, you can ask your students to review elements from the completed assignment, such as what they perceive to be the strengths of the assignment or areas for further improvement, or about the process of completing the assignment itself, such as reviewing the time and energy they put into their assignments. In reflective letters for portfolio assessments, students typically are asked to reflect on their rationale for including specific elements in the portfolio and to articulate growth or development over the time period represented in the portfolio.

You also can facilitate more informal reflection through group discussions. Ask your students pointed questions about where they felt successful and in which areas they felt less successful. This will allow you to incorporate your students' feedback into your own assessment of the lesson. Keeping track of your own thoughts and ideas about the lesson, either in the lesson plan or in a teaching journal, will allow you to revise your lesson to better meet the needs of your future students.

EXERCISES

1. Preservice teacher Lauren has written a lesson plan for a 9th- and 10th-grade biology class as her final assignment in her writing in education course. Her lesson requires her students to build "creatures" with random genetic mutations out of craft supplies. Students then write a letter to these creatures explaining their mutations from the position of a genetic counselor. In her overview of her lesson, Lauren states, "During this project, students will not only learn the basics of three different processes involved in genetic variation, but also how to write a formal letter. Additionally, they will explore the occupation of genetic counseling." Lauren's objectives for this lesson are listed below:

   Objectives:
   • *Processes of Genetic Variation:* Students will understand how genetic variation can occur through three different processes. They will

understand recombination during meiosis, the process of DNA replication and the types of errors that can occur, and different types of mutagens that can be found in our environment.

- *Formal-Letter Writing:* Students will learn about the formatting of formal letters, and they will know the different situations in which formal letters can be used. They will also be able to explain the difference in style between a formal letter and other types of writing. The ability to write a formal letter will become more applicable to students as they begin applications for college and jobs.
- *Audience:* Students will learn the importance of understanding who the audience for their writing is and how they can accommodate that audience. They will be able to adapt complex language into terms that are easily understandable for their audience. They will also ensure that their tone is appropriate for the situation. The skill of catering one's writing to a particular audience will be one that serves them as they continue in their education and writing careers.
- How specific are these objectives? Are these objectives open to interpretation?

Consult Table 6.5 to revise these objectives using more specific verbs.

2. What grade level or discipline do you plan on teaching? Investigate the standards or frameworks associated with your future teaching environment and consider how you will design an assignment that addresses two or three key standards in this area. What ideas for a creative and real-world assignment do you have that address these standards? Sketch out your ideas and share them with your classmates and professor to consider the feasibility of this assignment.

CHAPTER 7

Writing Teaching Philosophies

Preservice teachers write teaching philosophies as a means to articulate their philosophical or theoretical approaches to their developing pedagogical practices. Stribling, DeMulder, Barnstead, and Dallman (2015) note:

> The majority of pre-service teachers do not complete their teacher training without first writing a Teaching Philosophy Statement. The assignment affords new teachers the opportunity to articulate their beliefs and understandings about effective teaching and learning by including descriptive examples of how they teach and by providing theory and research-based justifications for why they make particular pedagogical decisions. (p. 37)

As a preservice teacher, you may write a teaching philosophy for your education professors, your cooperating teacher, or future administrators, often in conjunction with a lesson plan. Or, you may write a teaching philosophy after writing a lesson plan as a means of reflecting on your teaching practices for an outside assessment body.

EXAMINING THE RHETORICAL SITUATION: PURPOSE, AUDIENCE, CONTEXT, VOICE, AND GENRE

Regardless of when you write a teaching philosophy or for which audience, the *purposes* of the document remain the same: to name your core beliefs about education, to isolate the theories and research that have influenced your beliefs, to illustrate how these theories and research-based practices manifest in your teaching practices, and to articulate your vision of school communities. As you progress through your career as an educator, your teaching philosophy will evolve to reflect your experiences and your more nuanced thoughts on education, but the ultimate purpose will remain constant. The teaching philosophy offers a brief snapshot of who you are as an educator and is often a succinct method of representing your pedagogical philosophy to an audience beyond your students.

The audience for your teaching philosophy can vary, but most often it is someone looking to gain insight into your teacher identity. If you are writing a teaching philosophy as an assignment for an education course in your under-graduate or credential program, the audience is your professor for the course. With this audience, you will need to write your philosophy in a way that meets the requirements of the assignment. The teaching philosophy may be one of the few occasions when your instructor will be able to conceptualize the educator you will become. Thus, your teaching philosophy will allow your instructor to assess your ability to integrate the educational theories and research you are studying into your own pedagogical practices. Similarly, when you write a teaching philosophy for a school administrator as part of a job application, it is critical to articulate a descriptive and accurate representation of your pedagogical philosophy and practices. This audience may not have any prior knowledge about you as an educator, so your teaching philosophy will need to use descriptive language that illustrates your pedagogical beliefs rather than drawing on generalities of teaching and learning.

After you gain experience as a practicing teacher, you may need to craft a teaching philosophy for career advancement or leadership opportunities. In these cases, the audience for your teaching philosophy may be the adminis-tration of your school site or the administration of a district, state, regional, or national body with whom you are seeking leadership opportunities. When your audience is the administration of your school site, you may want to pay special attention to situating your philosophy in the core principles or beliefs at the site in order to demonstrate how your teaching philosophy aligns with them.

For example, if you were applying to become a teacher leader at your school site, your teaching philosophy might include your thoughts on the role of local collaboration and community in your pedagogical practices. If you were applying for a regional position in your teachers' union, you might want to conceptualize the role of community within the profession at large. Regardless of the audience for your teaching philosophy, your document must carefully consider the manner in which you are representing yourself as a teacher and to what extent that matches the philosophy of your audience.

The contexts surrounding the writing of your teaching philosophy can be similar to the contexts of lesson plans described in Chapter 6: a theoretical context, such as a classroom assignment, or a practical context, such as cur-riculum design or a career search. As a classroom assignment, the context of the teaching philosophy is often an introductory or culminating assignment. As supporting documentation for job placement or career advancement, the context surrounding the teaching philosophy can be similar to that of a cov-er letter in that you are articulating your core teaching beliefs as a means to introduce yourself to the hiring committee and demonstrate your fit with a position.

A critical element of the context of a teaching philosophy is reflection. The document requires that you carefully consider how you represent yourself as a teacher, including the theories and research-based practices with which you are aligned and how those theories and practices manifest in your pedagogy. Reflecting on these concepts in a teaching philosophy is a beneficial exercise for all educators (both preservice and practicing), as it forces you to articulate your professional values. Even if you don't find yourself in a context in which you are required to write a teaching philosophy, we encourage you to draft a teaching philosophy for yourself. Moreover, we recommend that you return to the document as a means to track your ongoing development as an educator and to help you articulate possible responses to questions in job interviews. The teaching philosophy is an evolving document that will grow and develop throughout the trajectory of your career in education.

The teaching philosophy, whether as part of an assignment or a job application, is a formal, professional document that requires a formal and professional voice. The teaching philosophy is the document that serves as the bridge between your writing in your credential program and the writing you will complete as a practicing teacher. Because the document is a representation of your teacher identity, your voice in your teaching philosophy must be clear, specific, and representative. Your word choice in your teaching philosophy will reflect your feelings toward key elements of the profession and should be made carefully so that there is no chance your audience will misinterpret your statements. You may choose to include specialized vocabulary or jargon to reflect your knowledge in the field. Your voice should project confidence in the knowledge you've accumulated as a preservice teacher as well as deference to your own learning process and position as a novice educator.

The genre of the teaching philosophy is most closely associated with higher education rather than K–12 education. When professors are looking for a position in a 2- or 4-year college, they often are asked to submit a teaching philosophy as part of their job application. In K–12 education, a teaching philosophy may be referred to by other names, such as a vision statement, philosophy of educational leadership, praxis pedagogy statement, or core beliefs statement. Teachers transitioning to administrative positions also may write administrative philosophies that articulate their core beliefs about leadership. In K–12 education, teaching philosophies may be used for different purposes than in higher education. Elements of a teaching philosophy may be required in a letter of introduction when applying for K–12 teaching positions or in supplemental questions to a job application. Despite the differences in educational contexts, the teaching philosophy has several stable characteristics as a genre.

The primary characteristic of the teaching philosophy is its brevity. The document is often a condensed overview of your core beliefs about teaching. It is frequently a one-page, single-spaced document. The brief nature of the document affects other stable characteristics of this genre. For example, instead of a detailed discussion of which educational theorists you align with, you might include in-text references to their seminal texts. Similarly, instead of describing every pedagogical practice you use in your classroom to foster a student-centered environment, you might describe one or two examples of how this practice may manifest in your classroom. The brevity of this genre gives your audience a brief insight into who you are as an educator.

BEFORE YOU WRITE A TEACHING PHILOSOPHY

Before you begin writing your teaching philosophy, we encourage you to take a moment to carefully reflect on the rhetorical situation surrounding the document. Table 7.1 is a graphic organizer that will lead you through an evaluation of the rhetorical situation of your teaching philosophy. You'll notice that Table 7.1 is similar to Table 6.2; that's because you may write lesson plans or a teaching philosophy in similar contexts, either as part of your coursework in education or for professional purposes.

WRITING A TEACHING PHILOSOPHY

Once you've examined the rhetorical context of your teaching philosophy, it is time to begin generating content for your document.

In this section, we'll take you through each potential element of a teaching philosophy as represented in Figure 7.1. You do not need to draft your philosophy in the order represented here. The organization of your teaching philosophy will depend on the context of your document. Novice educators

Table 7.1. Teaching Philosophy Rhetorical Situation Graphic Organizer

What is the **purpose** of this teaching philosophy? What are your reasons for writing this teaching philosophy?
Who is the **audience** for your teaching philosophy? Is there more than one audience? What are the needs of this audience? What steps will you take to meet the audience's needs?
What is the **context** surrounding your teaching philosophy? What are the circumstances or situations surrounding the document?
What **voice** do you want to establish in your teaching philosophy? How can your word choice and tone reflect the themes in your document?
What is the specific **genre** of your teaching philosophy? What is this document being called? What elements must be included in your teaching philosophy?

Figure 7.1. Elements of a Teaching Philosophy

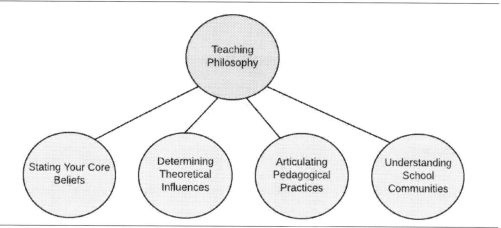

writing their first teaching philosophy may write more about their theoretical or research influences, due to their limited practical experience. Experienced teachers writing teaching philosophies as part of a job application or career advancement may include more details about their pedagogical practices or understanding of school communities in order to demonstrate their teaching ability or fit with a specific school community.

Sample Teaching Philosophy from a Preservice Teacher

Figure 7.2 is a sample teaching philosophy from a preservice teacher, Faith, whom we introduced in Chapter 6. Faith wrote her teaching philosophy as part of her education coursework for her single-subject English credential at Illinois State University. She has since revised the document and believes that at this point her teaching philosophy "is truly reflective of who I am and will be as an educator." As you read through Figure 7.2, we encourage you to refer to Figure 6.2 to evaluate the way in which Faith's teaching philosophy is represented in her lesson plan, and vice versa.

Because the teaching philosophy can function as a representation of your teacher identity, it can feel overwhelming to distill the many facets of who you are as an educator into one brief document. There are so many different choices educators can make in their pedagogical practices that when you write your teaching philosophy, it is necessary to choose representative examples of both your practices and the rationale behind them. No pedagogy is ideology-free; thus, consider which ideology (or ideologies) influences your pedagogy. For example, Faith's teaching philosophy (see Figure 7.2) reflects her ideology of culturally responsive teaching. As you review both her lesson plan (featured in Figure 6.2) and her teaching philosophy, you will notice how she

Figure 7.2. Sample Teaching Philosophy (written by Faith and annotated by the authors)

"We look to schools to solve problems facing our country—even problems that go beyond education. In order for education to play a role in getting us to play an equitable part of society, we need a different form of education."

—Pedro Noguera

Faith opens her teaching philosophy with a quote from a well-known researcher in the field of education who advocates for progressive change in education. With a preface to her teaching philosophy, Faith has shared her theoretical influences with her audience and aligned herself with a specific body of social justice research.

Learning takes place when teachers and students combine their talents to progress the content of a classroom. It happens when teachers diligently seek out inclusivity in their spaces, and when students are prepared to engage in the spaces that have been presented to them, as well as the spaces that have been created by them. Learning is fostered by the intent of the lesson, and the focus of accessing the worlds that exist around us. It happens when we realize that the classroom extends beyond our eight hour days.

In her opening paragraph, Faith articulates one of her core beliefs in education: where learning takes place. This discussion includes a discussion of her thoughts on school communities.

My philosophy, then, stems from that. And as I prepare to enter the classroom, I prepare to enter a world that is filled with young, eager minds, minds that are much more capable than some would believe. As I prepare to teach, I rebuke deficit model teaching, for it is restrictive of the abilities of all students, no matter their background.

Faith demonstrates her theoretical influences by stating which theories she does not believe in.

Pedro Noguera states, "We need a different form of education." We need teachers who are willing to address issues of race, ethnicity and nationality. Teachers who are willing to discuss classism, sexism, gender, identity, and socioeconomic status. We need teachers who realize the unfair past of this country, and our unwillingness to simply acknowledge it, is stifling to our children, and destructive in our classrooms. I decided to teach for one of the more traditional reasons: there was a deficit in my learning.

By quoting a scholar in the field of education like Noguera, who has an active research agenda surrounding issues of equity in education, Faith articulates her vision of a school community, and the role of a teacher in that community.

Faith briefly alludes to her own experience as a learner, and isolates her experience as motivation for pursuing a career in education.

I continue this journey for a less traditional reason: there is work to be done. Learning is an investment, and one that we all can afford. It is receiving information, and actively deciding what is consumable and what is not. What is worth perpetuating and what is not. What is worth keeping and what it is not. It's taking "canonical reads" like *The Great Gatsby* and addressing who the American Dream is reserved for. It's reading Kendrick Lamar lyrics and connecting them to African literary traditions. It's acknowledging the *Borders*, it's dissecting "the greats," it's sharing the microphone. It's accessing the Third Space.

Again, Faith alludes to a recurring theme of equity in education.

Faith transitions her discussion of equity into a discussion of curriculum, in her case that of a high school ELA.

In this section, Faith articulates specific pedagogical practices that reflect the issues and concerns she has raised earlier in the document.

Together is where learning takes place. My classroom will demonstrate reflexivity in practice. Every day will be a rough draft in the way that the next day will be an improvement. It will demonstrate accountability practices. Students will be as responsible as I for the energy they put out, and how it is received. In addition to the scores and rubrics, the letter grades and feedback, students will be assessed on their ability to plan and orchestrate, and on the effort they have driven into completing tasks. My goal as an educator is to prepare students for what is here, and what is to come, may that be college *or* career readiness. I hope to encourage pupils who are ready and willing to view their days through various lenses and perspectives. I hope that they recognize the dangers in single stories, and that they leave my classroom each day, each week, each year with a seed that has been planted and may only be fostered to grow by their drive. I hope that my students leave each day challenging everything that is presented to them with tact, empathy, and fervor. I want nothing more than to be a catalyst for change, a projector of dreams, and resource for hope.

> Here, Faith names a core belief that also reflects her pedagogical orientation to her classroom.

> Her understanding of school communities is clear in this section.

> In this section, Faith articulates her philosophy and approach toward assessment.

> Faith relates her goal as an educator to her understanding of the purpose of education.

> Faith's pedagogical goals for her students clearly reflect the pedagogical practices in her lesson plan.

> Faith closes her teaching philosophy with her goals as an educator, which are consistent with issues she raises earlier in her teaching philosophy.

represents herself as a reflective and well-informed preservice teacher. When you draft your own teaching philosophy, consider how your document will represent your teacher identity, by naming your beliefs, articulating your theoretical and research influences, describing your pedagogical approaches, and demonstrating your understanding of school communities.

Stating Your Beliefs

The most critical element of the teaching philosophy is your beliefs about teaching. When you name your beliefs, you provide your audience with specific, detailed evidence about the type of teacher you are or will be. Clear and specific core beliefs function as a foundation of your teaching philosophy. Each element included in your document should reflect or connect to your stated core beliefs. In this way, your core beliefs function as the theme of your teaching philosophy, which binds the content of the document together.

By this point in your education, you have thought a lot about what you believe about education, but you may have not yet had the opportunity to name these beliefs in a specific genre for a targeted audience. This is your opportunity to identify what you believe about teaching and how these beliefs manifest in your teaching. There are many ways to name your beliefs, but the primary goal of this element in the teaching philosophy is to give specific context about the environment in which you teach (or hope to teach) and then to outline the role and responsibilities of a teacher in that context.

For example, your teaching philosophy can include a direct statement about the age level, discipline, or type of student you hope to teach. If you are interested in becoming a middle school science teacher, then your teaching philosophy could include a statement such as: "As a middle school science teacher, I plan to open my students' eyes to the mysteries of the natural world all around them." Or perhaps you are passionate about teaching English language learners; in that instance, your teaching philosophy should include a direct statement articulating your passion for working with this population. You don't want to be too specific about the context you hope to teach in (for example, "I plan on teaching 2nd grade in this district and can't imagine doing anything else."), because this may shut the door to possible job opportunities if your teaching philosophy is going to be used as part of your job materials.

If you are not yet sure of the specifics surrounding the context in which you'd like to teach, your teaching philosophy can include general statements about the classroom environment you hope to create. Molly, a preservice teacher in a credential program, noted in her methods vision statement: "I want my class to be a place where students feel welcomed and safe, and where they can make mistakes, grow, and have their learning celebrated." Even though Molly has not specified an age level or discipline, she has provided an overarching description about the classroom environment she plans to create. Reflecting on the environment you hope to create in your classroom will help you to name your core beliefs. Use the graphic organizer in Table 7.2 (presented near the end of this chapter) to help you generate ideas about your core beliefs, and sample responses to help guide your responses. Once you have generated some ideas about your core beliefs in education, support and illustrate them with evidence from educational theories or research.

Determining Theoretical Influences

Another key element of your teaching philosophy is to articulate your theoretical background in education. In this genre, because of its brevity, this element usually means briefly alluding to or citing the work of educational theorists and researchers with whom you align. Ask yourself how this alignment occurred. You have already named your beliefs about education, and now you need to document the source of these beliefs. In order to do this, think back to a class or a reading that had a profound effect on the way you think about yourself as a teacher. Locate the source of that inspiration and refer to it in your philosophy with an APA in-text citation (APA citations will be covered in Chapter 10).

It may be tempting to rely only on evidence drawn from your own experience to support your core beliefs about education and not use evidence from educational theorists and researchers. After all, you have been a student for many years and no doubt have instructed others in your teaching, tutoring, coaching, or child care experiences. While these experiences may be relevant to include (particularly if you have extensive experience in one of these areas) in your discussion of your pedagogical practices, they may be less appropriate to discuss as part of your theoretical background. Often these personal experiences reflect a limited, or even biased, source of theoretical evidence for your core beliefs. That is, your personal experiences are not sufficient data to support a whole claim or theory. By drawing on research-supported beliefs and practices in your teaching philosophy, you are locating yourself within the large body of education research and validating the field of education as one based on research and not just experience.

Theoretical Influences. In your education and credential coursework, you will be or have been introduced to many educational theories that will influence you and your developing teacher identity. When writing your teaching philosophy, think back to any relevant coursework you may have completed in your studies, such as in psychology, child and/or human development, or ethnic studies, and consider how theories from these disciplines may have influenced how you see yourself as an educator. Stribling et al. (2015) outlined five major educational theories, "Behavioral, Comprehensive, Progressive, Humanistic, and Social Change" (p. 40), in their study of teaching philosophies, but there are many relevant theories with which you can align yourself. Alternatively, you can identify your theoretical influences in your teaching philosophy by articulating with which theories you do not align.

Research-Supported Influences. In the increasingly data-driven field of education, it is imperative that your teaching philosophy refer to research-supported pedagogical practices in addition to your past experiences or personal preferences in education. As we noted in Chapter 4, research in education is wide-reaching in its scope, so citing specific research or researchers in your teaching philosophy is one way to align yourself with a specific area of research. For example, Emily, a credential student, noted in her praxis pedagogy paper:

> Since I believe in learning that is student-centered and "contextualized" within the social and cultural realities of my students, the theoretical lenses that guide my teaching are social constructivism and social and ecological justice. (John-Steiner & Mahn, 1996)

In this statement, Emily not only names the pedagogical theories with which she aligns herself, but also includes a specific in-text citation to ground her beliefs in peer-reviewed research by education scholars.

Similarly, in Faith's sample teaching philosophy in Figure 7.2, she references noted education scholar Pedro Noguera at two points in the document.

Referencing Noguera, a scholar with a research agenda focused on issues of equity, achievement, class, and race, in her teaching philosophy, is consistent with Faith's pedagogical practices represented in the lesson plan in Figure 6.2. Her lesson on unbiased language in essay writing reflects the research-based practices of scholars working in the fields of equity and access in education. Together, Faith's lesson plan and teaching philosophy present a coherent and research-supported representation of her pedagogical practices.

Articulating Pedagogical Practices

Once you've articulated the core beliefs and theoretical influences of your teaching philosophy, it is necessary to also include evidence as to how the research-based theories and practices manifest (or will manifest) in your classroom. That is, based on the theories and research that you align with, what will pedagogical practices look like in your classroom? This element of your teaching philosophy is an appropriate place to use evidence from your experiences as an instructor or from your experience of observing others instruct. In addition, articulating specific pedagogical approaches provides evidence of your core beliefs.

You also may choose to articulate how your theoretical and/or research-based foundation will allow you to approach specific elements in your teaching, such as selecting one mode of assessment over another, effective classroom management, or differentiated instruction. Emily—a teaching credential student—was assigned to write a praxis pedagogy paper. In it, she first aligns herself with critical pedagogy theory, which she locates as pedagogy based on investigating authentic problems, and then highlights how this will influence her approach to crafting thematic units in class.

> Together, students explore these problems thematically as they relate to literature and life, socially constructing their questions and ideas and propelling each other's curiosity. Every unit begins with this collective drive to understand before students diverge for individualized inquiry through research and action projects.

By describing her approach to thematic groups through her alignment with critical pedagogy theory, Emily is giving her audience a clear example of how her theoretical background influences her pedagogical practices, and provides a clear insight into who she is as a teacher.

Another way in which you can articulate your pedagogical practices in your teaching philosophy is to describe the actual practices you enact, or plan to enact, in your classroom. This section may include describing what your classroom may look or feel like; how students might feel in your class (for example, about themselves as learners or about the subject matter); how students might feel when they leave your class; or what students might take with them when they leave. For example, if your goal is to create a collaborative classroom that is welcoming and safe for all students, which practices would you need to use to achieve this classroom community? Would you assign groupwork or facilitate whole-class check-ins?

In her methods vision statement, preservice teacher Molly articulated that her theoretical goal for her classroom was to create an equal-status classroom influenced by the work of Cohen and Lotan (1995). She then illustrated her attempts to enact that theory during her student teaching.

> During my placement, one of the things I focused on is getting all students engaged during my teaching. I had one student in particular who had low English abilities, but I noticed that she did an assignment exactly as I wanted the students to, so I displayed her work on the document camera as an example. Celebrating her strengths and having a safe class where mistakes are okay seems to help her be willing to share answers even if they are not correct, and she has improved a lot since the beginning of the year.

In her description of her attempt to create an equal-status classroom for an English language learner, Molly clearly and specifically describes the way in which she is enacting her theoretical influences in practice, and she also provides her audience with a clear example of what her students may experience in her class.

Understanding School Communities

You also may want to consider articulating your understanding of school communities in your teaching philosophy. Because effective teaching takes place within the context of a school community, you can use your teaching philosophy to convey what kind of member of this community you are or would like to become. This approach may be an essential element of a job application or letter of introduction for a teaching position. In discussing your understanding of school communities, you can articulate exactly how you envision a school working together and consequently what kind of colleague you will strive to be.

Collaboration. Because teaching is both an independent and a collaborative profession, your teaching philosophy is a place in which you can describe your approach to this dualistic aspect. As you describe the role of the school community in your teaching philosophy, you may want to answer questions like:

- How do you feel about collaborating with colleagues?

- What role do you see the school community playing in your teaching practices?
- How do you envision a school community, yourself included, supporting the development of teachers?

By answering these types of questions, you will give your audience clear insight into your understanding of the school community.

Community. Because your teaching takes place (or will take place) in a community comprising many different members and external elements, you also may want to describe any salient feelings you have about these considerations within the community. For example, in your teaching philosophy you may want to address some of the following questions:

- How do you see the role of students in your class?
- What are the roles of the parents of your students?
- What role does your local community play within your classroom?

If you are a single-subject teacher, you also may want to articulate your feelings about your discipline and the effects that learning this discipline will have on the lives of your students. Whichever elements you choose for your teaching philosophy, including a brief discussion about how you see your teaching practices functioning within a larger school community, is yet another way for you to convey your specific core beliefs about teaching to a larger audience.

Table 7.2 is a graphic organizer containing targeted questions and hypothetical, sample answers designed to generate content for each of the four potential elements of your teaching philosophy: core beliefs, influences from education theory and research-supported practices, preferred pedagogical practices, and understanding school communities. Use the questions and sample answers to guide your own responses in the space provided and add or remove content that is not relevant for the context of your own teaching philosophy.

EXERCISES

1. Jessica, a special education teacher in Paso Robles, California, has been teaching for many years, and after earning her administrative credential, she is looking to pursue leadership positions within her district. Below, she has written a draft of her administrative philosophy. Based on the contents of this chapter, what advice would you give Jessica for strengthening her philosophy?

Table 7.2. Teaching Philosophy Content Graphic Organizer

Element	Sample Response	Your Response
Core Beliefs • What is the educational context surrounding your teaching practices? What grade level, discipline, or student population would you like to teach? • What is the purpose of education?	• As a U.S. history teacher for students for whom English is not their first language, I want to introduce my students to the history of immigration in this country. • My approach to teaching history in this way allows me to demonstrate to my students that current events and policies surrounding immigration stem from a long history of immigration in this country, and that this history is relevant today. This approach allows me to promote positive social change in my classroom.	
Determining Influences from Education Theory and Research-Supported Practices • Which educational theories have influenced your core beliefs? • Which research-based practices have influenced your core beliefs?	• As a historian and an educator of students who are not native speakers of English, I have been heavily influenced by theory of culturally sustaining pedagogy (CSP) (Alim & Paris, 2015). • I teach history with a focus on socially just culturally sustaining pedagogy, based on the research of Lee and Walsh (2017). This approach allows my students to critically investigate social injustices within the history of immigration to the U.S. with the goal to facilitate positive social change in the future.	
Articulating Pedagogical Approaches • What kind of classroom environment do you want to create? Why do you want to create this? • What is a pedagogical practice you routinely employ in your classroom that facilitates your desired classroom environment?	• In my history class, I want my students to see that history matters in their everyday lives. As such, I regularly bring in current events to class to serve as the foundation for our active, collaborative classroom discussions. In my class, students are actively engaging with current events, rather than passively receiving them. • In all of my classes, I have my students tell their families' immigration stories, either through oral presentations or written histories. After we share our stories, we examine the role of governmental power within the immigration system of this country.	

Table 7.2. Teaching Philosophy Content Graphic Organizer (continued)

Element	Sample Response	Your Response
Understanding School Communities • What role does collaboration play within a school community? • How do you feel about the vision statement for the school in which you teach (or would like to teach)? • What are the role and/or responsibilities of the teacher in the classroom? • What are the role and/or responsibilities of the students in the classroom? • What is the role of parents in your classroom?	• Student learning takes place within dynamic communities, both in and out of the classroom. As such, my responsibility as an educator is to function as a committed member of these communities and collaborate with each stakeholder involved in student learning. From planning curriculum with my grade-level colleagues at my school site to attending conferences with fellow members of the Organization of History Teachers, I am committed to working with others to foster my students' understanding of U.S. history. • I believe that students learn best in collaboration with one another. Because of this belief, I am a strong proponent of project-based learning and well-prepared to teach history in this method. • In my classroom, I see myself as a guide for my students on this journey through American history. I point out landmarks on this journey, but do not make them arrive at any specific destination. • In my classroom, my students need to bring an inquisitive nature, and be open to making sense of the current events around them. • Because I reject the deficit model of education, I see parents as incredible resources who add value and knowledge to my classroom. I regularly invite parents to my class to share their expertise and experience with my students.	

Nelson Mandela once said, "Education is the most powerful weapon which you can use to change the world." Educational leadership is a platform to provide that positive change as well as continued guidance to a community of educators and students. Without clear leadership, education itself is in danger of falling short of its true potential to positively influence the world. Every successful educational leader possesses specific quality traits and must have a clear vision of both the desired goal and process needed to achieve it.

Though the job title of an educational leader may vary, there are several attributes that are necessary for success. These common traits include enthusiasm, knowledge, and respect. Enthusiasm toward the betterment of education and the success of children is mandatory. This excitement over the refinement of education will help support the drive and direction of the decision maker. An educational leader must also be knowledgeable in the law and mandated requirements of a school system. This information can then be used to make well informed, legally responsible, district supported decisions. Though respect is not something that can be forced, it is also essential for a leader to both possess and earn. Without this type of support, the integrity of the educational system can be in jeopardy. With these key traits, an educational leader is more qualified and better able to focus on the desired educational goal.

"A leader is one who knows the way, shows the way, and goes the way," John C. Maxwell. Every strong leader needs an objective to work toward, in order to give those they lead a path to follow. Once an end goal is acknowledged, it is the educational leader's role to delegate how to achieve it. This process utilizes the ambition of the leader to assess specific situations and determine the effectiveness of the educational system. In this process, it is crucial for a leader to master the delicate balance between consideration for others' opinions and making a decision that may be difficult, but best for students. Though it is essential to have a solid end goal, one can only be as successful as the process is clear. Educational leadership is ultimately a collaborative position, which relies on the support of others. Without a supported goal and process, an ineffective leader will stand alone.

The fundamental role of any successful leader is to guide others toward a positive end result. Through a combination of key virtues and transparent processes, a true educational leader will achieve the ultimate goal of increased student success. With this success, each student will make the world a uniquely better place.

2. Imagine that you have earned your credential, and that you are now looking for full-time employment as a teacher. After searching open teaching positions on your state's department of education website or an employment portal such as EDJOIN, you unexpectedly locate your dream job. Take a few moments and write the job ad for your dream job modeled on ads you see on these sites. After you articulate the specifics of this position, consider what steps you will take in your teaching philosophy to demonstrate how you fit this position. What elements must you include? What items can you leave out or mention at a later date? How can you use the draft of a teaching philosophy to represent who you are as a teacher?

CHAPTER 8

Writing Critical Reflections

In Chapter 7 you learned how to articulate the kind of teacher you want to be in a teaching philosophy. You likely will be asked to write this document during a credential program in anticipation of moving into the teaching profession. This chapter will cover another important genre you'll be asked to write during the student teaching phase of your credential program and as you transition from a preservice to practicing teacher: a critical reflection. In order to earn your credential, you will be required to demonstrate your teaching effectiveness on an assessment measure, such as the edTPA. To do this, you will submit a portfolio of your teaching practices to the assessment body. This portfolio may include many different elements, depending on which state you live in, but the focus will always be evidence of your teaching practices. In this chapter, we'll discuss how to select effective, representative evidence of your teaching from successful lesson plans (as we discussed in Chapter 6) that represent your core beliefs about teaching (as we discussed in Chapter 7). Whereas Chapter 5 focused on investigating and analyzing the teaching practices of other educators, critical reflection requires that you instead investigate and analyze your own pedagogical practices.

Critically reflecting on your teaching practices signifies your movement up the continuum of writing in education that we introduced in Chapter 1. Compiling a teaching portfolio for assessment is a task that is strictly for professional, not for academic, purposes. As you step into the role of a professional educator, you will notice that reflection is at the heart of teaching, as we explained in Chapter 1. Because more complicated and complex forms of reflective writing are required as a practicing teacher, it is imperative that you develop the skill of critical reflection. Only a few other professions use reflection as a mode of assessment the way we do in education; that is what makes teaching different, and that is what makes learning this skill so essential. As Barth-Cohen, Little, and Abrahamson (2018) note, developing your reflective practice as an educator is, and always has been, key to success in the profession, whether that includes journaling about your day or lesson, or evaluating a videotape of yourself teaching.

Critical reflections may be called different things in your teaching portfolio assessment, such as narratives, commentaries, or descriptions. In this chapter, we define critical reflection as the process of looking back on past teaching experiences with the aim of improving teaching and learning. With this understanding, you will be able to create and collect materials that accurately highlight your abilities as an educator, and present them to an outside audience.

EXAMINING THE RHETORICAL SITUATION: PURPOSE, AUDIENCE, CONTEXT, VOICE, AND GENRE

Students and teachers in education write critical reflections for several professional reasons. In most states, writing critical reflections is a requirement for getting a teaching credential. In these rhetorical situations, you are writing to those who will score your teaching portfolio, usually active and retired teachers. If you are writing critical reflections once you are in the classroom, your audience will be your school administrators, who make decisions about the quality of your teaching and whether you advance in your career.

But perhaps the most important audience for critical reflections is *you*, because analyzing and reflecting on questions such as "What am I teaching? Why am I teaching this to this particular group of students? What worked? What could I improve next time?" are all ways to develop, change, and grow as a professional teacher. The more awareness you have of the connections between your teaching practice and theory, research, knowledge of your students, and your personal values, the more you will be able to articulate and advocate for the best practices within the field. So, when writing a critical reflection, ask yourself about the purpose of the reflection. What do you hope to achieve? Do you want to:

- Demonstrate to outside evaluators that you are ready to teach?
- Demonstrate your teaching excellence to your school administrators?
- Reflect on your teaching practices in order to facilitate your professional growth?
- Create and refine your professional vision and values in order to effect change?

Knowing your audience and purpose will enable you to make other rhetorical choices, such as how much description of your teaching practices to include, how best to write about your pedagogical choices and how they reflect current knowledge of the field, and how to choose evidence that supports your instructional choices.

The context for a critical reflection can vary depending on the circumstances in which you are writing it. Portfolio assessment measures, such as the edTPA, for example, are considered a high-stakes testing environment because you cannot earn your credential without passing them. Likewise, writing a critical reflection of your teaching for career advancement is also a high-stakes situation, as you may be trying to keep your job or advance on the pay scale. The context in which you are writing the critical reflection may change, as may the audience and the specific genre or form the resulting writing takes, but the purpose will always be to demonstrate growth as a practicing teacher. Thus, you want to approach all of these writing situations very thoughtfully, since critical reflections are a very writing-intensive genre.

When you write critical reflections, your voice should come across as professional, confident, and aspiring to work toward positive change in your teaching pedagogy. Reflecting critically on your teaching requires you to be introspective and open to finding areas that can be improved. You want to be able to point to what you are doing well, as well as to areas that need improvement. You also want to come across as a credible professional—an educator who is examining evidence you've collected about your teaching practices and your students' learning, and who is using this evidence to articulate ideas for pedagogical growth.

The length of a critical reflection will vary depending on purpose, audience, and context. The critical reflection that credential students write for the edTPA is many pages long and dictated by certain required sections. When you write a critical reflection as part of a review while a practicing teacher, however, you will write a much shorter piece that often has required elements as well. As with all of the other genres we've discussed in this book, when faced with a writing task, you'll want to first examine the rhetorical situation at hand and then review samples of the genre before attempting to write it yourself. Understanding how the genre is written is key to being able to write the genre.

TEACHING PORTFOLIO ASSESSMENTS: DEMONSTRATING TEACHER READINESS

According to Noel (2014), "The American Association of College Teacher Educators (AACTE) reports that 34 states and the District of Columbia currently participate in teacher candidate performance assessment" (p. 357). One of the most frequently used assessments, the edTPA, was developed at the Stanford Center for Assessment, Learning, and Equity and is administered through Pearson, a publishing company.

While the edTPA requires extensive reflection by teacher candidates and is rooted in a portfolio model of assessment, many educators remain critical of the edTPA for various reasons. For example, educators object to the high cost of the exam and its connections to Pearson, which outsources the scoring to current and past teachers who are not familiar with local teaching contexts. Other teacher educators and preservice teachers compiling their portfolios, particularly those "working with emergent bilinguals in bilingual, bilingual special education, or TESOL classrooms" (Kleyn, Lopez, & Makar, 2015, p. 104), argue that the focus on English as the language in the assessment disregards the importance of bilingualism and bilingual education.

The edTPA reflects the next iteration of school reform focused on accountability within U.S. education. It is part of a nationwide push for the standardization of teacher knowledge and is related to other nationwide reform movements, such as the Common Core standards, Race to the Top, and No Child Left Behind. While we agree that the edTPA has drawbacks, and that assessments are best evaluated within local contexts, if you are planning to become a teacher in this country, you will need to know how to write a variety of critical reflections for these different assessments.

THE edTPA FORMAT

The version of the edTPA you complete will vary depending on your chosen subject and which state you live in. In your portfolio, you'll need to submit a lesson plan, two 5- to 10-minute videos of you teaching lessons, classroom artifacts (handouts and other teaching guides), and student samples, along with your feedback and assessments. You'll also need to "explain and defend different aspects of [your] pedagogical practices" (Clark-Garcia, 2015, p. 212) by writing critical reflections or commentaries that address evidence of student learning and are grounded in data, education theories, and research.

Writing Critical Reflections for the edTPA

In the edTPA, you will critically reflect on your pedagogical practices in three different areas: planning commentary, instruction commentary, and assessment commentary. The planning commentary justifies the choices in your lesson plans. To effectively write this section, refer to the strategies discussed in Chapter 6 about writing rationales. The instruction commentary focuses on your videos and includes classroom artifacts. The assessment commentary addresses how you evaluated student learning and provided feedback. Each of these reflections requires you to describe what you have done and explain how your choices reflect current knowledge of the field by using a variety of evidence to support your instructional choices. In the following sections, we provide guidance about how to approach these writing-intensive sections of the edTPA.

Choosing Representative Lessons. In order to demonstrate your teaching efficacy, think back to what you learned in Chapter 6 and carefully choose your most effective lessons—those that best facilitate student learning. Teaching portfolio assessments will require you to use a prescribed lesson plan template.

This template will include items such as state standards, central focus, learning targets, and academic language. Therefore, as you consider which lessons to include in your portfolio, choose those that include a strong understanding of these elements. Your selected lessons should effectively highlight relevant state standards that facilitate a clear central focus (or outcome) of your lesson, and you should have a clear rationale for choosing these standards.

Analyzing Your Lessons. In a teaching portfolio assessment, your audience is looking for evidence of your teaching efficacy based on student learning. You will demonstrate this efficacy through two short video clips of you teaching specific lessons. As you carefully review the videos, what do you notice about your teaching practices and your students' learning? Are students interacting with the lesson in the manner you had planned? Are students using the artifacts in the way you anticipated? Do you see evidence of student learning? Do you see ways in which you could improve opportunities for student learning? Your audience also may want to see how your pedagogical practices reflect the educational theories and research-based practices you have been learning in your education courses. How does your lesson do this?

After reviewing your teaching videos, you need to analyze and reflect on how the different elements of your lesson worked together. Were the teaching artifacts (lesson plans, materials, and student assessments) from the lesson aligned with your goals and assessments for the lesson?

Using Evidence in Reflections

When writing the commentary sections of the edTPA, you need to use evidence to support specific claims about the efficacy of your teaching. As we discussed in Chapters 4 and 5, evidence in education can take many forms, and in the case of your reflections, it may be best to use a variety of evidence to support your claims. You probably will draw the most evidence from your videos and teaching artifacts: learning targets, central focus, instructional materials, state standards, preassessment and postassessment data (represented through narratives or graphs), and student work. You also can use the evidence from your teaching artifacts in conjunction with key educational theorists and researchers to support the claims you are making about your own practices. Refer to the section "Determining Theoretical Influences" in Chapter 7 for how to align yourself with educational theorists and researchers.

The following two sections provide an overview of some of the reflective writing you are expected to do in the edTPA.

Instruction Commentary. The instruction commentary of the edTPA requires preservice teachers to describe, defend, and reflect on short video clips of their chosen lesson. These commentaries are extremely detailed, thorough, and lengthy (edTPA, 2015a). Figure 8.1 includes a sample excerpt of one instructional commentary for a 9th-grade history class covering a unit on the role of women in U.S. history. In this instruction commentary written by Preet, the class is engaged in reading a complex primary source, "The Declaration of Sentiments and Resolutions," written in 1848 by Elizabeth Cady Stanton and Lucretia Mott. This lesson aims to meet standards for reading a complex text, as well as speaking and listening when working collaboratively with a partner.

   Assessment Commentary. The assessment commentary section of the edTPA asks students to explain the results of their pre- and postassessment data on evaluations of the learning targets and critically reflect on the level of student learning achieved during the lesson (edTPA, 2015b). In Figure 8.2, Preet analyzes her students' comprehension of the "The Declaration of Sentiments

Figure 8.1. Sample Instruction Commentary (written by Preet and commented on by the authors)

The second video clip captures my interactions with pairs of students as they discuss "The Declaration of Sentiments and Resolutions." This video was taken during Lesson 4, and I began by reminding students that, by this point, they have previously worked with primary historical documents. That day, the instructional goal was to analyze the declaration and discuss the historical context for the text. At the beginning of this lesson, I modeled how to do a close reading of the document with my cooperating teacher as my pretend partner. Students in the video are partnered and have moved their desks, which are typically in rows, so that they either sit side-by-side or across from their partner. Once their desks were together, I passed out a set of definitions for some of the unfamiliar or archaic language in the declaration. With partners, they translated these terms into modern-day language. Immediately after this second video clip, we regrouped for a whole-class discussion of the meaning of the declaration in today's language and I asked students to share what they discussed in pairs. I knew to move on to this discussion when many students' hands are raised for me to check their accuracy and progress. You can hear me say, "That's my cue." In reflecting on this clip, I realized that I had not made the learning targets as clear as I could to the students. Therefore, in the future, I will need to make the connections between prior lessons and learning targets clearer.

> Preet is addressing Common Core State Standards: CCSS.ELA-Literacy.RH.9-10.1 and CCSS.ELA-Literacy.SL.9-10.1A.

> Here Preet is clearly establishing the goals for the lesson.

> She provides a detailed description of the learning activity.

> She could have supported the rationale of her learning activity by bringing in a credible source.

> Finally, Preet critically reflects on what could be improved in future iterations of the lesson.

Figure 8.2. Sample Assessment Commentary (written by Preet and commented on by the authors)

Patterns in content show that most students demonstrated knowledge of the essence of the "Declaration of Sentiments and Resolutions" in their modern-day declaration of the rights of teenagers well enough for someone listening to understand. Most students also demonstrated their ability to successfully translate the archaic language into contemporary language. The lowest scores here, a two out of four, were given when students wrote a modern-day translation, but failed to represent the essence of the original. Work Samples 1 and 2 showcase strong content because they named specific, relevant ageist conditions that they face as teenagers in the United States. However, as seen in my written feedback, both Work Samples 3 and especially 4 could have improved in the specificity of their descriptions of their ageist conditions, a pattern I noted across student work. In Work Sample 3, the student didn't articulate fact-based criterion for ageist conditions, while in Work Sample 4, the student's declaration was based entirely on narrow personal experience rather than more universal facts. These Work Samples and the rubric results tell me that all students would have benefited from more formal written feedback.

> Here the student teacher reflects on what her students have learned as a result of her lesson.

> In her analysis of the data, she discusses how her students' efforts to comprehend the primary text were successful.

> To show that your students have achieved the learning targets, you must be able to point to specific assessment data that you have gathered from your teaching.

and Resolutions." In order to do this, she had her students write their own declarations of the rights of teenagers. Students then read their declarations to the class and received oral and written feedback from the teacher and their classmates. Figure 8.2 represents one small excerpt from Preet's extensive assessment commentary.

WRITING CRITICAL REFLECTIONS IN FORMAL ANNUAL EVALUATIONS

In addition to the reflective writing you are asked to do in the edTPA (or other multiple-measure teaching portfolio assessments), you will write critical reflections as a practicing teacher. When you first become a teacher, you also will likely be required to complete a new teacher induction program in your state that involves working with a mentor teacher, administrator, or coach who supports you in assessing and reflecting on your professional growth. In these programs, new teachers work closely with their mentors to conduct observations of both student learning and teacher practices, as well as create action plans for improving teaching and learning conditions. Practicing teachers also must critically reflect on their teaching practices as part of their review process. Whether you undergo a review every year, multiple times a year, or once every 3 to 5 years depends on whether you are a temporary, probationary, or permanent employee. These reviews are high-stakes in that they determine whether you will be promoted to probationary or tenured status and whether you earn a salary increase.

Formal evaluations can take different forms, but usually they consist of some variation of the following: a goal-setting meeting, a preobservation conference, a formal classroom observation, and a reflection plan.

Goal-Setting Meeting

At the beginning of the school year, a teacher usually meets with an administrator for a goal-setting meeting to discuss their state's professional teaching standards. Typically, the teacher and administrator agree on a couple of standards for the teacher to focus on during the year, with the end goal being satisfactory performance. They may even draft a specific action plan in which the teacher articulates detailed plans for focusing on a particular teaching standard. For example, New Jersey has 11 standards for the teaching profession, ranging from standards focused on the learner, content, instructional practice, and professional responsibility (New Jersey Department of Education, 2014). At the end of the year, teachers are assessed on whether they are performing satisfactorily on all state-mandated teaching standards. Administrators often will note where on a sliding scale of achievement within the standard they think the teacher is. California uses the following ratings within each of the California Standards for the Teaching Profession: emerging, exploring, applying, integrating, and innovating (California Commission on Teacher Credentialing, 2012).

Preobservation Conference

During the preobservation conference, teachers meet with the administrator who will observe their teaching to discuss the review process. Following this meeting, teachers write the lesson plan they will follow on the day of the observation (teachers should choose lessons they feel will show professional growth) and/or fill in a prepared form that typically asks the purpose of the lesson and standards to be addressed, the planned instructional strategies, expected learner behaviors, and how the teacher will monitor or assess student progress (see Chapter 6 on writing lesson plans). The teacher gives this to the administrator before the scheduled classroom observation.

Formal Classroom Observation and Reflection Plan

During the formal classroom observation, the administrator takes notes of what is happening in the class and whether evidence of the stated components of the lesson plan is observed. Following the class observation, the teacher spends time reflecting on how the lesson went and usually will be asked to write a postobservation reflection responding to the following questions:

- Did the lesson go as you anticipated? Why or why not?
- Did you teach the lesson as planned? What changed?
- Did the students respond to your lesson the way you anticipated? Why or why not?
- If you were going to teach the same lesson again, what would you do differently?
- How did you incorporate goals/objectives in the lesson plan? (Woodland Joint Unified School District, 2016)

For example, Dave, who teaches 8th-grade social studies and life skills in Redding, California, identified California Standard for the Teaching Profession 1 (engaging and supporting all students in learning) and subgoal 5 (promoting critical thinking through inquiry, problem solving, and reflection) as his focus for the year. To meet this objective, he wrote the following Teacher Action Plan in his goal-setting meeting with his administrator:

> My objective is to build a rigorous curriculum that emphasizes critical thinking. I have implemented many aspects of the Common Core social science skills but would like to "up my game" to engage struggling students more and push students more toward analysis and synthesis rather than straight identification and examination. I hope to achieve this through inquiry-driven units and PBL (project-based learning) units.

In this goal-setting writing for the year, Dave reflects on how he envisions his teaching developing.

In a lesson for his life skills class, Dave asked his students to work together in groups to accomplish a difficult task and practice communication strategies they had been discussing. The exercise was meant to prepare the students to communicate with different kinds of people once they entered the workforce. In this excerpt from his reflection plan, Dave critiques how the lesson went and articulates how he might change his teaching methods in the future to increase student engagement and learning. He writes:

> My goal/objective of creating lessons that engage critical thinking and problem solving was evident in the task itself. Students had a stated goal and had to work collaboratively to solve the problem of putting up the tent. Students struggled to do this and were able to discuss how those struggles either contributed to a breakdown in communication or how positive communication contributed to successful outcomes. It

did not go the way I intended in that we ran over time, not all students participated, and the discussion turned into a "blame" game between students. Next time, I would provide more detailed instructions. My initial goal was for the students to do their best with little input from me. However, due to the foreign nature of the task, the students needed more scaffolding and direction to be successful. Had that been provided, then students would have struggled less—reducing frustration. For example, in the future I would assign roles so that students knew exactly what they were to do.

As you can see, Dave reflects on the different aspects of the lesson, including student engagement, instructional strategies, learning goals, and lesson modifications for future use. While writing his reflection, Dave utilized information from his administrator's observation that described what different students/groups were doing during the lesson. As a reflective teacher like Dave, you need to always be thinking about why a lesson didn't go the way you intended. What can you add to or change about your instructional strategies to engage the students more effectively the next time?

WRITING CRITICAL REFLECTIONS FOR PROFESSIONAL GROWTH

As we noted earlier, writing critical reflections does not have to be for an outside audience or assessor. Maintaining a personal, reflective teaching journal for yourself is an important way to facilitate your professional growth as an educator. When you are your own audience, you determine the content and format of your reflections: You can track the success of specific lessons over time, mull over the climate in your classroom or at your school site, or even contemplate local, regional, and national issues in education that can influence and affect your teaching practices.

When you write for yourself, try to maintain a balance between objective reflections on your teaching practices and your personal feelings about an issue. Review a lesson or experience with the aim of making improvements in the future. Consider reflecting in a method similar to how you might ask your students to reflect on a lesson. The list of questions below is adapted from an Edutopia (2011) resource educators can use to facilitate student meta-reflection in four ways: "backward-looking," "inward-looking," "outward-looking," and "forward-looking."

1. Backward-looking:
   a. How much did you know about the subject before you taught it?
   b. What process did you go through to design this lesson?

    c. In what ways have you gotten better at this kind of work?

    d. What problems did you encounter while you were working on this lesson? How did you solve them?

    e. What resources did you use while working on this lesson? Which ones were especially helpful? Which ones would you use again?

2. Inward-looking:

    a. How do you feel about this lesson? What parts of it do you particularly like? Dislike? Why?

    b. What was especially satisfying about the process and/or the products of the lesson?

    c. What did/do you find frustrating about it?

    d. What does this lesson reveal about you as a teacher and as a learner?

    e. What did you learn about yourself as you created this lesson?

3. Outward-looking:

    a. What is the one thing you particularly want administrators or parents to notice about this lesson?

    b. In what ways did your lesson meet its stated standards or goals?

    c. How did students respond to the lesson? Was it what you anticipated? Why or why not?

    d. If someone else was looking at your lesson, what might that person learn about your professional values?

4. Forward-looking:

    a. What one thing would you like to improve upon in this lesson?

    b. What would you change if you had a chance to teach this lesson again?

    c. Are there any strategies other teachers use that you would like to incorporate the next time you teach this lesson?

    d. What's one goal you would like to set for yourself for the next time you teach this lesson?

    e. What would you like to spend more time on in your school community?

    f. What things might you want more help with in your professional development?

Responding to these types of reflective questions will not only isolate areas for professional growth in your teaching, but can also create and refine your vision as an educator. An awareness of your vision, and the values associated with it, will allow you to formulate opinions about issues in education that are based on your observations of your teaching practices. This awareness may make you curious about whether the patterns you notice in your own classroom are representative of other teachers (or students) in your district, state, or the nation. For example, as a new teacher, you may notice from your reflective journaling that you are spending a lot of classroom time lecturing, and as a consequence students are losing interest in the course topics. This might lead you to research the best practices for fostering engagement in your student population. This could then lead you to make suggestions for improvements in classroom design or class size in your district. For an example of how you might write a critical reflection for your own professional development, see teacher Leslie Young's (2018) reflective piece "Age of Resistance" published in *California Educator*. In the next chapter, we'll discuss how to translate your professional reflections about teaching practices into well-researched arguments for change in education.

EXERCISES

1. Reflect on a lesson you've designed or taught recently. Justify the choices you made in your lesson plan, describe the success of the lesson, and apply some of the meta-reflective questions we discussed in the "Writing Critical Reflections for Professional Growth" section.
2. Not every state assesses teachers in the same way. However, many use a teaching portfolio assessment to evaluate teacher readiness. Do some research to determine how your state assesses preservice or practicing teachers. Compare what you find with what we have discussed in this chapter.

CHAPTER 9

Writing Proposals for Educational Policy Change

So far in this guide we have focused on written genres you will need to be most familiar with in your undergraduate and graduate career in education. This chapter brings together the skills and rhetorical concepts you've learned in the preceding chapters to discuss writing for change once you enter the profession. The field of education is, in many ways, inherently political; you may have noticed that assignments you've encountered in your education classes have asked you to analyze inequitable learning conditions within the education system and to articulate plans for change. For example, you may have interviewed teachers about how they adapt lesson plans in order to meet the needs of diverse learners in their classes. You may have researched current theories for how to address the achievement gap, which spurred you to think about a new or innovative approach. Or you may have read an Op-Ed in a national or local newspaper about an issue in education, which inspired you to think of solutions. In the course of your career as an educator, you may encounter problems, or shortcomings, with teaching or learning conditions that could be fixed or improved. Writing policy proposals and similar genres can be your vehicle for changing those conditions.

EXAMINING THE RHETORICAL SITUATION: PURPOSE, AUDIENCE, CONTEXT, VOICE, AND GENRE

In an article in *U.S. News and World Report*, Brown (2015) reports that "the number of opportunities through which teachers can engage in policy has grown significantly in recent years." She points out that in addition to teachers' unions supporting teachers in engaging in policy conversations over the years, many new organizations are on the rise, with the aim of "launch[ing] initiatives to train current or former teachers in policy analysis and content and to provide them with opportunities to use their voices to influence policy." Because teachers work so closely (and often alone) with students, and because reflective practice is integral to the field of teaching, teachers are usually the best equipped to propose changes, to either policy or practices, that result in better teaching or learning conditions. In fact, we would argue that the written voices of teachers are critical to improving the American education system. When teachers identify and articulate current problems within a district, school, program, or classroom, and then formulate well-researched solutions, we all benefit.

Why Teachers Write for Policy Change

There are many reasons why educators may want to write for change. They may discover a problem with an existing policy that they would like to change in order to improve teaching/learning conditions. Alternatively, they may want to create a policy for an educational problem or school/district issue that they have observed but that doesn't yet have existing documentation.

As a teacher, you must comply with many different types of policies that are written at the federal, state, district, and school levels. At the state level, for example, teachers have to follow and integrate curriculum standards and student assessment criteria that were designed by outside bodies and implemented by state legislatures. State departments of education also develop professional teaching standards that teachers must demonstrate during their evaluation reviews. The states also determine requirements for teaching credential programs, which you may be experiencing firsthand right now. Additionally, states decide on the amount of funding for K–12 schools and establish key priority spending areas—such as pupil achievement or school climate.

At the district level, numerous school board policies exist on topics ranging from amount and type of homework allowed to special program master plans (e.g., gifted and talented, English language development, special education) to bullying and sexual harassment. At the school level, there are policies on reading programs, school discipline, counseling services, and bell schedules, for example. The existence (or lack) of a particular policy or program may be preventing you from becoming a better teacher or may be compromising your students' abilities to achieve their highest potential. It is up to you, the teacher, to use your voice, through your writing, to articulate changes that hopefully will bring about improvements in education.

Potential Audiences and Contexts When Writing for Policy Change

So far, this guide has helped familiarize you with writing for your professor, students, future administrators, and assessment bodies. Here, we will expand that list of audiences to include a variety of stakeholders who serve as site and district decisionmakers, such as principals, school board members, superintendents, directors of curriculum, and coordinators of special programs. In addition, there are legislators at the state level who create and pass bills that affect K–12 education. Your target audience will depend on who would make the decision to revise or implement your proposed policy change.

Principals make site-specific decisions that impact how a school runs. They decide how to staff classes, how the school day will run, and what specific discipline policies will govern student behavior. They, along with teachers and parents at school-site council meetings, make decisions about how some earmarked funds are spent at the site level. They work closely with teachers to address student issues in the classroom, and they are responsible for listening to and communicating with parents about their children's education and any policies affecting that education.

School board members are elected by the community to provide oversight of district administrators and ensure that the district is listening to community members/teachers/students and implementing the district's stated mission. In this role, the board can put pressure on district administrators to make changes to policies and/or adopt new policies. Many district policies are approved by the board and are meant to be followed by all school sites. Keep in mind that school board members may or may not have a background in education, and they may have their own personal or professional agendas. For example, many who end up in public office at higher levels get their start as school board members. When board members run for office, they write candidate statements that explain their background and vision of education and/or their goals for the district.

Superintendents and others in higher administrative roles in district offices have a lot of decisionmaking power. They decide how to spend the money the state has given them; they decide what schools or issues are going to be prioritized; they can set brand-new policies to be approved by the board. They are also responsible for listening and responding to the concerns of teachers, staff, and parents about existing programs and policies, and making adjustments when necessary.

At the state level, decisionmakers are often lawmakers. In order to propose a policy change at this level, you should research your state's legislators and current Senate bills that more broadly affect K–12 education throughout the state. You likely would write directly to a state legislator or chosen members of the state department of education. Every elected official has a website with a space for comments and responses. You can propose changes to Senate bills or legislation by close-reading the bill and then writing directly to the legislator. You also can visit your state's board of education website to get information about key people working at the state level in positions that affect K–12 education.

If you are a teacher, you also can get involved in your state's teachers' union (local affiliation of the American Federation of Teachers or National Education Association, for example) and/or the local union affiliated with your school district. Unions bargain with school districts for stronger contracts that include better pay and improved working conditions, among other things.

Table 9.1. List of Common School District Departments

General District Departments	Jurisdiction
Business services or chief business and operations manager	Budgets
Facilities/Maintenance and operations	Building/classroom repair, building projects
Health services	Food allergy policy, lice policy
Human resources	Personnel matters, induction program
Instructional services	Special programs, English language learners
Instructional technology services	Student use of technology policy
Public information office	Emergency communications policy
Special education services	IEP process, eligibility for special services, procedural safeguards
Student nutrition services	Menus
Student support services	504 plans, school discipline policy
Superintendent and board of education	Board policy

Because your audience can vary significantly when it comes to writing for policy change, it is important to research your audience's background, knowledge of the topic at hand, likely attitude toward it, and what the audience might need from you, the writer. Your overarching goal in gathering this information about your audience is to get a clearer sense of how you need to frame your argument so that your audience is compelled to act. When thinking of whom you might need to write to at the local level, you can consider the general district departments listed in Table 9.1.

For all of these audiences, your voice needs to be professional, confident, and educated. You can use the graphic organizer in Table 9.2 to help you organize information about your audience.

Table 9.2. Audience Analysis Graphic Organizer

Who is this decisionmaker? What can you find out about the person's experience in the education field?
What major issues or policies has this decisionmaker been involved in before? How has the person **voted/or what has the person's stance been** on these issues?
What does this person likely **know** about my topic?
How is this person likely to **feel** about my topic?
What does this decisionmaker likely **need from me**, the writer, in order to be convinced that a change to this policy/program (or an additional policy/program) is necessary?

USING DIFFERENT GENRES TO WRITE FOR CHANGE

Writing for change can take many different forms, depending on whom you need to reach and what your purpose for writing is. You might argue for policy change by writing and delivering a presentation to the school board at their monthly meeting. You may want to write a letter to the superintendent. You also may write a white paper—a well-researched, short position statement. White papers can be written by educators who are affiliated with organizations or educational institutes, as demonstrated by Pigg and Grabill's paper, *The Writing Lives of College Students: Revisualizing Composition Study Group* (2010), or by teachers in a district, such as Austin Independent School District's *Single Gender Education: A Review of Current Issues and Practices* (2011). Often, white papers are commissioned by companies or education think tanks to advance a particular political, philosophical, or commercial agenda. White papers often lack more formal elements, such as a table of contents or appendix, and instead employ attractive visuals or formatting to capture their audience's attention.

This chapter introduces you to a more formal genre for writing for change—the proposal—because it brings together all of the strategies you've learned so far in this book to articulate detailed solutions to problems you find in your local teaching context. Effective policy proposals convince an audience that a change is necessary and suggest a viable, well-researched solution to the problem.

BEFORE YOU WRITE A PROPOSAL FOR POLICY CHANGE

To get started on your proposal, you'll need to first identify an educational problem at the state, district, school, or classroom level. For help doing this,

Figure 9.1. Current Educational Issues/Policies to Consider

Arts education	High school dropout rates	Standardized testing and
Behavior and discipline	Home schooling/unschooling	accountability
policies	movements	Teacher collaboration time
Bullying/cyberbullying	Online education	Teacher evaluation/salary
Charter schools	Physical education	Teacher professional
Common Core State	Professional learning	development
Standards	communities	Teaching with technology
Curriculum	School funding	Tracking in schools
Differentiated instruction	School reform	Writing across the curriculum
English language learners	School-to-prison pipeline	in K–12
For-profit education	Special education	
Gifted education	Special programs	

see the listing of current educational issues and policies in Figure 9.1. Once you have identified a problem, you should search for any existing policies that pertain to it, to gain a better understanding of its context. See Table 9.3 for examples of policies and URLs where you can read them. You may find that the problem has an official existing policy, or you may find that the problem exists because there is no current policy in place. If it is a problem with no

Table 9.3. Examples of Policies from School Districts

Policies	School District and URL
Bullying policy	San Bernardino City Unified School District (San Bernardino, CA)
	sbcusd.com/UserFiles/Servers/Server_59869/File/Student%20Resources/Restorative%20Justice/SBCUSD%20Bullying.pdf
Class size	Austin Independent School District (Austin, TX)
	pol.tasb.org/Policy/Code/1146?filter=EEB
English learner master plan	Woodland Joint Unified School District (Woodland, CA)
	1.cdn.edl.io/nih6qTK89xxrWkn5VN32n4nvglLwe3pXS5WLZOqF3tz1qAP4.pdf
Homework policy	Davis Joint Unified School District (Davis, CA)
	gamutonline.net/district/davis/DisplayPolicy/683105/
Parent and family involvement	Brooklyn City School District (Brooklyn, OH)
	boarddocs.com/oh/brooklyn/Board.nsf/Public?open&id=policies#
School discipline policy	Davis Joint Unified School District (Davis, CA)
	djusd.net/departments/student_support_services/behavior_interventions_
Secondary student technology use agreement	Woodland Joint Unified School District (Woodland, CA)
	1.cdn.edl.io/WwkLbfGcxl8wJGbcqSnSfUQFvylKNozRmenXW6a5iTLH7g5y.pdf
Staff freedom of speech	Washoe County School District (Reno, NV)
	wcsdpolicy.net/
Strategic plan	Sacramento City Unified School District (Sacramento, CA)
	scusd.edu/sites/main/files/file-attachments/board_adopted_strategic_plan_0_0.pdf
Student dress	Madison School District (Rexburg, ID)
	msd321.com/docs/district/policies/3000/3255.pdf?id=1252
Use of peace officers to remove students from school grounds	Wayzata Public Schools (Wayzata, MN)
	drive.google.com/file/d/1vmRk3-qO6dxjv8_9vSJA3k2WB5DU8x94/view
Wellness program	Banks County School District (Homer, GA)
	simbli.eboardsolutions.com/SB_ePolicy/SB_PolicyOverview.aspx?S=4008

existing policy, you will want to research whether other districts have policies in place for the matter, since you may want to propose a new initiative, policy, or practice. If you are interested in changing an existing policy, it is imperative to locate and read the entire policy so that you will be able to suggest specific changes. This also will help you determine your audience.

Many, if not most, local policies are available on school or district websites. Since all district websites are organized differently, finding the policy that concerns you may take some time. You usually can browse by departments (student support services, student nutrition, etc.) or by instructional services (different district programs). There also should be a tab that provides information about the school board, leadership team, and district's mission statement. You can browse through the minutes of prior school board meetings, which often contain links to important policy documents. You also can try gamutonline.net and search by district to find all of the policies affecting a specific district (see Table 9.3 for examples of policies/program descriptions). Be prepared to spend a good amount of time looking through a variety of documents on the district's website so that you can be better informed about the policy, where it originated, and who is involved with it. Another good source will be your state's Dashboard website for a district or a school within it.

The proposal organizer in Figure 9.2 may be helpful as you begin to brainstorm how to write your proposal.

WRITING A PROPOSAL

We will now walk you through a successful proposal. Figure 9.3 presents a student sample of a proposal written for our Writing in Elementary and Secondary Education course annotated to help prepare you to write your own. Most of the students enrolled in this course are junior or senior undergraduates interested in careers in education, and the goal of the class is for them to gain experience writing in genres they most likely will encounter as graduate students or future educators. The assignment asks students to identify a significant problem with an existing policy or program in a local school district and propose an innovative, well-informed solution. We encourage students to frame the local issue in a broader national debate about education early on in their introduction and propose solutions based on sound primary and secondary research. Deanna was troubled by Sacramento City School District's policy on school discipline and its lack of a focus on restorative justice. Her proposal identifies problems with the policy and proposes some solutions. We include detailed annotations of how Deanna successfully uses rhetorical knowledge to appeal to her audience.

Figure 9.2. Proposal Organizer

Identify the Problem
• What is the educational problem? Why is it a problem?

Research Existing, Relevant Policies
• Are there existing policies that address the problem?

Determine Your Audience
• Who will I need to write to in order to make this argument for change?

Choose Your Genre
• What is the best genre for me to use to facilitate change? What are the conventions of the genre that I need to follow?

Types of Research/Evidence
• What research will I need to conduct so that I can support my statement of the problem and proposed solutions?
• What research will be most appealing/necessary for my audience?

Method of Organization
• How can I most effectively organize the different sections?
• Where/how should I incorporate my research? Is a visual needed?

Voice
• How can I ensure that my tone comes across as professional, well-informed, and thoughtful?
• What kind of field-specific vocabulary/jargon will my audience be expecting?

The typical components of a formal proposal include a letter of transmittal, a title page, a table of contents, an abstract, an introduction and statement of problem, a solution(s)—with costs, feasibility, and limitations considered—a conclusion, works referenced list, and an appendix.

(text continues on p. 168)

Figure 9.3. Sample Student Proposal (written by Deanna and annotated by the authors)

Deanna Gallegos
1 V. Street
Davis, CA 95618

February 26, 2018

Superintendent Jorge A. Aguilar
Sacramento City Unified School District Office
5735 47th Avenue
Sacramento, CA 95824

Dear Superintendent Aguilar:

There is no doubt that you, as the Superintendent of schools for the city of Sacramento, are committed to promoting equitable school environments and supporting students' overall well-being. During your previous appointment with the Fresno Unified School District, you had splendid results in improving graduation rates and reducing dropout rates. Your combined twenty-plus years of work in education is admirable, to say the least. Though this is your first school year working for the Sacramento City Unified School District, the public is confident in your ability to improve Sacramento schools. Given your background of focusing on equity and access in schools, you surely understand the importance of creating a supportive school community and responding to the needs of students.

Successful letters of transmittal usually begin by pointing out what the decisionmaking body has done well. This sets a positive, constructive tone and builds common ground between the reader and the writer, enticing the reader to read the proposal.

However, traditional disciplinary practices, such as suspensions and expulsions, are heavily enforced in Sacramento schools, but yield little in positive results. In the SCUSD's "Annual Parent and Student Right Notification and Standards of Behavior for 2017-2018," there are policies surrounding in school and out of school suspensions and expulsions, but little discussion on student support resources. It is a concern that the mentoring and counseling services listed in the handbook "may not be available at all sites" (2017, p. 10). With this proposal, I hope to express the faults of solely using traditional disciplinary policies, as they disrupt students' academic and social growth, and overall emotional well-being. Rather, I propose implementing restorative justice practices to all schools within the SCUSD. Restorative justice practices would take the place of many suspensions that could be better worked out through effective communication by teachers and administrators who strive to understand their students.

Deanna quickly explains the problematic lack of counseling services provided to students and moves to why her solutions would be beneficial for students.

The introduction of widespread restorative justice practices will be beneficial for entire school communities as teachers and administrators will be able to guide students through thinking about their actions and disrupt the cycle of harm that persists in school environments. Restorative justice practices will encourage positive interactions between teachers and students and make sure that students' voices and perspectives are heard and validated. Furthermore, I know that schools in the SCUSD have the fortitude and motivation to implement restorative justice practices and create school communities that will prepare their students for their futures.

> Deanna provides a key reason for why her target audience should read her proposed solutions.

Respectfully,
Deanna Gallegos
Deanna Gallegos

> She ends on a positive note to further compel her reader to read her proposal.

Proposal for Reducing Traditional Disciplinary Procedures and Implementing Restorative Justice Practices, 2017-2018

Prepared for Superintendent Jorge A. Aguilar, Sacramento City Unified School District, Sacramento, California
By Deanna Gallegos, University of California, Davis
[Reprinted by permission of UC Davis, UWP]

> Follows the typical layout for a title page. Titles should be succinct and specific.

INFORMATIVE ABSTRACT

The Sacramento City Unified School District (SCUSD) has high rates of suspensions and expulsions; furthermore, there is racial disparity in which students are disciplined. In particular, black students are suspended at rates that are four to five times greater than their white classmates. Overall, taking students out of the classroom has negative consequences; students fall behind their peers academically, have less opportunities to learn important social-behavioral skills, as well as unfortunate effects on students' emotional well-being. I propose that SCUSD schools reduce the amount of suspensions and expulsions they hand out in favor of implementing restorative justice practices. Entire school communities, including teachers and administrators, must be adequately trained on how to introduce restorative justice practices into their classrooms and school environment. It is important that teachers and administrators not shy away from discussing how racism and hierarchical power dynamics shape school climates and how discipline is applied. A major goal of restorative justice practices is to promote positive interactions between teachers and students and build community. Further discussion on the details surrounding implementing this paradigm shift are included in the methods, feasibility, and personnel sections of this proposal. Executing restorative justice practices take time and energy to do properly, but such an investment will be well worth it when students benefit from a more communal school culture.

> The abstract summarizes the major components of the proposal. Abstracts are generally short, usually 250 words or less, and provide the reader with a sense of the scope of the project.

Figure 9.3. Sample Student Proposal (written by Deanna and annotated by the authors)
(continued)

INTRODUCTION

Overview

Disciplinary practices in U.S. schools have been largely discussed for many generations of students. For decades, our nation's public schools have turned to suspensions and expulsions to "correct" student misbehavior. Fisher, Frey, and Smith (2016) state that "Since 1974, suspension and expulsion rates have doubled in the United States" (p. 54). Additionally, students of color, students with disabilities, those who are in poverty, foster care, and homeless are most at-risk of being suspended or expelled (Fisher et al., 2016). Moreover, traditional disciplinary practices do little to change student behavior, but rather, often have the adverse effect of continuing a cycle of harm and contributing to dropout rates and the fracturing of school communities.

One approach to disrupting the cycle of harm perpetuated by suspensions and expulsions is through implementing restorative justice practices. Restorative justice practices focus on restoring wellness within a school community by giving a voice to those who are harmed, repairing relationships, and encouraging accountability through collaborative decision-making (Mullet, 2014). A goal of restorative justice practices is to promote better communication and interactions between students, teachers, and school administrators.

> The proposal opens by using relevant and necessary secondary sources to situate the author's primary concern (suspension/expulsion rates) within a broader educational context in order to give it a sense of urgency. Deanna shows her reader why the local problem she's uncovered matters in the bigger picture.

BACKGROUND

The Sacramento City Unified School District's "Annual Parent and Student Rights Notification and Standards of Behavior for 2017-2018" handbook includes details of the district's disciplinary practices, including suspensions and expulsions. In their handbook, SCUSD states that their in-school suspensions "mea[n] that the student is removed from class, but remains on campus *isolated from the other students*" (emphasis mine, 2017, p. 10). To put this policy into perspective, during the 2014-2015 school year, the Sacramento City Unified School District had 5,579 in-school and out-of-school suspensions (Education Data Partnership).

When isolating students through suspensions and expulsions, teachers and school administrators fail to recognize that "students who present with social-emotional deficiencies need connectedness and belonging, not exclusion" (Riley, 2018, p. 16). One way to focus on students' well-being is through restorative justice practices. Restorative justice practices "utilize a problem-solving approach to school discipline issues [through a] proactive approach that builds community around common infractions through discussions and

> The Background section provides the reader with pertinent information about the district, the program, or the people who created this policy. This section also provides specific information about the policy itself. Deanna provides her readers with background information they will need to understand her proposal.

exploration" (Riley, 2018, p. 16). Furthermore, restorative justice practices can improve teacher-student interactions, and thus create a better classroom and schoolwide environment for everyone in the school community.

STATEMENT OF THE PROBLEM

There is an overreliance on traditional disciplinary practices, such as suspensions and expulsions, in the Sacramento City Unified School District. When students are taken out of the classroom, they are not able to learn and thus: one, fall academically behind their peers and two, do not learn the social-behavioral skills they should experience in the classroom. In addition, students of color are more likely than their white peers to be suspended or expelled. Overall, there is a problem surrounding the way teachers and administrators view discipline as correcting student behavior and ordering student compliance. Regulating student behavior through punitive measures does not change students' actions in the long run; if anything, repeated suspensions and/or expulsions push students further away from the academic setting while ignoring the root causes of the initial "misbehavior" and thus perpetuating a cycle of harm.

> Deanna provides a very brief summary of the problem before going into more detail on the specific aspects of it.

Problem I: An Overuse of Suspensions and Expulsions Hurts Students' Academics, Social-Behavioral Skills, and Emotional Well-Being

> Deanna uses specific subheadings to organize her discussion of the different problems with the existing policy.

When students are suspended from school, they miss out on valuable instruction time in their classes. As a result, students miss lessons and fall behind their peers in their academic goals. Ultimately, when students are not present in the classroom, they are not able to learn (Fisher et al., 2016). Additionally, students are not given opportunities to develop their social-behavioral skills when they are removed from the classroom setting. When a teacher or administrator confronts a student and scolds them for "misbehavior," the student may feel that they are being singled out and interpret the interaction as a negative one. A pattern of multiple negative interactions with adult figures at school can cause a student to pull away from the school environment that fails to understand the student's perspective.

The overuse of suspensions and expulsions further harms students' emotional well-being. When students are suspended, they are no longer around their peers, friends, and teachers. This course of action dramatically decreases the number of people the suspended student has surrounding them to act as mentors, companions, and supporters. Hopefully, students have people they can turn to outside of school, such as parents, guardians, extended family members, and other friends and peers within their neighborhood; however, this ideal cannot be applied to all students,

Figure 9.3. Sample Student Proposal (written by Deanna and annotated by the authors)
(continued)

as many surely have few other adult figures in their lives (besides their teachers) who are able to support and advise them. So then the question is raised of who can support students' emotional well-being? Schools can tackle this task through the resources they provide their students. In the Sacramento City School District, some student support resources are said to be offered, such as, "counseling . . . conflict resolution . . . [and] mentoring" (Sacramento City School District, 2017, pp. 10–11). However, the accessibility and availability for these resources can be further improved upon. The district's handbook includes a disclaimer that these types of counseling and mentoring resources "may not be available at all sites" (Sacramento City School District, 2017, p. 10). The lack of any mention of a number of minimum required student support resources per school campus is also an issue.

> To illustrate the problem, Deanna incorporates data gathered from district and school websites and reports.

Problem II: A Disproportionate Number of Students of Color Are Being Suspended and Expelled

In the Sacramento City Unified School District, a disproportionate number of students of color are suspended and expelled compared to their white peers. Comparing specifically black students and white students in the district during the 2014-2015 school year, the demographics show that white students made up 18.1% of the student population, and black students made up 17.3% of the student population (Education Data Partnership). During the same school year, black students were given 599 in school suspensions, and white students had a total of 143 in school suspensions (Education Data Partnership). A similar pattern holds up for out of school suspensions. Black students had a reported 2,156 out of school suspensions, and white students had 455 out of school suspensions (Education Data Partnership). By looking at the numbers, it is clear that there is a discrepancy in which students are disciplined. Although there are roughly the same number of white and black students within the SCUSD, it is clear that there is an issue with how black students are suspended at rates that are four to five times higher than white students.

The overrepresentation of students of color being disciplined speaks to a greater issue of racism in schools. Whether schools are using traditional discipline models (like suspensions and expulsions) or restorative justice practices, it is important to have conversations surrounding how racism affects students and the school community as a whole. If such racism goes unchecked, schools "will maintain racial disproportionality in discipline, regardless of what particular discipline practices are used" (Lustick, 2017, p. 685). It is not simply enough to cut out suspensions and expulsions; doing so will only be reflected in statistics on paper wherein the number of suspensions drop. Rather, it is crucial that talking about racial inequities be included in discussions about school discipline policies.

Problem III: The Hierarchical Power Structures in Teacher Student Relationships

The disciplinary practice of suspending and expelling students creates an uneven power dynamic between teachers and students. The problem stems from generations of schooling reinforcing the notion that teachers must command their classrooms in an authoritarian manner in order to gain students' respect and compliance. In fact, it can be said that the "social reproduction and education for control and compliance are deeply embedded in schooling and highly resistant to change" (Vaandering, 2014, p. 65). This problem makes it even more difficult for teachers to form positive relationships with students and promote effective communication within the classroom.

However, it must be noted that restorative justice practices face the same issue of reproducing hierarchical power structures. If restorative justice practices are practiced with a focus on classroom and behavior management, teachers may "inadvertently reinforce an agenda of compliance and control rather than [restorative justice's] intended purpose of building relational, interconnected and interdependent school cultures" (Vaandering, 2014, p. 65). Thus, the issue of unequal power dynamics must be addressed and dealt with, regardless of what disciplinary practices a school uses.

PROPOSED PLAN

First, I propose to change the Sacramento City School District's approach and view of discipline at its numerous schools by decreasing the number of suspensions and expulsions by only exercising these practices for the most extreme cases where student and teacher safety is an issue. Second, I propose a two-part plan to implement restorative justice practices at all schools in the SCUSD. Part A acts to input new district wide policies surrounding implementing restorative justice practices at all schools in the SCUSD. Part B acts to properly train teachers on restorative justice practices; multiple trainings, workshops, continued education, and culturally responsive pedagogy education would be utilized to best support teachers, and subsequently, all students.

> Deanna provides a brief summary of the two solutions she is proposing.

METHODS

I. Dramatically Reduce the Reliance on Suspensions and Expulsions as the Primary Form of Discipline

I propose a change in the Sacramento City Unified School District's "Standards of Behavior" handbook regarding the manner in which

Figure 9.3. Sample Student Proposal (written by Deanna and annotated by the authors)
(continued)

suspensions and expulsions are considered. In the handbook, there
is a section that outlines whether suspension and/or expulsion may
be considered for particular circumstances; circumstances include
"acts of violence," "theft or stealing," "attendance truant," "sexual
assault or sexual battery," "willful defiance or disruption of school
activities" and "bullying" to name a few (Sacramento City Unified
School District, 2017, pp. 12–14). I propose an addition to this
handbook stating that suspensions and expulsions be considered
for circumstances that cause alarm for the immediate danger to
student and teacher safety. Suspensions and expulsions could be a
last resort for when principals are faced with situations that involve
violence and weapons on school campus, for instance. If there is an
emergency, such as if a student has a weapon on campus, it would
be within reason for the acting principal and their colleagues to
require that student not be allowed back on campus, around the
rest of the student population, in order to ensure campus safety.
This policy, then, would advise administrators to only dish out
suspensions and expulsions in the most extreme cases in which the
safety of students and teachers is at risk.

II. Implement Restorative Justice Practices

A. Introduce a New District-Wide Policy Committed to Focusing on Restorative Justice Practices

The current SCUSD handbook lacks any mention of restorative
justice practices. I propose that a section be added to the District
handbook stating the District's commitment to incorporating
restorative justice practices at all school sites.

The new section would include information about restorative
justice, such as how it is a mind set and approach that focuses on
repairing harm done to relationships through identifying the causes
of the ongoing cycle of harm (Mullet, 2014). The handbook would
also identify examples of restorative justice practices, including
"restorative circles," developing re-entry plans, and encouraging
teachers to build positive relationships with students. Creating a
re-entry plan with a student might entail having a teacher rehearse
an apology with a student, helping a student identify a lifeline (a
person who the student could go to for advice), and scheduling
follow-ups with students to make sure they're adjusting well to
entering the school space after they caused harm (Fisher et al.,
2016). Providing students with the opportunity to reflect on their
actions and craft an apology demonstrates restorative justice's goal

> Deanna incorporates secondary research to support her proposed solutions throughout this section.

of promoting accountability for students' actions, while supporting positive interactions between teachers and students (Tyler & Perez, 2015).

Through restorative justice practices, students will not be sent out of the classroom nearly as often as before. As a result, students remain in the classroom and are thus able to keep up with the school curriculum while practicing social skills and maintaining their own emotional well-being.

B. Provide Teachers with Continual Training on Restorative Justice Practices

In order for restorative justice practices to work, it is of the utmost importance that teachers are adequately trained. Recalling from her own experience of working with preservice teachers, Maisha T. Winn found that, "most of the emerging teachers experienced academic success in classrooms and schools with little or no understanding of what it is like for students who struggle socially and/or academically" (Winn, 2018, p. 253). Winn's story demonstrates the disconnect that teachers may have from their own students' experiences. Therefore, it is in the best interest of the entire school community to make sure that teachers are trained on how to employ restorative justice practices in their own classrooms.

However, it is not enough to only do *one* restorative justice workshop with teachers and expect incredible, instantaneous results. Implementing restorative justice practices across an entire school (and an entire school district at that) will require adequate, continual training and support throughout the school-year; a one-off meeting or workshop simply won't cut it (Winn, 2018). Furthermore, it is significant to note that "Restorative discipline is not a scripted program to be applied similarly across groups" (Mullet, 2014, p.159). Each particular school will need to adapt to their own students' needs.

To put it simply, teachers need to understand their students. Through restorative justice practices, students and teachers can use narratives to humanize both themselves and others (Winn, 2018). Teachers can build positive relationships with students by knowing all students' names, eliminating sarcasm, showing respect for students' perspectives, and knowing at least one thing about a student's story (Fisher et al., 2016). To help aid in the process, teachers should also be trained on culturally responsive pedagogy (Lustick, 2017). By learning about how to employ culturally relevant tactics in the classrooms, teachers will be better prepared to engage with students of various backgrounds. Having teachers be trained on culturally responsive pedagogy would further help

Figure 9.3. Sample Student Proposal (written by Deanna and annotated by the authors)
(continued)

to bring about discussions surrounding racism and authoritarian structures embedded within school cultures.

FEASIBILITY

Implementing restorative justice practices would not put a strain on Sacramento City Unified School District's budget. Teachers and administrators are already involved in trainings and meetings that discuss the procedures surrounding suspending or expelling a student; some time that would normally be allotted to the topic of traditional disciplinary procedures could go towards training teachers and administrators on restorative justice practices. Furthermore, the time that would normally be spent with students in the principal's office being scolded and told they are suspended could instead be time spent utilizing restorative justice practices, such as a restorative circle.

> Deanna demonstrates she has thought through all necessary components of a good solution to the problem.

More than anything, implementing restorative justice practices across the Sacramento City Unified School District will cost time, effort, and energy. But many education scholars and researchers argue that restorative practices "are worth the investment of time and energy" as they have the power "to disrupt inequitable applications of school discipline" (Fisher et al., 2016, p. 58).

> Here, Deanna discusses the feasibility of her plan. You may also want to address cost here if your audience would be wondering about your proposed solution's effect on the school/district budget.

PERSONNEL

Teachers and principals would be largely responsible for keeping up to date on how to best practice restorative justice in their schools. However, teaching in and of itself is a career that involves continuous growth as teachers better learn their craft (Winn, 2018). In order for restorative justice practices to reach their full potential at a school site, it is essential that *all* teachers and administrators reevaluate their views surrounding discipline and punishment. It simply won't do to introduce restorative justice practices but continue to view discipline through a hierarchical lens. Restorative justice practices require active listening on behalf of everyone (but especially for adults working in a school) so that students who caused harm or were harmed are able to have a voice and share their perspective and feelings. Teachers and administrators must be willing to take on the task of utilizing restorative justice practices to positively influence the emotional well-being of all students.

CONCLUSION

Overall, this proposal hopes to inspire Superintendent Aguilar to consider the needs of students in the Sacramento City Unified

School District. In a time when our country is divided on numerous matters, one common ground we all have is that our children's education and well-being is a priority. Taking students out of school through suspensions and expulsions does little to change long-term behavior, and causes more harm to students' academic progress, social skills, and emotional well-being. Restorative justice practices are rooted in humanizing people and creating a positive community atmosphere. When school communities engage with restorative justice practices and review how they perceive discipline, teachers and administrators are then able to "see the full humanity of all children" (Winn, 2018, p. 260). If we genuinely want to reach every student, we must be willing to put in the time and energy to disrupt the cycle of harm where "over time, hurt people tend to hurt other people" (Mullet, 2014, p. 158). Speaking with students, understanding their stories, and validating their perspectives will make for more motivated learners and more talented teachers.

> Deanna reaffirms the need for her solution and encourages the decision-making body to act.

END MATTER

References

Education Data Partnership. (n.d.). *Sacramento City Unified School District demographics, suspensions and expulsions.* Retrieved from ed-data.org/district/Sacramento/Sacramento-City-Unified

Fisher, D., Frey, N., & Smith, D. (2016). After sticks, stones, and harmful words. *Educational Leadership, 74*(3), 54–58.

Lustick, H. (2017). Making discipline relevant: Toward a theory of culturally responsive positive schoolwide discipline. *Race Ethnicity and Education, 20*(5), 681–695.

Mullet, J. (2014). Restorative discipline: From getting even to getting well. *Children & Schools, 36*(3), 157–162.

Riley, B. (2018). A better approach to school discipline: How restorative practices can help decrease disciplinary referrals and increase students' social-emotional skills. *Principal, 97*(3), 14–17.

Sacramento City Unified School District. (2017). *Annual parent and student right notification and standards of behavior.* Retrieved from scusd.edu/student-hearing-and-placement-department

Tyler, B., & Perez, B. H. (2015). A restorative approach to student discipline. *Leadership, 45*(2), 24–26.

Vaandering, D. (2014). Implementing restorative justice practice in schools: What pedagogy reveals. *Journal of Peace Education, 11*(1), 64–80.

Winn, M. (2018). Building a "lifetime circle": English education in the age of #BlackLivesMatter. *Urban Education, 53*(2), 248–264.

> The End Matter includes a references page for those who would like to read up on the sources cited in the paper, and appendices (possibly transcripts of interviews or notes of observations (if you conducted them), policy documents, etc.).

As you can see, Deanna identifies specific problems with the existing school discipline policy and discusses why these problems matter, all the while showing that she is clearly passionate about her topic. She integrates research to argue for a restorative justice approach to discipline across the district. Her solutions are practical, innovative, and grounded in education research. Furthermore, she discusses the feasibility of her solutions and provides her readers with a sense of closure and a call to action in her conclusion.

After they have written their arguments for policy change, we encourage our students to submit their proposals to their intended audience. This is usually a local decisionmaker, such as a principal or a superintendent of a district. We want our students to remember that there is an authentic audience for the assignment. Depending on what genre or form your argument for change ends up taking, you should submit or send your piece to the target audience in the hopes of having it published or recognized by the decisionmaker. For a list of possible venues committed to publishing works by teachers writing for change, see Figure 9.4.

EXERCISES

1. Look back at the student sample in Figure 9.3: How does Deanna appeal to her audience? What information does she use to argue her point in the different sections of the proposal? How does she organize information, use sources, and shape her voice/tone throughout the piece?
2. Think about a problem at your local school, within your district, or at the statewide level that needs to be changed to improve student learning or teacher effectiveness (see Figure 9.1 for ideas). See whether you can find any policies that address the problem. Whom would you write to concerning this policy? What kind of research would you need to do to propose a solution to the problem(s)? Why is modifying, adding to, or deleting sections from this policy or program important?

Figure 9.4. Possible Venues for Publishing

American Federation of Teachers

AFT e-newsletters: aft.org/action/subscribe-aft-e-newsletters
AFTVoices: aftvoices.org/

Connecticut Writing Project Op-Eds

cwp.uconn.edu/c3wp-op-eds/

Educational Leadership

ascd.org/publications/educational-leadership.aspx

Heinemann Publishing Company

medium.com/@heinemann/
why-teachers-need-to-write-for-the-public-b44ac3b5083f

Language Arts

www2.ncte.org/resources/journals/language-arts/

National Council of Teachers of English

Literacy & NCTE Blog:
www2.ncte.org/get-involved/write-for-ncte/write-for-the-blog/_

National Education Association

NEA Today: neatoday.org/

National Writing Project

www.nwp.org/

Teacher/Writer/Researcher Newsletter

cwp.uconn.edu/teacher-writer-researcher/

Writers Who Care: A Blog for Authentic Writing Instruction

writerswhocare.wordpress.com/

CHAPTER 10

Crediting Sources in APA Style

In Chapter 9 we discussed how to write a proposal for an educational policy or program change. We emphasized the importance of using research to create a well-informed description of the current problem and a specific and feasible solution. As you have seen throughout this book, conducting research and incorporating it effectively into your writing are integral to writing in education. This chapter provides you with the tools necessary for understanding the important role that APA Style has in making that research clear to your audience. Leverenz (1998) noted that by understanding APA Style, you learn "the values of the American Psychological Association and other social sciences" (p. 187). Armed with this knowledge, you will be well-prepared to make, and support, your arguments.

WHY USE SOURCES: BUILDING KNOWLEDGE IN THE FIELD

Professors ask you to find and use sources prior to writing your education papers in order to orient you to the predominant theories and knowledge of the field before you enter it. When you write a paper in education, knowing what researchers have said about a topic and being able to use this discussion to shape your own argument demonstrate to readers that you should be taken seriously: that you, indeed, have earned a place at the table. In this way, using sources builds your ethos as a writer.

In addition to the rhetorical function of building your credibility as a writer in education, using sources in your work also helps you to avoid plagiarizing the words or ideas of others. When you write about educational theories, pedagogy, or policy in your work, you need to constantly think about where your information is coming from and how it shapes your stance. Referring to sources in your papers lets your audience know where your ideas come from and how you are using scholarly sources to shape your thinking. It also lets your readers know where they can find more information on the research to which you are referring.

Whether plagiarism is intentional or unintentional, it most often reflects a lack of understanding of the conventions of using sources, and it is treated as a serious academic offense. Providing readers with proper source documentation is necessary to ensure an ethical approach to writing in education. Whether you decide to quote, paraphrase, or summarize your source, you must give credit to the originator of the idea. If you have a question or concern about how to avoid plagiarism, be sure to ask your instructor or an academic librarian.

HOW DOES APA DIFFER FROM FORMATTING STYLES YOU ALREADY KNOW?

As an advanced undergraduate or master's student, by this point in your academic career you are probably familiar with the citation style of the Modern Language Association (MLA). Your upper-division education courses may be your introduction to APA Style. At first, the differences between MLA and APA may be confusing, and the rules guiding each citation style seemingly random. However, this is not the case. The citation guidelines actually reflect the underlying beliefs of the disciplines: English and the social sciences. Examining these beliefs before we discuss the specific citation guidelines will make these guidelines less confusing.

The MLA and the APA, both as organizations and as citation styles, value different things and create knowledge in different ways. Thus, they hold different epistemologies. The field of English studies the written word; therefore, the text is the source of all data. Because of this focus on the text, MLA privileges the author and the text in its citation style. MLA in-text citations include the author and the page number because the data source (the text) is stable and does not change over time. The "timelessness of texts" (Leverenz, 1998, p. 190) valued by MLA is also apparent in the verb tense used to describe texts: the literary present. The literary present requires that you use the present tense when discussing texts, related research, and analysis of texts. Similarly, the focus on the text means that when you are writing about texts, and their related research, you rely on an abundance of quotes from the texts to support your analysis.

APA Style reflects the values of a research-driven field. The different fields within the social sciences rely on research as sources of data (as discussed in Chapter 4). Trends in research build upon the results of past research. Accordingly, APA Style values the names of the authors (as researchers) and the publication date of the research in its in-text citations. Often, the most recent research is prioritized, as it can be the most relevant. However, the value of publication dates in research may be dependent on context; thus, it is important to always consult your professor before eliminating a source due to its publication date—it might be a foundational source for your topic. The focus on the results of research, and the researchers themselves, often results in fewer quotations and more frequent use of paraphrasing. Whether you are quoting or paraphrasing, APA Style recommends including the page number of the document whenever possible.

EFFECTIVE METHODS FOR INTEGRATING
SOURCES AND SUPPORTING ARGUMENTS

In order to effectively integrate sources into your work, you should avoid simply "dropping in" quotes without providing your reader with some context or analysis of your citation. In MLA, it is common to introduce each source with the author's name and the full title of the piece you are quoting. For example, if you were writing a research paper in MLA, you might introduce a quote like this:

Introducing a quote in MLA:
In the article titled "A Collective Effort to Make Yourself Feel Better: The Group Process in Mindfulness-Based Interventions," Cormack, Jones, and Maltby stress the importance of instructor-led mindfulness-based approaches to stress reduction. They state, "instructor quality is very important for successful mindfulness programs" (4).

The same quote in APA Style might look like this:

Introducing a quote in APA Style:
Cormack, Jones, and Maltby (2017) state that "instructor quality is very important for successful mindfulness programs" (p. 4).

Notice that in APA Style, the authors and date are foregrounded, not the title of the article. Although you sometimes may include the article title when introducing quotes, this type of introduction is not the norm unless you have a need to emphasize the article title for rhetorical reasons. Your reader is expected to find the title of the article in your reference list. In order to integrate the source into your text, use the sentences before and after your source to

Figure 10.1. Integrating Sources in APA Style (written by Kevin and annotated by the authors)

To best ensure that our students are receiving beneficial resources regarding mental health, we must also ensure that our teachers are educated in such matters. Cormack, Jones, and Maltby (2017) note the importance of the instructor in the Mindfulness-Based Stress Reduction (MBSR) program. The researchers found that teachers who personally practiced mindfulness exercises, and those who remained nonjudgmental and supportive during group discussions, were the most effective in delivering successful MBSR interventions (Cormack, Jones, & Maltby, 2017). Because teachers are often the first to know about distressed students, professional development in how to best use mindfulness techniques with students is imperative.

> Kevin integrates two paraphrased sentences from a recent source to support his topic sentence.

> Kevin reiterates his argument about the importance of professional development.

provide context and analysis. See Figure 10.1, a paragraph from a proposal for educational change, for an example of integrating sources.

APA DOCUMENTATION: CREDITING SOURCES

Tables 10.1 and 10.2 provide valuable information about how to cite your sources both in the reference list and in the in-text citation.

For more information on citing additional sources not covered in this chapter, please refer to the *APA Publication Manual*, 6th edition (APA, 2009).

Table 10.1. Reference List Citations

Source	Basic Format and Examples for Reference List
Book	AuthorLastName, A. A. (Publication year). *Title of book: Subtitle* ([ordinal number] ed.). Publication city, Publication state abbrev.: Publisher.
1 author	Ayers, W. (2010). *To teach: The journey of a teacher* (3rd ed.). New York, NY: Teachers College Press.
2 to 7 authors	Ferris, D. R., & Hedgcock, J. S. (2014). *Teaching L2 composition*. New York, NY: Routledge.
Edited collection	Paris, D., & Alim, H. S. (Eds.). (2017). *Culturally sustaining pedagogies*. New York: NY: Teachers College Press.
Chapter in a book	Murphy, S., & Smith, M. A. (2015). Integrating the language arts. In *Uncommonly good ideas: Teaching writing in the common core era* (pp. 10–42). New York, NY: Teachers College Press.
Essay, article, or chapter in an edited book	Rhea Coy, D., & Zimmerman, S. (2008). Time management and the school counselor. In J. M. Allen (Ed.), *Empowering the 21st century professional school counselor* (pp. 305–316). Ann Arbor, MI: Counseling Outfitters.
2 works by the same author	Yin, R. K. (2003a). *Applications of case study research*. Thousand Oaks, CA: Sage. Yin, R. K. (2003b). *Case study research: Design and methods* (3rd ed.). Thousand Oaks, CA: Sage.
Journal article	AuthorLastName, A. A., & Author, B. B. (Publication year). Title of article. *Title of Publication, volume number*(issue), page–page.
Journal article with two authors	Boon, R., & Barbetta, P. (2017). Reading interventions for elementary English language learners with learning disabilities: A review. *Insights into Learning Disabilities, 14*(1), 27–52.
Journal article with DOI available	Lustick, H. (2017). Making discipline relevant: Toward a theory of culturally responsive positive schoolwide discipline. *Race Ethnicity and Education, 20*(5), 681–695. doi: 10.1080/13613324.2016.1150828

Table 10.1. Reference List Citations (continued)

Journal article with more than 2 authors	Use same author formatting as for book source.
Newspaper article	AuthorLastName, A. A., (Publication month day, year). Title of article. *Title of Publication.* Retrieved from webaddress.com
(retrieved electronically)	Kaufman, J. (May 24, 2008). High school's worst year? For ambitious teens, 11th grade becomes a marathon of tests, stress and sleepless nights. *Wall Street Journal.* Retrieved from search.proquest.com/docview/399061049?accountid=14505
Magazine article	Follows formatting for basic journal article
(retrieved electronically from database)	Heitin, L. (2016). Publishers get poor marks on common-core math texts. *Education Week, 35*(36), 4. Retrieved from search.ebscohost.com/login.aspx?direct=true&db=eue&AN=116937476&site=ehost-live
Website or webpage	Alber, R. (2011). *6 scaffolding strategies to use with your students.* Retrieved from edutopia.org/blog/scaffolding-lessons-six-strategies-rebecca-alber
School policies (cite as a website/webpage)	Sacramento City Unified School District. (2017). *Annual parent and student right notification and standards of behavior.* Retrieved from scusd.edu/student-hearing-and-placement-department
Policy report or white paper from an organization	National Education Policy Center. (2017). *Community schools: An evidence-based strategy for equitable school improvement.* Boulder, CO: Author.
Standards	National Governors Association Center for Best Practices & Council of Chief State School Officers. (2010). *Common core state standards for English language arts: Speaking and listening grade 9–10.* Retrieved from corestandards.org/ELA-Literacy/SL/9-10/
Government document	Government Department (publication year). *Document title* (pub. no. if found). Retrieved from webaddress.com Example: Michigan Department of Education. (2018). *Educator staffing strategic plan: In support of Michigan's top 10 in 10.* Retrieved from michigan.gov/documents/mde/Educator_Staffing_Strategic_Plan_612221_7.pdf
Legislation	Individuals with Disabilities Education Act, 20 U.S.C. § 1400 (2004).
Motion picture (theatre, DVD, video)	Producer, P. P. (Producer), & Director, D. D. (Director). (Year). *Title of motion picture* [Motion picture]. Country of origin: Studio or distributor. Example: Chilcott, L. (Producer), & Guggenheim, D. (Director). (2010). *Waiting for superman.* United States: Paramount Vantage.

Table 10.2. In-Text Citations

Citation for	Example
Basic format	Lustick (2017) believes that schools "will maintain racial disproportionality in discipline, regardless of what particular discipline practices are used" (p. 685).
	If such racism goes unchecked, schools "will maintain racial disproportionality in discipline, regardless of what particular discipline practices are used" (Lustick, 2017, p. 685).
2 authors	Zaval and Cornwell (2017) discuss the critical psychological and social barriers that prevent the education of conservation and the motivation to live a more sustainable lifestyle.
	Critical psychological and social barriers prevent the education of conservation and the motivation to live a more sustainable lifestyle (Zaval & Cornwell, 2017).
3–5 authors	In first mention:
	According to Campbell, Nayga, Part, and Silva (2011), compared to children from 1999–2000, where only 14% of students ages 2–19 were overweight or at risk of being overweight, the obesity rate had nearly doubled in the following three years (p. 1099).
	In first mention:
	Compared to children from 1999–2000, where only 14% of students ages 2–19 were overweight or at risk of being overweight, the obesity rate had nearly doubled in the following three years (Campbell, Nayga, Part, & Silva, 2011, p. 1099).
	In subsequent citations:
	According to Campbell et al. (2011),
	(Campbell et al., 2011)
6 or more authors	Roth et al. (2011) noted that compared to students of teachers who were only content trained, the students of this experimental group of teachers performed significantly better between pre and post-tests.
	Compared to students of teachers who were only content trained, the students of this experimental group of teachers performed significantly better between pre and post-tests (Roth et al., 2011).
Organization as an author	The United States Department of Agriculture (USDA, 2017) reported that, with 7.1 million children participating, the National School Lunch Policy (NSLP) is one of the many programs responsible for the food and nutritional services in the United States.
	With over 7.1 million children participating, the National School Lunch Policy (NSLP) is one of the many programs responsible for the food and nutritional services in the United States (United States Department of Agriculture [USDA], 2017).

Table 10.2. In-Text Citations (continued)

Work cited in another source	The National Commission on Excellence in Education's *A Nation at Risk* outlined the declining state of the U.S. education system in 1983: "Our once unchallenged preeminence in commerce, industry, science, and technological innovation is being overtaken by competitors throughout the world" (as cited in Golinkoff & Hirsh, 2016).
Two works by the same author in the same year	This research is classified as an explanatory case study, rather than an exploratory, descriptive, or evaluative case study, because of context surrounding the data collection (Yin, 2003a). Yin (2003b) highlighted the method's rigor.
Interviews, emails, and personal communications (these are not included on the references page)	**Basic format:** (communicator's name, personal communication, date of communication) Examples: The addition of a physical education curriculum has helped to improve the discipline in the second grade at Pine Street Elementary School (A. Brown, personal communication, August 25, 2018). Ms. Brown, a second grade teacher, noted that "discipline in my classroom has improved with the addition of physical education into my daily curriculum" (personal communication, August 25, 2018).

Conclusion

As we draw this text to a close, we hope that you've developed a stronger understanding of how writing is a crucial responsibility of teachers and part of their intellectual work. As a teacher, you will write on a regular basis. And even if writing is not an activity you envisioned as part of your work as an educator, we hope that this guide will allow you to approach your writing tasks with more confidence.

Writing is a recursive process, which means that as a teacher you will regularly return to the practice and process of writing. Therefore, the goal of this guide is to start you on this journey as a teacher-writer, not to predict your journey. In your career as an educator, you will encounter writing tasks and genres that extend beyond the scope of this text. Approaching these unfamiliar rhetorical situations with the skills and techniques outlined in this guide will allow you to effectively achieve the varied purposes of these unfamiliar writing situations.

Similarly, you may find that you do not encounter the genres covered in the guide in the order that we've presented them here. We organized the genres in a manner that moved from academic to professional. This does not mean that you have to read the guide sequentially in order to benefit from this text. It is our hope that you will use this guide as a writing resource throughout your career and regularly return to the guide whenever you need it.

We also hope that by conceptualizing writing as one of your primary responsibilities as a teacher, you will approach writing tasks not as chores but as opportunities. The varied rhetorical situations in which you will write as a teacher will be didactic, helpful, instructional, and often joyful. You will write to parents to communicate the achievements of your students, and to your principal to reflect on your continued growth as a teacher.

It can be easy to get discouraged about the status of education, which often highlights the deficits of our educational system. However, you have a voice in this country's discussion about education, and as an educator, your voice matters. Writing is the vehicle through which you can make your voice heard. Instead of accepting the status quo in education, consider employing the skills outlined in this guide to observe, research, and propose positive change. Writing is the way in which you can enact the changes you want to see.

In order to make your voice heard, develop a daily writing practice. Start a teacher journal, email curriculum ideas to your colleagues, or post regular updates on your school's learning management system. When you write every day, writing tasks become less daunting and you will be better prepared to share your voice with others.

Happy writing!

References

Ackerman, E. (2014). Analyze this: Writing in the social sciences. In G. Graff, C. Birkenstein, & R. Durst (Eds.), *They say, I say: The moves that matter in academic writing, with readings* (pp. 187–205). New York, NY: Norton.

Alber, R. (2011). *6 scaffolding strategies to use with your students.* Retrieved from edutopia.org/blog/scaffolding-lessons-six-strategies-rebecca-alber

American Civil Liberties Union of Northern California. (2003). *Sex education in California public schools.* San Francisco, CA: Burlingame Press.

American Educational Research Association. (2018). What is education research? Retrieved from aera.net/Education-Research/AERA-Education-Research

American Psychological Association. (2009). *Publication manual of the American Psychological Association* (6th ed.). Washington, DC: Author.

Andersen, L., Myers, L., O'Malley, K., Mundorf, A. R., Harris, D. M., & Johnson, C. C. (2015). Adolescent student use of school-based salad bars. *Journal of School Health, 85*(10), 722–727. doi:10.1111/josh.12302

Applegarth, C., Varley, P., Bacon, L., Edwards, A., Kennedy, K., Schieffer, S., & Yang, L. (2010). An inspired model . . . or a misguided one? Oprah Winfrey's dream school for impoverished South African girls. Retrieved from case.hks.harvard.edu/an-inspired-model-or-a-misguided-one-oprah-winfreys-dream-school-for-impoverished-south-african-girls/

Austin Independent School District. (2011). *Single gender education: A review of current issues and practices.* Austin, TX: N. Ibanez.

Ayers, W. (2010). *To teach: The journey of a teacher* (3rd ed.). New York, NY: Teachers College Press.

Barth-Cohen, L. A., Little, A. J., & Abrahamson, D. (2018). Building reflective practices in a pre-service math and science teacher education course that focuses on qualitative video analysis. *Journal of Science Teacher Education, 29*(2), 1–19.

Bassok, D., & Latham, S. (2017). Kids today: The rise in children's academic skills at kindergarten entry. *Educational Researcher, 46*(1), 7–20. doi: 10.3102/0013189X17694161

Bean, J. C. (2011). *Engaging ideas: The professor's guide to integrating writing, critical thinking, and active learning in the classroom* (2nd ed.). San Francisco, CA: Jossey-Bass.

Bitzer, L. (1968). The rhetorical situation. *Philosophy and Rhetoric, 1*(1), 1–14.

Brown, C. E. (2015). Making classrooms work: Why teachers need to be involved in education policy decisions. *U.S. News and World Report.* Retrieved from usnews.com/opinion/knowledge-bank/2015/06/24/why-teachers-should-be-involved-in-education-policy-decisions

California Commission on Teacher Credentialing. (2012). *Continuum of teaching practice*. Retrieved from ctc.ca.gov/docs/default-source/educator-prep/ca-ti/final-continuum-of-teaching-practice.pdf

California Department of Education. (2018). *Acronyms and initialisms*. Retrieved from cde.ca.gov/re/di/aa/ap/

California State Department of Education. (2017). *History-social science framework for California public schools: Kindergarten through grade 12*. Sacramento, CA: California State Department of Education.

California State University, Sacramento Online Writing Lab. (2011). The rhetorical square. Retrieved from csus.edu/owl/index/read/rhsqr.htm

Clark-Garcia, B. (2015). Where practicum meets test preparation: Supporting teacher candidates through edTPA. *CATESOL Journal, 27*(2), 211–220.

Cohen, E. G., & Lotan, R. A. (1995). Producing equal-status interaction in the heterogeneous classroom. *American Educational Research Journal, 32*(1), 99–120.

Common Core State Standards Initiative. (2018). *Standards in your state*. Retrieved from corestandards.org/standards-in-your-state/

Creme, P. (2008). A space for academic play. Student learning journals as transitional writing. *Arts and Humanities in Higher Education, 7*(1), 49–64.

Dean, D. (2008). *Genre theory: Teaching, writing, and being*. Urbana, IL: National Council of Teachers of English.

Dee, T. S., & Penner, E. K. (2017). The causal effects of cultural relevance: Evidence from an ethnic studies curriculum. *Educational Research Journal, 54*(1), 127–166. doi: 10.3102/0002831216677002

Delaware Department of Education. (2017). *Instruction and assessment/standards and assessment/English and language arts*. Retrieved from doe.k12.de.us/site/handlers/filedownload.ashx?moduleinstanceid=6017&dataid=15771&FileName=Gr2 Narrative%20R.pdf

Devitt, A. (2009). Teaching critical genre awareness. In S. H. McLeon (Series Ed.), C. Bazerman, A. Bonini, & D. Fifeuiredo (Eds.), *Genre in a changing world* (pp. 337–351). Anderson, SC: Parlor Press.

Dirk, K. (2010). Navigating genres. In C. Lowe & P. Zemliansky (Eds.), *Writing spaces: Readings on writing* (pp. 249–262). West Lafayette, IN: Parlor Press.

Dyson, A. H., & Genishi, C. (2005). *The case: Approaches to language and literacy research*. New York, NY, & London, UK: Teachers College Press.

edTPA. (2015a). *Exemplar instruction commentary: elementary mathematics*. Retrieved from passedtpa.com/wp-content/uploads/2016/12/Elementary-Mathematics-Instruction-Commentary.pdf

edTPA. (2015b). *Perfect secondary English language arts assessment commentary*. Retrieved from passedtpa.com/wp-content/uploads/2015/06/Perfect-Assessment-Commentary.pdf

edTPA. (2018). About edTPA. Retrieved from edtpa.com/PageView.aspx?f=GEN_About EdTPA.html

Edutopia. (2011). *Free resources and tools for replicating project-based learning*. Retrieved from edutopia.org/stw-replicating-pbl-resources

Efrat, S. E., & Ravid, R. (2013). *Action research in education: A practical guide*. New York, NY: Guilford Press.

Ferris, D. R., & Hedgcock, J. S. (2014). *Teaching L2 composition*. New York, NY: Routledge.

Flower, L. (2012). Writing for an audience. In G. Goshgarian (Ed.), *Exploring language* (pp. 91–93). Boston, MA: Pearson.

Gay, L. R., & Airasian, P. (2003). *Educational research: Competencies for analysis and applications*. Upper Saddle River, NJ: Merrill Prentice Hall.

Giroux, H. (1985). Teachers as transformative intellectuals. In K. Ryan & J. Cooper (Eds.), *Kaleidoscope: Contemporary and classic readings in education* (pp. 35–40). Belmont, CA: Cengage Learning.

Graff, G., Birkenstein, C., & Durst, R. (2014). *"They say, I say": The moves that matter in academic writing, with readings*. New York, NY: Norton.

Hicks, T., Whitney, A., Fredricksen, J., & Zuidema, L. (2017). *Coaching teacher-writers: Practical steps to nurture professional writing*. New York, NY: Teachers College Press & National Writing Project.

Hines, B., Henze, A., Ivanova, C., Rowland, L., Waggoner, L., & Lisak, M. (2016). *Action research in education*. Oxfordbibliographies.com. doi: 10.1093/obo/9780199756810-0140

Jaradeh, K. (2015). *Teacher's holistic approach works*. Davis Enterprise. Retrieved from davisenterprise.com/forum/opinion-columns/teachers-holistic-approach-works/

Kamenetz, A. (2015). 5 big ideas in education that don't work. *National Public Radio*. Retrieved from npr.org/sections/ed/2017/01/14/508991615/5-big-ideas-in-education-that-dont-work

Kleyn, T., Lopez, D., & Makar, C. (2015). What about bilingualism? A critical reflection on the edTPA with teachers of emergent bilinguals. *Bilingual Research Journal, 38*(1), 88–106.

Kolln, M. (2003). *Rhetorical grammar*. New York, NY: Longman.

Krajcik, J. S., & Blumenfeld, P. C. (2005). Project-based learning. In R. K. Sawyer (Ed.), *The Cambridge handbook of the learning sciences* (pp. 317–333). Cambridge, UK: Cambridge University Press.

Kvale, S. (2008). *Doing interviews: An introduction to qualitative research interviewing*. London, UK: Sage.

LePan, D., Buzzard, L., & Okun, M. (2017). *How to be good with words*. Peterborough, Ontario, Canada: Broadview Press.

Leverenz, C. S. (1998). Citing cybersources: A challenge to disciplinary values. *Computers and Composition, 15*(2), 185–200.

Lindsay, C. A., & Hart, C.M.D. (2017). Exposure to same-race teachers and student disciplinary outcomes for black students in North Carolina. *Educational Evaluation and Policy Analysis, 39*(3), 485–510. doi: 10.3102/0162373717693109

Martin, L. (2017). *Observation assignment* [Edu 110 Class assignment]. Davis, CA: University of California, Davis.

Miller, C. (1984). Genre as social action. *Quarterly Journal of Speech, 70*(2), 151–167.

Murphy, S., & Smith, M. A. (2015). *Uncommonly good ideas: Teaching writing in the common core era*. New York, NY: Teachers College Press.

Nast, P. (n.d.). Authentic assessment toolbox. Retrieved from nea.org/tools/lessons/57730.htm

National Governors Association Center for Best Practices & Council of Chief State School Officers. (2010a). *Common core state standards for English language arts &*

literacy in history/social studies, science, and technical subjects: Appendix C: Samples of student writing. Retrieved from corestandards.org/assets/Appendix_C.pdf

National Governors Association Center for Best Practices & Council of Chief State School Officers. (2010b). *Common core state standards for English language arts: Speaking and listening grade 3*. Retrieved from corestandards.org/ELA-Literacy/SL/3/

National Governors Association Center for Best Practices & Council of Chief State School Officers. (2010c). *Common core state standards for English language arts: Speaking and listening grade 6*. Retrieved from corestandards.org/ELA-Literacy/SL/6/

National Governors Association Center for Best Practices & Council of Chief State School Officers. (2010d). *Common core state standards for English language arts: Speaking and listening grade 9–10*. Retrieved from corestandards.org/ELA-Literacy/SL/9-10/

National Governors Association Center for Best Practices & Council of Chief State School Officers. (2010e). *Common core state standards for English language arts: Speaking and listening grade 11–12*. Retrieved from corestandards.org/ELA-Literacy/SL/11-12/

National Governors Association Center for Best Practices & Council of Chief State School Officers. (2010f). *Common core state standards for English language arts: Speaking and listening kindergarten*. Retrieved from corestandards.org/ELA-Literacy/SL/K/

National Governors Association Center for Best Practices & Council of Chief State School Officers. (2010g). *Common core state standards for English language arts: Writing grade 9–10 1d*. Retrieved from corestandards.org/ELA-Literacy/W/9-10/1/d/

National Governors Association Center for Best Practices & Council of Chief State School Officers. (2010h). *Common core state standards for English language arts: Writing grade 9–10 2d*. Retrieved from corestandards.org/ELA-Literacy/W/9-10/2/d/

National Writing Project & Nagin, C. (2006). *Because writing matters: Improving student writing in our schools*. San Francisco, CA: Jossey-Bass.

New Jersey Department of Education. (2014). New Jersey professional standards for teachers alignment with InTASC NJAC 6A:9-3.3. Retrieved from state.nj.us/education/profdev/profstand/ProfStandardsforTeachersAlignmentwithinTASC.pdf

No Child Left Behind Act of 2001, P.L. 107-110, 20 U.S.C. § 6319. (2002).

Noel, A. M. (2014). Teacher performance assessment (edTPA): An instructor's development and evaluation of an embedded signature assessment in an early childhood literacy course. *Journal of Early Childhood Teacher Education, 35*(4), 357–372.

Pigg, S., & Grabill, J. (2010). *The writing lives of college students: Revisualizing composition study group* (A WIDE survey and white paper). East Lansing, MI: The Writing in Digital Environments Research Center.

Purdue Online Writing Lab. (2018a). *APA stylistics: Avoiding bias*. Retrieved from owl.purdue.edu/owl/research_and_citation/apa_style/apa_formatting_and_style_guide/apa_stylistics_avoiding_bias.html

Purdue Online Writing Lab. (2018b). *APA stylistics: Basics*. Retrieved from owl.purdue.edu/owl/research_and_citation/apa_style/apa_formatting_and_style_guide/apa_stylistics_basics.html

Rinard, B. J. (2010). *The persuasive and evaluative essays of adolescent English learners: How context shapes genre* (Unpublished dissertation). University of California, Davis.

Rinard, B. J., & Masiel, D. (2017). Carolyn Miller: "A set of shared expectations." In D. Masiel, E. Schroeder, & L. Sperber (Eds.), *Teachers on the edge: The WOE interviews, 1989–2017* (pp. 462–471). New York, NY: Routledge.

Romano, T. (1995). *Writing with passion: Life stories, multiple genres.* Portsmouth, NH: Heinemann.

Romano, T. (2000). *Blending genre, altering style: Writing multigenre papers.* Portsmouth, NH: Heinemann.

Romano, T. (2013). *Fearless writing: Multigenre to motivate and inspire.* Portsmouth, NH: Heinemann.

Shulman, L. S. (1986). Those who understand: Knowledge growth in teaching. *Educational Researcher, 15*(2), 4–14.

SMART Technologies. (2004). Interactive whiteboards and learning: A review of classroom case studies and research literature. Retrieved from peremarques.net/pdigital/es/docs/Research%20White%20Paper.pdf

Stribling, S. M., DeMulder, E. K., Barnstead, S., & Dallman, L. (2015). The teaching philosophy: An opportunity to guide practice or an exercise in futility? *Teacher Educators' Journal*, 37–50.

Subban, P. (2005). Differentiated instruction: A research basis. *International Education Journal, 7*(7), 935–947.

Swanborn, P. (2010). *Case study research: What, why and how.* Los Angeles, CA, & London, UK: Sage.

Vygotsky, L. S. (1978). *Mind in society: The development of higher psychological processes.* Cambridge, MA: Harvard University Press.

Vygotsky, L. (2012). *Thought and language* (rev. & expanded ed.). Cambridge, MA: MIT Press.

Warren, V. L., & APA Committee on the Status of Women in the Profession. (1986). *Guidelines for nonsexist use of language.* Retrieved from jstor.org/stable/pdf/3131589.pdf

WestEd Justice & Prevention Research Center. (2018). *What do we know about the effects of school-based law enforcement on school safety?* Retrieved from wested.org/resources/effects-of-school-based-law-enforcement-on-school-safety/

Wharton, S. (2012). Presenting a united front: Assessed reflective writing on a group experience. *Reflective Practice, 13*(4), 489–501.

Wiggins, G., & McTighe, J. (2005). *Understanding by design* (2nd ed.). Alexandria, VA: Association for Supervision and Curriculum Development.

Wilson, M. (2006). *Rethinking thinking rubrics.* Portsmouth, NH: Heinemann.

Winegarden, B. (n.d.). *Writing instructional objectives.* Retrieved from training.nwcg.gov/pre-courses/m410/Writing_Instructional_Objectives.pdf

Woodland Joint Unified School District. (2016). *Performance evaluation manual for certificated staff.* Woodland, CA: Author.

Yin, R. K. (2003). *Case study research: Design and methods.* Thousand Oaks, CA: Sage.

Young, L. (2018). Age of resistance. Retrieved from californiaeducator.org/2018/06/18/age-of-resistance

Index

About the Authors

Katie O. Arosteguy is a lecturer in the University Writing Program at UC Davis, where she teaches a variety of upper-division courses in writing in the disciplines—including Writing in Education. For 3 years she directed the Writing Ambassadors program and prepared some 100 undergraduates per year to intern as writing assistants in K–12 schools in the region. Before UC Davis, Katie taught composition in community colleges in the Sacramento area as well as junior high and high school English. She has published on teaching audience awareness on the *Writers Who Care* blog and presented her work on designing multimodal writing projects at the Conference on College Composition and Communication. A National Writing Project teacher-consultant, Katie works with high school and community college teachers to better understand writing instruction at all levels. She holds a PhD in English from Washington State University, an MA in English and secondary teaching credential in English from California State University, Sacramento, and a BA in English from the University of California, Davis.

Alison Bright is a lecturer in the University Writing Program at UC Davis and a teacher-consultant with the National Writing Project. She serves as the University of California representative on the Advisory Board for the California Writing Project. Her research interests include writing program administration, writing across the curriculum, writing centers, tutor preparation, teacher identity, and the professional development of teacher/writers. She has published the results of these research interests in *English Education* and *Teaching/Writing*. Alison and several of her colleagues collaboratively co-authored the *English Education* article "Beyond Strategies: Teacher Practice, Writing Process, and the Influence of Inquiry," which was the recipient of the 2009 NCTE Janet Emig Award. She holds a PhD in Education from the University of California, Santa Barbara, an MA in English (with an emphasis on rhetoric and the teaching of writing) from Sonoma State University, and a BA in Spanish literature from the University of California, Santa Cruz.

Brenda J. Rinard is a lecturer in the University Writing Program at UC Davis, where she teaches Writing in Elementary and Secondary Education and a variety of other writing courses across the professions and disciplines. From 2013–2016 Brenda served as the assistant director of the UWP's Writing Across the Curriculum Program and worked extensively with graduate students and faculty to integrate best practices in writing instruction across campus. Before coming to UC Davis, Brenda directed Stanford University's Pre-Collegiate Studies Writing Program and developed writing curricula for international students. As a teacher-consultant for the Area 3 Writing Project, Brenda works with high school teachers from the Davis and Sacramento area to discuss the writing transitions from high school to college. Brenda holds a PhD in education from UC Davis, an MA in rhetoric and composition from San Francisco State University, and a BA in English from UC Berkeley.